POETICS OF CHANGE

The Texas Pan American Series

POETICS OF CHANGE
The New Spanish-American Narrative

JULIO ORTEGA

Translated from the Spanish by **GALEN D. GREASER**
in collaboration with the author

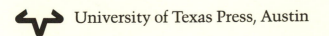 University of Texas Press, Austin

First paperback printing, 1988

Requests for permission to reproduce material
from this work should be sent to:
   Permissions
   University of Texas Press
   Box 7819
   Austin, Texas 78713-7819

LIBRARY OF CONGRESS CATALOGING IN PUBLICATION DATA
Ortega, Julio.
   Poetics of change.
   Includes index.
   1. Spanish American fiction—20th century—History
and criticism—Addresses, essays, lectures.   I. Title.
PQ7082.N7073   1984   863   83-26110
ISBN 0-292-76488-X
ISBN 0-292-76508-8 pbk.

*The Texas Pan American Series is published with the assistance
of a revolving publication fund established by the Pan American
Sulphur Company.*

Contents

Acknowledgments

The translation of this book has been made possible thanks to the assistance of the University of Texas's University Research Institute, and I want to express special gratitude for the opportune support I have received from URI and Vice-President William S. Livingston, and from Robert King, Dean of Liberal Arts, and William Glade, Director of the Institute of Latin-American Studies.

Special recognition is due to the John Guggenheim Memorial Foundation for the 1974 grant that allowed me free time for research.

Part of the essay on José Lezama Lima and the essay on José María Arguedas's last novel were translated by Susan Jean Pels and William L. Siemens, respectively, and published in *Review*. The Center for Interamerican Relations kindly permitted us to reprint those essays with minor revisions.

"Morelli on the Threshold" was published in *The Review of Contemporary Fiction* (Fall 1983).

The essays on *Pedro Páramo*, *Hopscotch*, *Paradiso*, *One Hundred Years of Solitude*, *A Change of Skin*, *Three Trapped Tigers*, and *From Cuba with a Song* were first published in Spanish in my book *La contemplación y la fiesta* (Caracas: Monte Avila Editores, 1969). They appear here in translation by permission of Monte Avila.

The manuscript was prepared thanks to the help of the typist pool of the Department of Spanish and Portuguese of the University of Texas at Austin. Instructor Johanna Emmanuelli Huertas assisted in the checking and proofreading of some of the essays. Professor Robert Brody's assistance was very valuable in the revision of the translation. Department Chairman Merlin H. Forster has always been helpful, as have staff members Raquel Elizondo and Sue Lawn.

J.O.

I. A CRITICAL MODEL

1. The New Spanish-American Narrative

In attempting to construct a critical model and to discover the lines of convergence of the "new Spanish-American narrative," we must start from the practice and interaction of the key, or modeling, texts. The works of Borges, Rulfo, Cortázar, Lezama Lima, and García Márquez propose different models of writing within the modern literary discourse of Latin America. At the same time, however, "The Aleph" (1945), *Pedro Páramo* (1955), *Hopscotch* (1963), *Paradiso* (1966), and *One Hundred Years of Solitude* (1967) create an interrelated space, and the textual operations in this space form a literary paradigm. We should, therefore, start with the texts and their specific practice.

In "The Aleph" we find an initial theory of writing in the contrasting notions of literature held by Carlos Argentino, the protagonist, and Borges, the narrator. Carlos Argentino, we are told, has access to the Aleph and has been writing a monstrous poem that is a duplication of the world. Through this iridescent sphere, which contains the entire universe, he reproduces the entropic diversity of the world. On the other hand, when Borges sees the Aleph, he reports that what amazed him most was that the multiplicity of the universe could occupy such a small, vertiginous space. Instead of the successive presence of things, he sees their simultaneous presence. He refuses to use the Aleph to duplicate reality, as Carlos Argentino does, and simply registers his amazement at the existence of this fantastic instrument. If we allow that the instrument in this story is a metaphor of the literary phenomenon itself, we find that we have uncovered an implied theory of literature. Borges's criticism of representational, descriptive literature reflects his preference for a different type of literary model that, rather than referring to the logic of reality, refers to its own existence, that is to say, to the logic of its own discourse. Literature begins with an examination of the functions of language in order to question its own function. Within

Latin-American literature of the 1940s, Borges's is probably the most rigorous theoretical postulation of an autonomous, self-sufficient writing with regard to the referential functions of language. We might say, then, that Borges introduced a model of *critical writing* into Spanish-American literature.

We know that "The Aleph" is a story, as well as an indirectly autobiographical report in the form of a chronicle, and a speculative essay. We also know that Borges has written many narratives in the form of reviews. Thus, the movement that transcodifies the narrative repertoires produces both "fiction" and "criticism" in this writing. In short, in Borges's critical writing, fiction shapes a deconstruction: the mechanisms of literature themselves create a fictional and critical model of reality whose meaning becomes relative in the act of being formulated. This model assumes that fiction is a form of criticism and vice versa, that criticism is a form of fiction.

Turning to Juan Rulfo, in *Pedro Páramo* we can speak of *mythical writing*. In the first line of this novel we are told, "I came to Comala because I was told that my father, a certain Pedro Páramo, was living here," but we soon realize that Comala has disappeared and is inhabited only by the voices of death; in other words, there is no "external world" in the novel. Everyone is or will be a ghost in a barren landscape. Place has disappeared, and we are left only with words. The single underpinning of the novel is its nominal character: "land," "moon," "night," are the realities that names provide, that names and language construct. It is thus a text supported solely by itself. Its power of representation is remarkable, but it has a somewhat phantasmic quality because the reference is purely verbal. On the other hand, we also find in *Pedro Páramo* a different systematic representation, a construction of reality derived from the Catholic code. The characters live the popular ideology of Catholicism as though it were real. Here this ideology has become a natural world: there is an afterlife, sins must be atoned for, conscience is guilt and punishment, death extends the suffering of guilt, etc. Thus, a popular ideology is coherently designed as a natural world, and it is here that the text shapes its cohesive paradigm: the "real" is produced in a code carried to an extreme. This ideology is not a mere illusion; rather, it creates for the subject his only possible world. In brief, this mythical writing assumes that "reality" and "fiction" cannot be distinguished. Myth is a reformulation of language; the representation of a *Weltanschauung* based on an ideology is sustained by the syntax of the narrative.

In the case of *Hopscotch* we encounter a model based on *colloquial writing* because this novel, as we know, attempts to reformulate literature on the basis of a new dialogue between the text and the reader. For Cortázar literature, like our other formalizations of reality, is defective. This idea falls directly in line with the surrealist tradition, but for Cortázar a new founding of the text requires that literature be remade and that the reader be changed.

The demand that life be changed goes through the reconstruction of the text to change the reader, who now becomes in effect the main character of the novel. The experience of reading decides the place of literature and our perception of other discursive series, starting from the speculative debate on signification and its demands; but a system of dialogue must be reestablished if communication is to flow between the text and the reader. By reconstructing the dialogue between the book and literature, between fiction and meaning, between the narrative and its own production, *Hopscotch* designs a complex system of communication. The actors unfold in the changing textual space of the newly convoked legitimacy. A new language, characterized by polyphonic communication, emerges from this debate. This language refuses to be a written, literary language, and can only be the reemergence of a spoken language, of a new colloquy. Replacing the shattered established literary and rationalist language, the new one is announced as an Adamic language: speech assigns names once again.

We could say that in this novel "reality" needs "fiction" in order to be more authentic, or simply to be. The series of discursive and formalized practices that our perception questions in order to genuinely express significance is a model reconstructed as "reality" in the work of the text and in its system of communication. The fictional nature of this practice authenticates and generates the fullest and freest meaning of the integrative language that the new speaker, who is a new man because he is a new reader, has reconstructed with the text or in its operations. Finally, this model of critical reading is what produces the alternative and the imminency of a restored colloquy. Speaking as though for the first time, the text states its question and awaits us within it.

The model of writing in *Paradiso*, by Cuban novelist José Lezama Lima, is *poetic writing*. In the first place, *Paradiso* is a novel about poetry. In a sense, the accomplished language of poetry is a paradisaic language sought through a long apprenticeship. *Paradiso* is a *Bildungsroman*, a novel of education. José Cemí, whose name alludes to the image, is the "young artist" in this ritualization of poetry understood as resolution and as a paradigm of meaning. Poetic knowledge implies, therefore, successive rites of passage by means of the image and an understanding of the image's unfolding and incorporating dimensions. Starting from poetry, language, which is a modalization of reality, produces in this case a "totalizing" model. The gap between natural language and poetic language is closed; in its transmuting code poetic writing does not recognize disjunctions, and its integrating power is unrestricted. In this writing, which fuses time and reintegrates a space of convergencies, "fiction" expands our perception of what is "real" and shapes it as an appropriation of language. Poetry as a path of knowledge and incorporation is held to be superior to reason. It forms a suprarational perception starting from the image, in which names surrender their referential root to a new space: the text of the world is thus made real in the production of a new reading.

This writing is "poetic" because it expands the possibilities of charting and inscribing a broader figurative space within language itself. The triad is one of the expanding mechanisms weaving the incorporations in the text. We see it at work, for example, when José Cemí contemplates two objects close to each other and discovers that they generate an opening, which establishes a third object. Thus, two images summon a third. Figuration establishes a space that Lezama calls gnostic, and this is the space of new knowledge. "Reality" is, therefore, a configuration generated by poetry; the image supplements this polysemous dimension that is the center of a restored perception.

These triadic configurations presuppose a substratum: the metaphor. In effect, in a metaphor two terms refer to an implicit third term. In the triad, however, we find that the third term is now present as a signifier of a sign whose sense rests in the very density of the configuration. Apart from this, the triad is also present in the organization of the text. Thus, the first character convokes a second, and that character in turn summons a third, producing in this way a syntax of unfolding combinations and oppositions and the development of the ritualized text. In short, the text progressively generates its own referents through the hyperbole of its configurations. Hence its baroque practice, but also the celebrating search of its free association.

"Fiction" reveals the latent text of "reality." There is no distinction between these terms because poetic writing produces and reproduces a sufficient text and an open-ended model that reconstructs the world as integral poetry. "Literature" is thus a radical act: it gives form to knowledge through the proliferating image in a reuniting language.

Finally, the writing in *One Hundred Years of Solitude*, the extraordinary novel by Gabriel García Márquez, is, in the last instance, *fictitious writing*. The associative dynamics of this writing reconstructs the natural world, transforming it into metafiction, especially since this associative dynamics has language itself in its favor. We find here that language has broadened its associative capacity and that, based on its own code, it converts the utterance into a proliferation of the denotative level. The natural world is thus changed into metafiction: the language is still the same but the act of its utterance is different. Language surrenders its referents to a writing that, upon uttering it, transforms it into fictional space.

In this case denotation—the representational and referential character of language—finds its code changed into a mechanism of proliferation. This writing could go on endlessly, not because we are being told the story of a legendary family or village, but because what is being reread is the discontinuity of a culture, the Latin-American culture, and this rereading implies an open-ended text. But we also discover another rereading, the comedy of language as metafiction; in other words, we find that almost all discursive series can be carnivalized. This intrareading implies an intertext: the traditional notion of the narrative as the fiction of language. The tradition of writing (of what is spoken and of what is written: of what is inscribed) is therefore the horizon of this text, which, not by chance, is also a fable about narration.

In the end, the code of this text refers to the book itself. This code is, as we know, the book we have read and the book that the last character in the novel reads. The text as a book is also a metaphor of this proliferating writing, but above all it is a code of enunciation. Literature speaks in this case. In other words, the utterance, as well as the references and fiction, derives from literature, from the paradigm of a transmuted and liberated language. In this writing the world and time have a written existence: reading itself forms part of the syntagm of the book. Based on the tradition of the world as writing and of the book as an image of the world, *One Hundred Years of Solitude* reconstructs a writing that is a new and sufficient space, entirely fictitious and entirely true.

"Reality" and "fiction" are thus a single writing whose source is the book. We can characterize this as fictitious writing because its language is transformed by a greater fiction, that of the book. This accounts for the impossibility of distinguishing between "reality" and "fiction." The referent of this fiction is another fiction, a fiction sustained by the enunciating book, which is a fantastic code and a generating source. García Márquez, who is closer to Borges than he might at first appear, thinks of fiction, criticism, and writing as a book, as a fictitious space. What is most fictitious is not the "book of the world" but this new "book of writing."

Now then, through the specific practice of their textual operations, which represent a systematic questioning, the texts we have characterized above also produce a systematic deconstruction of traditional writing, of the tradition of modernity itself and, therefore, of the role of the text and of our cultural and natural perception of language.

On the other hand, we should not forget that these texts—which are among the most accomplished examples of the resurgent Spanish-American narrative—are also shaped by their peculiar historicity. This is what defines them as objects that adopt, discuss, and resolve a theoretical and practical set of diverse formulas, operations, and debates that modernity—and the dialogue of each text with the literary tradition, the Spanish-American culture, and the social practice itself—has displaced, as a debate, to the space of writing. This accounts for the resolving nature of these major texts, which are summations and proposals, true paradigmatic reconstructions of the very discourse of literature, in other words, of poetics. This "poetics of change," this transitive practice and remodeling of literature implies, for this very reason, both a process of deconstruction and a practice of reconstruction. In the first place, this poetics deconstructs the notion of the text within the literary tradition and, second, it deconstructs its role in the natural language.

If we turn again to Borges, we discover that his works tend toward what we may call the deconstruction of culture, because Borges approaches culture not as a monument, but as a text. Culture for Borges is not historiographic (in other words, it is not a source of truth), but a free alternation of texts in the space of the narrative, a space in which these texts are placed on the same level and decentered. Borges deconstructs the idea of the stability of culture, the idea of information as a museum, as a hierarchical, exemplary, hegemonic monumentality. The same thing had been done already by Joyce, Picasso, Stravinsky, and, of course, Pound. The formal repertoires change their stable order in the changing space of the text, which is why we can state that the Borgian text begins the construction of a decentralized space of culture. Culture ceases to be stable information derived from a hegemonic center and is transformed into a textual construction. Within culture, the notion of "truth" thus becomes a formal operation that is no less fantastic than the literary act itself. Using the formalized materials and repertoires of culture, Borges produces the narrative of a vast deconstruction.

In this same vein, it is perhaps not merely by chance that following this Borgian foundation *Pedro Páramo* produced a deconstruction of social life, while at the same time constructing the ideological space of a social hell. Rulfo deconstructs society as a natural model and constructs instead an allegory of ideology as a sort of hell. In the case of *Hopscotch*, the deconstruction involves, in the first place, the genre itself, the naturalized space of the novel. At the same time, however, this work constructs reading as the restructuring code of the new literary dialogue. The fabric of communication is transformed into a text dramatizing the place of the speakers and the flow of meaning. In *Paradiso* we cannot escape the conclusion that what is being deconstructed is the notion of referentiality, the denotation that supposes a natural world and a language that states it. This impression is not created because Lezama Lima exceeds the norms of verisimilitude, which he in effect transgresses as just another convention, but because the connotations—and their free interweaving—are the expanding model of a world restituted by a suprarational writing. This enables Lezama Lima to construct a text of meaning and to represent the abundance of meaning as a text. Lezama has discovered the inexhaustible connotation of reading: sense articulates, functioning as an Eros that supplements its possible space and its expansive trace. García Márquez, on the other hand, deconstructs history, not only because *One Hundred Years of Solitude* outlines a version of history that is free and altered, although still central to the development of the narrative, and not only because the novel occupies the space of Latin-American history as defined by its mythical origins, but above all because history is shifted, as narrative, to a reconstructed subject, to the critical consensus of popular culture. We might say that in *One Hundred Years of Solitude* popular culture is being produced as a material subject that restructures historicity, while in *The Autumn of the Patriarch* the collective subject of popular culture has fused, through the historicity of its construction, the carnival aspects of its "materiality" with the critical activity of its political role.

Historicity is on the other horizon of this Spanish-American writing; its social dimension is defined by its critical practice. This is true from the questioning power of Borges's texts, which in the 1940s began demonstrating the specificity and maturity of our literature and liberating it from the colonial cast of regional thematics, to *Pedro Páramo* and *Hopscotch*, which as texts of change obviously imply a broader questioning of thematic, ideological, and cultural forms. In this sense, *Paradiso* is a demand for a more radical liberation of the subject through the critique of language and the search for meaning. In this novel art seeks to impose a more genuine communication as its social function. And in García Márquez the text internalizes and carries on the social discourse; the subject is shifted toward the text itself and thus becomes the narration of critical knowledge, of critical restitutions and liberations.

At that point in which history conceals or falsifies, this polyphonic writing reestablishes a space that, shattering the conditions of empirical reality, begins a reconstruction of language as a critical instrument and as emancipated social matter.

2. The First Letter

The dialogue between tradition and change, which in Borges's work is to a great extent a paradigmatic dialogue, and which had a productive influence on the new Latin-American literature, is a key to re-reading "The Aleph" as a literary theory.

Some critics have read "The Aleph" as a parody of Dante's *The Divine Comedy*. They have stated that Carlos Argentino Daneri parodically evokes Dante Alighieri, and that although here the significance of Beatriz is less obvious, it is no less central to the narrative.

Argentine critic Daniel Devoto has made an erudite, intriguing, and perhaps excessive reading of the possible connections with *The Divine Comedy*, and Roberto Paoli, an Italian critic, has also called attention to the ambiguous associations with that classic work. Borges, however, has played down this discussion in the notes he wrote to *The Aleph and Other Stories.** He maintains there is no connection with *The Divine Comedy* and that Beatriz Viterbo is a woman who actually lived and whom he loved with no hope of being requited. But as Emir Rodríguez Monegal has shown, that does not mean that this connection does not exist; and the fact that Borges denies it may make it even more likely.[1] Obviously, what Borges is criticizing is a direct connection, because the reading itself inevitably leads us to allegorize one. Any suggestion of a connection must start from the fact that, in the story, Beatriz has died. In *The Divine Comedy*, as we know, Beatrice is the highest emblem of a way of knowledge that leads through intellectual love to a higher revelation and that postulates a reading that summarizes and culminates a spiritual apprenticeship. On the other hand, "The Aleph" confronts us with a world in which the first thing of which we are made aware is

*The Aleph and Other Stories, *1933–1969*, edited and translated by Norman Thomas di Giovanni in collaboration with the author (New York: E. P. Dutton, 1970).

the death of Beatriz. We are abandoned in a world that in some parallel way is marked by the emptying from this emblem of what Beatrice represents in the literary tradition. If we attempt to represent
to ourselves the atmosphere, marked by the absence of Beatriz, that
Borges induces in this text, we find a series of substitutions, parodies, and duplications, a world we could at least call false, a world
in which things do not seem real and in which the people, ideas, and
relations seem devoid somehow of meaning and, above all, of authenticity. What remains of it in the rereading is its artificiality, its
ungenuine condition. The drama is somehow placed in a form of reality that we can call degraded. This means, perhaps, that what tradition promises and maintains, a life of meaning, has been lost. That
is, the void left by Beatriz confirms a broader meaninglessness. The
world now seems ludicrous, profusely grotesque, and, at the same
time, ghostly.

The center of the farce is Carlos Argentino Daneri. Carlos Argentino is a sort of Dante of our times: vacuous and also grotesque. Instead of a divine *comedy* of tradition, Carlos Argentino writes an
earthly *comedy*, a poem as base as his world, which he entitles *The
Earth*. Literature, it might be said, has lost its meaning in the hands
of the Carlos Argentinos of this world. It is not, as tradition promises, a life of knowledge, but an impoverishing duplication of reality.

The drama of meaning takes on the ironic form of a report in
which the author goes so far as to become the narrator. In other
words, through the authorship of the report he underlines the irony
of the witness, of the protagonist, of a substitutive world in which
the notion of the fantastic, of transferred desire, must sustain the
restitution of meaning. Irony is, thus, a form of nostalgia.

The house where the Aleph is found is going to be torn down. Upset, Carlos Argentino calls Borges and tells him about the Aleph.
Borges immediately responds: to respond is his sign. The drama is
precipitated and begins again with a question about language:

> I arrive now at the ineffable core of my story. And here begins
> my despair as a writer. All language is a set of symbols whose
> use among its speakers assumes a shared past. How, then, can I
> translate into words the limitless Aleph, which my floundering
> mind can scarcely encompass?

The approach to the center—of the narrative, of the stating of a
possible meaning—requires this examination of the very nature of
language; language is obviously a cultural creation and serves to
identify a world modeled in communication. When in tradition we
enounter the experience of certain situations that supposedly lack

a name, such as the mystical experience, we fall back on the analogical languages. Analogy provides this supplementary expression, which is a configuration of symmetrical connections. In that space, the equivalent object announces an abundance of meaning.

This, then, is an alternative of expression sanctioned by tradition. But it also presupposes a greater agreement, that of a saturated meaning. On the other hand, Borges finds himself with another center without agreement:

> Really, what I want to do is impossible, for any listing of an endless series is doomed to be infinitesimal. . . . What my eyes beheld was simultaneous, but what I shall now write down will be successive, because language is successive.

In the face of this questioning of the very nature of language, Borges recognizes the path of tradition, which offers the analogical language of the mystics; but by rejecting it he can only look for another type of language, another way of stating again, although recognizing that the successiveness of language conspires against the simultaneity of his vision, which is why he concludes by saying, "Nonetheless, I'll try to recollect what I can." This precipitates the brilliant enumeration we know. The drama of the text is in stating the fiction. The utterance begins again as a ritual of the name, with the alarm and pleasure of wonder. The associative speech seeks here to saturate with its apparent dispersion that wonder, that joint birth of the name and the object in this sort of renaissance of the subject in the space of fiction. The language of testimony (I saw this or I saw that) authenticates the irruption of the unusual by verifying it, which again is the fortuitous life of the letter—in this case the first—at the beginning of the discourse of the fiction that is recorded. Not by accident, the verb at the beginning of the phrase reiterates the importance of the action, the renewal of another world in its very axis: the action of beginning to see it.

The new thus recovers tradition because something completely different is being seen in the narrative; for the first time the world is being seen through the Aleph, in the implicit literary discourse. But this is an experience that opens in tradition, first, because it is proposed as a mystical experience; second, because the rhetoric of wonder is found in various discourses, from Revelation to Rabelais. It is a rhetoric of excess, an accumulation of naming the object in the act of its constitution by the subject. This device of naming also reappears in the associations of One Hundred Years of Solitude.

What did Borges see? The "unimaginable universe," again in the world, liberated now by fiction:

I felt infinite wonder, infinite pity.

"Feeling pretty cockeyed, are you, after so much spying into places where you have no business?" said a hated and jovial voice.

The contrast between the restitutive language of the narrator and Carlos Argentino's reducing dialogue intensifies the antagonism between these two readers. Carlos Argentino holds one position, Borges holds another, and the Aleph is the center that determines the antagonism. Carlos Argentino has been using the Aleph to write his poem. For him, to look through that small sphere is to register everything he sees. Paradoxically, this suggests that Carlos Argentino represents a literary option, a style of writing we can call duplicative of reality in literature; in other words, reality enters the text with no modification other than its tedious and grotesque repetition in language.

Not by accident is Carlos Argentino's poem entitled *The Earth*. This is clearly a literary joke by Borges. He is poking fun at a type of writer and at a particular notion of literature and, probably, at a certain type of national literature. The extraordinary thing, however, is that from the very same fantastic source of the Aleph—from the first sign of writing—this type of writer has been produced. In some way, then, Carlos Argentino is the loss of tradition. The other literary option, the one that reinitiates the change, is introduced in this statement by Borges:

> In that single gigantic instant I saw millions of acts both delightful and awful; not one of them amazed me more than the fact that all of them occupied the same point in space, without overlapping or transparency.

The difference here is clear. Carlos Argentino has gone through the Aleph toward things, while Borges has remained before the Aleph, amazed by the very existence of this fantastic instrument. The difference infers a reading from this change. As opposed to a duplicative, proliferating attitude, we encounter a critical, laconic attitude. One resorts to metonymical enumeration, while the other selects synecdochically, giving evidence of the very existence of this instrument of seeing, saying, and inscribing.[2]

What is the Aleph? In the story it is a small iridescent sphere, a fantastic object that materializes in a cellar. It is also, of course, the first letter of the Hebrew alphabet, and in the Kabbala it is the letter that represents the godhead. It is, therefore, an object of tradition that is given new functions in the narrative. If we start from the two attitudes about the act of writing, we can propose that in this story the Aleph somehow postulates the literary instrument; in other words, the Aleph—first letter, the letter of the enigma, access, and prism—emblematically implies literature. This story deals not with a religious experience but with a literary experience that speculates on the mystical tradition of the Aleph. If the Aleph in this story is a metaphor of literature—because in it the world is also virtual—we come back to the origin of its options. Whereas Carlos Argentino has turned to literature to duplicate the world, Borges announces another possibility, that of again posing the very existence of the literary fact. This, naturally, implies criticism and, through criticism, the operation of change, because whenever an irruption of change opposes tradition, literature is redefined. Each time that change responds to tradition there is a new literary practice, a new reflection that poses again the main purpose of the act of writing. Through change the world is revised with the materials of tradition, because now, from another perspective, literature is a rebeginning of reality. And this revision is necessarily criticial, starting with the fact that the story itself constructs its reading as a critical text, as a text critical of a model of literature, of a type of writer and of a society degraded because it does not have a place for literature aside from its false literary life. In this sense, the story is a satire that begins with the substitutive literary life.

There is a deeper criticism, however, a criticism of language itself. To remake literature, to make a new literature, language must be used in another way. This is what the story tells us. The degraded tradition that Carlos Argentino represents uses language in an impoverishing manner, and the postulation that Borges represents in the story, proposing a use of language that, in the first place, is critical, reacts against that tradition. That is why the postulation of another language emblematically represents Borges's work, which is a rereading of tradition through criticism. Criticism in this case is polyvalent, as is poetry in other postulations. This has to do as much with the fact that Borges refuses to engage in extensive discourses, in the novel, as with his conversion of metaphysics into fantastic speculation. And it has to do above all with the series of operations by which the cultural dimension of tradition is reduced by irony, by the game, and by paradox; the recodification, in short, that imposes the materials of tradition.

Now then, the tradition/change dialogue is not limited to a break that denies a tradition, which is what the avant-gardists generally do. In this case the elements of tradition are implicit and present in the very act of breaking and impugning tradition. Also, the relationship of tradition and disruption is not a mechanical polarity or even a symmetrical opposition, but forms a complex scheme in which a new perspective is determined for the same materials. It can be said that a new tradition is constituted when its figures, in other words, its "tropes," have become "topos," when the impugning quality of the images is pacified in the end by their circulation and consumption. The disruption that opens a new space starts with the fragments of that tradition, with its criticism. In this story about change we find both a nostalgia for and mockery of the fragments of tradition.

The complexity of these relations is perceived in this story when we verify that the postulation that the making of literature demands that we start by posing the very existence of literature is followed by a return to tradition, a characteristic of these texts that are, we could say, at the center of change.

Let us see how this return to tradition occurs. Borges reminds us of the analogical speech from which he departs, and at the same time he tells us of a magic instrument that is materialized in the story but is totally fantastic. For that very reason, if literature is postulated by the Aleph, this means that even if we read and make literature in some other way, in this case starting from the change opened by criticism, the very nature of the Aleph will conclude by returning us to tradition. Because what the Aleph announces is literature as myth. Carlos Argentino's mistake is not having realized that the Aleph is fantastic. He perceives the Aleph as just another household object, only more valuable, and has proceeded straight through it to arrive at the world serialized as natural. But if we must begin again, and begin by the amazing fact of the existence of the Aleph, we will return to a source of tradition, because the natural language used by Carlos Argentino is insufficient, when what is required is the search for another language, the metalanguage of literature, which begins in its criticism and culminates in its myth.

The myth of literature is obviously a promise of language, because the Aleph not only contains all things, but all languages, which means that it contains the promise of stating more than the language. That is the literary promise. The possibility of saying more is in fact one definition of literature. Literature says what natural language is not capable of saying. If natural language states the world, literature states another world. This is the critical position of Borges as opposed to that of Carlos Argentino, but this is also the return of Borges to the first source of tradition. Thus, an act of disruption is sustained by tradition, it returns to the literary virtuality par excellence, to the literary utopia.

Borges has stated that the esthetic act is like an imminency that is not fulfilled, in other words, like a promise of language that is not realized. Therein lies the defective derivation of his criticism that reduces the repertoires of knowledge to forms of fiction, and the very notion of truth to an operation of language. But lying behind these reductions is the other tension of his work, marked by the epiphany of the Aleph.

In the Postscript the story returns to the falsest of all worlds, the world of literature, which is treated as such several times. Earlier in the story, when Carlos Argentino explains himself, Borges says, "So foolish did his ideas seem to me, so pompous and so drawn out his exposition, that I linked them at once to literature and asked him why he didn't write them down." In the Postscript we read, "I want to add two final observations: one, on the nature of the Aleph; the other, on its name." This begins another phase of the narrative from that which we could call a scholastic rhetoric about the Aleph. The interesting conclusion for us is that the Aleph he has seen in Carlos Argentino's house is a "false Aleph." He asks himself, "Does this Aleph exist in the heart of a stone? Did I see it there in the cellar when I saw all things, and have I now forgotten it?" But what we are given in this Postscript, as always in Borges's postscripts, are bits of information that question what we have just read by introducing a second fantastic instance. Everything that has been said is fantastic, but an "Aleph" that "we have seen" becomes derealized. With this twist, the narrative—by an erudite path—escapes its own poly-semous density. But by turning again to the Aleph as a religious ob-ject, Borges is concealing the dimension of the Aleph in the narra-tive, its dimension as an object emblematic of literature. Because if this is what is involved, the Aleph could not be real. Like the other objects, it would be "false." As an object of literature, it can only ex-ist as a metaphor of writing, as a condensed figure. Starting from the kabbalistic tradition that sustains the mediation of the Aleph, the narrative returns to the inscription of the sign at the beginning of the alphabet, of literature. It is a real object only in the gratuitous measure in which it is an equivalent object.

We can now return to the representation that the narrative erects. The world of this story is a desubstantiated world. It is a parodical world in which literature is no more than the business of prizes and honors and external recognitions. It is also a world devoid of stan-dards, of morals; good and evil cannot be distinguished. Therefore, the notion of genuineness does not exist, and, precisely, the experi-ence of literature, which has been devalued, is recovered as an access to certainty. This is the moral postulation of criticism; to relive real-ity genuinely is the other promise of literature. If the other forms of living the world, including literature, have been falsified, then the dimension of certainty that literature remakes in language must be recovered. It is nothing but a very isolated genuine life of the world. Let us remember that the Aleph was discovered in a marginal space of the house, in other words, outside the social spaces, in a semidark corner. The house is also soon to be destroyed because the world is changing, but it is changing for the worse, progressively degenerating. We should remember also that when Beatriz dies the first thing that Borges observes is that a billboard has been changed. The world changes trivially and imperturbably. Literature becomes something marginal, and not only because it reveals itself in the cellar. Borges himself and his text *The Sharper's Cards* are not recognized; he remains on the fringe, like a somewhat domestic character who melancholically alludes to the impoverishment of reality. Literature is a possible and fortuitous way of seeing the world from a dimension of certainty. However, literature is improbable: the criticism that liberates it, returning it to myth, also questions it and makes it relative. Its marginal function is also stoical, because there is a final stoicism in cultivating this writing against a world in which its place is precarious. Living in a world in which Beatrice is no longer possible gives the measure of the deep agony of meaning that underlies the narrative. That contaminated and emptied world is, however, inhabited by the demand of the Aleph, by the other literature, that which leaves its trace in this delayed report.

Notes

1. "The Aleph" was first published in *Sur* (Buenos Aires), September 1945, and was included in *El Aleph* (Buenos Aires: Losada, 1949). Daniel Devoto's study is found in a special issue of *L'Herne* devoted to Borges: "Aleph et Alexis," No. 4 (Paris, 1964): 280—292. Roberto Paoli's study is entitled "El Aleph: Bifurcarzioni di lettura" (Florence: Università degli Studia di Firenzi, 1977), pp. 7—49. Emir Rodríquez Monegal analyzes the parodical level of this narrative in comparison with *The Divine Comedy* in his book *Jorge Luis Borges: A Literary Biography* (New York: E. P. Dutton, 1978), pp. 413—417. The relation of this narrative to the Kabbala has been noted by Saul Sosnowski in his study *Borges y la Cábala* (Buenos Aires: Hispamérica, 1976), pp. 77—81. See also Ana María Barrenechea, *La expresión de la irrealidad en la obra de Borges* (Buenos Aires: Paidos, 1967) and Jaime Alazraki, *La prosa narrativa de Jorge Luis Borges* (Madrid: Gredos, 1968).

2. From this "allegory of reading" the following postulation could be elaborated: "Carlos Argentino Daneri" represents metonymy (notation, extension, repetition, cause-effect relationship), while "Borges," who leaves out the metaphor (the analogy), represents synecdoche (the part for the whole).

Tradition, in effect, is metonymical, while change is synecdochical. But the option is produced between the metaphor and the synecdoche, not only in confrontation with tradition, whose topology is more obvious. Simultaneity, we know, is codifiable by the equivalence of the metaphorical substitution. On the other hand, selection (the strategy of exclusions) produces the discursive eruption that postulates the totality. This strategy is a genuine disruption, because it is fulfilled in the same successive order of language. In this way, it postulates a microcosm ("I'll try to recollect what I can") of the narrative to allude to the macrocosm of the universe of simultaneity. The "Aleph" configurates that interaction, that supplementary correlation of the discourse. More "phantasmic," "Carlos Argentino" and "Borges" are figures in approximation to the center of the "Aleph" and, therefore, the ironic treatment of the drama of the text. (See Harold Bloom, "The Breaking of Form," in De-construction and Criticism [New York: Seabury Press, 1979].)

3. Borges and the Latin-American Text

A reading of Borges's writings from the perspective of the Spanish-American cultural system would seem, at present, to go against the prevailing trend, since our critics prefer to study them as a cosmopolitan by-product. Nevertheless, this may be the opportune time to begin asking ourselves about the Spanish-American nature of this writing and about its functions within our cultural discourse.

Obviously, like any major oeuvre, Borges's works operate within an international literary context. But they also operate within the creative dynamics of Spanish-American culture and respond to its formulations and discontinuities. Thus our analysis concentrates on the productive mechanisms of Borges's writing rather than on establishing a disjunction between what some critics have taken to be the Spanish-American and European levels in these works, an approach that frequently has led to a mere cataloguing of themes. An analysis of these works will show that, regardless of the themes of his works, the productive mechanisms of Borges's writings are consistent with the practice of textualization that characterizes Spanish-American writing. This initial reading is not an attempt to question the many critical studies that have focused on the broadly-based museum of Borges's cultural references, nor is it a discussion of the arguments used, especially in Argentina, to oppose his cosmopolitanism. It seeks instead to examine Borges's works starting from the contention that writing is externalized in the productive context of a cultural horizon and that this analysis is needed to forestall the forfeiture of a major body of work important to our understanding of Spanish-American discourse, especially if we are convinced that one aspect of this writing is produced within the dynamics of that cultural discourse.

The persistent debate on the presumed cultural "foreignness" of Borges's work has clouded, rather than clarified, the discussion of its Spanish-American configuration. Some critics, such as Néstor Ibarra, have proclaimed that "there is no one more countryless than Jorge Luis Borges,"[1] a statement that only reinforces the accusation of "foreignness" generally advanced in Argentina to dismiss and forfeit these works.[2] Nevertheless, some critics have already proposed a reading of Borges's works that goes beyond the scope of this polarization. Humberto M. Rasi, for instance, has made the following accurate observation: "The general direction of the studies devoted to Borges's writings, as well as the preferences of certain of his translators, has contributed, for various reasons, to create the image of a countryless writer, one foreign to the literature and realities of his homeland."[3] Many of these studies have chosen to overlook the obvious fact that, beginning with *Fervor de Buenos Aires* (1923), Borges has developed and reiterated in his writings numerous themes and problems specifically related to his particular perception of the history and reality of Argentina. These themes range from the elegiacal presence of the city to the elaboration of a historical realm revolving around his ancestors and around figures such as Sarmiento, Quiroga, and Rosas, figures whom he evaluated and judged one way in his early works and another way in his mature writings. We could also analyze Borges's literary experience, starting with a study of his initial, polemical *criollismo*, his disquisitions on the Latin-American writer and the European tradition, and the demarcations and options he outlines in his prefaces to Argentine works, but an analysis of the sources of his themes would not give us an integral view of his writings. On the other hand, a study of the mechanisms of this writing will show that the themes of Borges's works only seem to be incompatible, and in fact are not.

Emir Rodríguez Monegal suggested, in 1962, that by their nature Borges's writings could be nothing other than Argentine, precisely because of their unabashed interest in cosmopolitan culture, their nostalgia for violence, and their perception of a peculiar urban landscape.[4] In the same vein, Carlos Fuentes has written: "Can there be anything more Argentine than this need to verbally fill the voids, to consult all the libraries of the world in order to fill the blank book of Argentina?"[5] Fuentes goes on to explain his Latin-American perception of these works:

> The end effect of Borges's prose, without which there simply would not be a Spanish-American novel, is to attest, first of all, that Latin America lacks a language and, consequently, that it should create one. To do this Borges shuffles the genres, rescues all traditions, eliminates the bad habits, and creates a new order of rigorousness on which irony, humor, and play can be based,

yes, but also a profound revolution which equates freedom and imagination and with them a new Latin-American language which, purely by contrast, reveals the lie, the submission, and the falseness of what traditionally passed as "language" among us. Borges's prose lacks, as we know, a critical intent. But the transition from writings of denunciation to a critical synthesis of society and of imagination would not have been possible, without this central, *constitutive* fact of Borgian prose.[6]

These observations are incontrovertible, but the differences noted by Fuentes tend to reinforce, in the end, the notion of the extraneous character and insularity of this prose. In Borges's writings there is a clear and persistent criticism of the indistinct or indulgent use of literary language, and a satire—as in the chronicles of Bustos Domecq—of certain stylistic standards, but the mechanisms that produce this writing confirm, in fact, an operative tradition that is characteristic of the Spanish-American text. In this sense the novelty of Borges's prose is not its negation of previous Spanish-American languages but, on the contrary, its privileged manifestation of these languages.

᛫ Let us look, for instance, at the interaction of various genres. At least since Inca Garcilaso de la Vega's *Royal Commentaries of the Incas*, Spanish-American writing has been constituted through the polyvalence of its formalization. Beginning with that text, Spanish-American writing has reflected the following characteristics: it dramatizes its manifestation in a textual space based on history understood as politics (the Incan utopia as the realized projection of the Neoplatonic order); it is formalized through a critical sum of texts (chronicles that are refuted or inserted as a probatory intertext); it is self-referring as a way of producing itself (the narrative that unfolds, splits, and is rechanneled); it shares frontiers with novelistic and philosophical treatises and with criticism; and, finally, it reveals the web of history and fiction in a context that generates the cultural discourse of a Spanish America whose first existence is as a textual drama.

These traits deconstruct the orthodoxy and verisimilitude prescribed by classical writing and produce, instead, a writing based on a virtual model, one which postulates a meaning that is to be resolved in the new order of its formal heterodoxy. These traits of Spanish-American writing allude to the productive forms of imagining and knowing reality that have been derived from our own historical and social experience. While it is true that these forms (the intertextual conjunction, the self-generation of writing, the montage of different cultural levels, the plurivalence of genres) are, in the end, universal, it is no less true that in a typology of discourse they would define a Latin-American heterodoxy, just as an "archaeology" of language would uncover the recurrence of a decodification that has dialectically reacted to its models in a hegemonic culture and enacted its own code, the discourse from which we, although within western culture, are distinct. As in the writings of Inca Garcilaso, in the works of Martí, Rubén Darío, and Vallejo (and in writing movements such as the chronicles of the Indies, the Spanish-American baroque, Modernism, and our avant-garde movements) we can also recognize the traces and mechanisms of this convergence of genres in a recodified textual space and the departures, incorporations, and answers that constitute this distinct Spanish-American writing.

As Fuentes has observed, Borges's writings are nurtured by various traditions, but these same traditions are found throughout multiple levels of Spanish-American writing. Although ours is a tradition of discontinuity, as Octavio Paz has noted, it is also an incorporating tradition, not simply because it needs to fill an empty cultural space, which would force us into successive dependencies, but because the mechanisms of Spanish-American writing imply an expansive dynamics—as reflected by the work of José Lezama Lima—that does not act by mere accumulation but by displacement and formalization, as in Borges's own work. In Borges this mechanism is constitutive; different traditions converge not as passive repertoires but as a restructuring of the transitive subjects of cultural discourse and of the formalized narrative, relieved of their original cultural density, in the web and space of a debate. Since Borges, and since Paz and Lezama, our reading of tradition—our reading of Garcilaso, Martí, or Darío—reveals the operative dynamics of this Spanish-American writing, its historical process, and its cultural horizon.

The mechanisms of textual formalization in Borgian writing act by deconstructing the repertoires of culture. Because of this, an enumeration of his cultural references would only give us the sum of his sources, in other words, the indeterminate space in his works. On the other hand, the mechanisms that act on these sources inform us of the very productivity of his writing. We should not lose sight of the fact that the analogy of the library and the universe, the equating of one book to all books, and the many other figures and ideas characteristic of Borges are incorporated in a process of textualization that transforms them into a formal and speculative repertoire removed from the totalizing meaning of its cultural origins. The probatory and teleological condition of culture is decodified by a fictional space sustained by critical speculation, although in the case of Borges we are dealing with several cultures located in the same flat space of his textual conversion. This differential decodification, which fractures the grammar of culture and introduces an element of discontinuity to it, also acts through parodical reduction, analogical induction, and through paradoxes and equivalencies based on a radical inquiry into the imaginary nature of knowledge itself. This process transforms into literature the repertoires of culture, fictionalizing its need for truth and meaning. In the end, this radicalism recodifies the systems of meaning that sustain the mediations and disciples of culture, interjecting into them the critical activity of fiction. It does so by using the repertoires of idealism and pantheism, displacing them from their ideological corpus (as so many other instruments of a logical operation of "reduction to absurdity") and stripping them of their referents and certainty. This playful and lucid activity uses the methods, models, and analytical schemes advanced by those systems of thought to transmute into fictional writing their notion of faith or truth.

Although these mechanisms are characteristic of our notion of writing, the radicalism of the Borgian inquiry, which culminates in autonomous images, in texts that are unique, universalizes this practice. But even in this expanded, radical writing we can observe the action of these mechanisms. His essay entitled "New Refutation of Time,"[7] for example, is not only a speculation on the mystical experience of nontemporality and an analysis of the textual tradition of this theme, of the philosophical and literary repertoire that serves as its reference, but is also a text in which Borgian writing takes its deconstructing passion to its ultimate consequences.

The radical intent of this essay is also paradoxical. The negation of the spirit and of matter, the negation of space, leads to the negation of time. This induction is speculative, but also ironic. Its argumentation evokes the intellectual conjectures of the baroque. But Borges goes beyond this to a totalizing postulation of the imaginary. He states: "If the reasons I have indicated are valid, then matter, the ego, the external world, universal history, our lives also belong to that nebulous orb of imaginary objects";[8] in others words, to this orb belong the subjects par excellence of culture, those that sustain and are the foundation of the repertoires of knowledge and consciousness. But more than a postulation, more than another philosophy, Borges's conclusion—reproduced by the narrative in its negation of the "I," in the notion of historical recurrences, in the anachronisms and interference of time, in the duplications of space, in the illusion of dreams—exposes the reductive practice of his writing. As a result of this decodification, reality is perceived as cultural. But this writing also produces a reversal of the correlations established by language, which culture has fixed as the site of knowledge. Thus, the imagination transcends culture, and literature becomes tantamount to the pure consciousness of the world, in other words, to a consciousness free from postulations and demands. Human nature is, perhaps, laconically tragic, but its cultural elaboration appears to be imaginary; meaning is to be found in fiction, that is, in the power through which fiction occasionally mediates an experience transcending us—be it mystical, esthetic, or ethical, words that, in turn, are equivalent—and provides systems that parallel the world.[9]

In this realm of codifications, individual experience cannot overcome the discord or aimless course of a destiny, but in history or in culture—and perhaps in literature—this destiny sometimes attains the glimpse of a meaning that, if not total, is at least sufficient for a stoical recognition of the absence of final explanations. Located between imagination and skepticism, the presence of this writing implies the dilemmas and enigmas of its unanswerable inquiry. Hence the last lines of "New Refutation of Time" ("The world, alas, is real; I, alas, am Borges") not only confront the speculations and promises of the imaginary with the skepticism of our human destiny, but also allude, in their return to the elementary names—time, the river, fire, the "I," which are equivalent to the other names of the mystical experience described—to a first day of language on a first day of the world, only in this case their critical derivation implies as well the last day of culture, a world without explanations.[10]

Again we are left only with words and with their critical dynamics in the fiction of writing. After the "refutation" of time—at the end of the categories of culture—time returns through nominative speech, but this speech is no longer Adamic or apocalyptic, as it is in Neruda and Vallejo, sensorial as in Darío, or constitutive of consciousness, as in Octavio Paz. It is a reductive speech, the voice of utopia at the end of all utopias, that is, the imagination that manifests its constructive intelligence in the realm of a culture whose reason can only be imaginary. Thus Borges carries to its ultimate consequences the cultural deconstruction that animates Spanish-American writing, revealing in it a polarization that produces the imaginary. Our culture has traditionally constructed a response that universalizes imagination as an analytical activity and as a transcodifying practice, but in Borges this response finds its radical, critical limit at the point where Western culture dissolves and where the language that expresses us returns with the lucidity of its questioning adventure and creative power.

It has been said, and this is one way of expressing it, that Borges could only be Spanish-American. In fact, the radicalism of his writings is no less heterodox than that of Joyce, an Irishman, or Kafka, a Czechoslovakian Jew, and perhaps Pound. Borges himself has referred to the role of Irish writers in English literature and history and to the parallel attitude that this vindicates for our writers. He has said in this regard: "I believe that Argentines and South Americans in general, are in a similar situation; we can draw on European themes, we can deal with them free from superstitions, with an irreverence which can have, and already has had, fortunate consequences."[11] This "irreverence" is central to our mechanisms of incorporation and disjunction; it implies the recodifying process and the dynamics of a dissolving and differentiating writing. It is revealing, therefore, that in their readings of Borges, French and American critics have also expressed their surprise at the cultural heterodoxy it promotes.[12] Borges's writings create this impression because, in spite of their obvious modernity, they do not acknowledge an organic history behind their cultural museum. Instead, they act on the cultural landscape as though it were a field generated by groups of images, plots, and ideas; in other words, they act in a preeminently textual space. Hence these works do not imply for European readers a rediscovery of their literary sources but, on the contrary, the free, sometimes anachronic, sometimes extravagant use of them. Perhaps the ironic literary modesty of Borges (who playfully concedes to the English the expressiveness of English, to the French the effectiveness of French, and to the Italians, who are ignorant of it, the nonexistence of Argentine literature) is not unintentional, since his relationship with the central cultures that praise his work is, to a great extent, a relationship based on a gloss and parody of them, on the mystifying, ludic, and critical processes of a heterodox decodification. When Nabokov, whose novels are also a criticism of signification based on the brilliant predominance of argumentation as a formal adventure, observed that Borges's literature is similar to a doorway behind which nothing is to be found, he erred in not following his intuition. Behind that doorway is another doorway, in other words, a labyrinth of forms that deconstructs the traditional site assigned by cultures to literature.

This writing transforms the signifieds of the cultures it encompasses into signifiers of the new cultural sign in which it is embodied. Rather than being the fullest sense of an ideology, the notions of time and infinity, of the book and the universe, and of pantheism and idealism are formal instances of speculation in a specular order, because they are produced in a sequence that simultaneously promotes and dissolves them as fantastic elaborations of a no less imaginary truth. These are notions that, like Tlön, emerge for the sake of meaning, construct their analogy of the world, and then dissolve as ultimate illusion, because the Borgian utopia—the self-sufficient space of the imaginary—generates its own antiutopia, the evidence of the illusory, the agnostic end that reveals the fiction of the labyrinth it has constructed. A postulation recognizes its contradiction, and through these tensions culture becomes a new signified. In this way a new sign emerges: the critical meaning of the imaginary. Writing retraces the path and begins again in its constructive practice, liberating its own space, realizing itself in its questioning dynamics.

Therefore, even though Borges's venture brings to mind other, no less radical ones—we could go all the way back to *Don Quixote*, but perhaps the most important are the modern efforts of Joyce and Pound—his is clearly distinguished by a dynamics internalized in the Spanish-American text. Beyond the mechanics of the text, and through its analytical reduction, this writing rejects the illusion of the narrative by revealing the mechanisms of its processes. Borgian writing thus extends the intertextual processes that were already present in Garcilaso, the heterodox incorporations verbalized by Darío, the mythopoetical reductions of José María Eguren, and the polar expansions explored by Huidobro. A deconstructing venture similar to that of Borges can be found in the break with the nominal referent that characterizes the writing of Vallejo, whose poetry questions the statute of language in order to generate its "materiality," its modern nature as an impugning consciousness. Similar efforts can be detected in *Pedro Páramo*, in which the religious culture is deconstructed from its natural order; *One Hundred Years of Solitude*, in which history is recodified by fiction; and especially in *Hopscotch*, in which the elements of signification and the very meaning of culture are deconstructed through a deliberative inquiry. In the case of *Hopscotch*, the meaning proposed by culture is not resolved in speculative forms, as in Borges, but is examined through the exhausted or partial alternatives that the "Spanish-American experience" questions from the perspective of its search for a language capable of reestablishing a new liberating meaning. Thus, in the proliferation of culture, a Spanish-American consciousness is shaped as a questioning and potentializing discourse. Through its new openings and disjunctions this writing probably answers—and corrects—the Borgian operations and dissolutions.[13]

James E. Irby's excellent analysis has demonstrated the continuity of the utopian idea in Borges's writings.[14] The utopian impulse is, in fact, another example of the radical constructs of these works. The library that is the universe and its infinitude, the sects and organizations that reshape men's lives, the intellectual adventures that forge coherent and total versions, as well as the moments of insight that triumph over the successive nature of language allude to the dynamics and forms of utopia. Because of its materials, this utopia is cultural, but its broader space is a first day of imagination.

In "The Analytical Language of John Wilkins"[15] we find the source of this utopian activity: the recodification of language itself as the alternative for another referential order capable of transcending the arbitrariness of the sign and of reformulating signification. The illustration of this argument, its manifestation and its parody, is found in the double universe of Tlön.

Michel Foucault's observations on Borges expand on this central aspect of Borgian writing. *Les mots et les choses*, he tells us, comes from one of Borges's phrases in "The Analytic Language of John Wilkins." Quoting "an alleged Chinese encyclopedia," Borges writes that

> animals are divided into (a) those that belong to the Emperor, (b) embalmed ones, (c) those that are trained, (d) suckling pigs, (e) mermaids, (f) fabulous ones, (g) stray dogs, (h) those that are included in this classification, (i) those that tremble as if they were mad, (j) innumerable ones, (k) those drawn with a very fine camel's hair brush, (l) others, (m) those that have just broken a flower vase, (n) those that resemble flies from a distance.[16]

Foucault's commentary is the following:

> That passage from Borges kept me laughing a long time, though not without a certain uneasiness that I found hard to shake off. Perhaps because there arose in its wake the suspicion that there is a worse kind of disorder than that of the *incongruous*, the linking together of things that are inappropriate; I mean the disorder in which fragments of a large number of possible orders glitter separately in the dimension, without law or geometry, of the heteroclite; and that word should be taken in its most literal, etymological sense; in such a state, things are "laid," "placed," "arranged" in sites so very different from one another that it is impossible to find a place of residence for them, to define a *common locus* beneath them all. *Utopias* afford consolation: although they have no real locality there is nevertheless a fantastic, untroubled region in which they are able to unfold; they open up cities with vast avenues, superbly planted gardens, countries where life is easy, even though the road to them is chimerical. Heterotopias are disturbing, probably because they

secretly undermine language, because they make it impossible to name this *and* that, because they shatter or tangle common names, because they destroy "syntax" in advance, and not only the syntax which causes words and things (next to and also opposite one another) to "hold together." This is why utopias permit fables and discourse: the fundamental dimension of the fabula; heterotopias (such as those to be found so often in Borges) desiccate speech, stop words in their tracks, contest the very possibility of grammar at its source; they dissolve our myths and sterilize the lyricism of our sentences.[17]

He later adds:

Yet our text from Borges proceeds in another direction; the mythical homeland Borges assigns to that distortion of classification that prevents us from applying it, to that picture that lacks all spatial coherence, is a precise region whose name alone constitutes for the West a vast reservoir of utopias. In our dream-world, is not China precisely this privileged *site* of *space*?[18]

We must remember first of all that Borges himself says that this classification is "arbitrary." In his own words, "there is no classification of the universe that is not arbitrary and conjectural. The reason is very simple: we do not know what the universe is." And he adds: "But the impossibility of penetrating the divine scheme of the universe cannot dissuade us from outlining human schemes, even though we are aware that they are provisional."[19] His purpose in recording these "hopes and utopias" of language is characteristic of his central speculation surrounding the original names, a simultaneous language, and a utopian writing previous to culture. "Theoretically, a language in which the name of each being would indicate all the details of its destiny, past and future, is not inconceivable," he has written.[20]

For Borges, arbitrariness is inherent in culture. This is also the starting point for Foucault's complex intuition, but the consequences that Borges extracts from this idea follow a different direction. In Borgian writing the "heteroclite" does not belong to the order of significations but to that of formalizations. Because it is arbitrary, meaning becomes conjectural and is reduced to an unusual or ironic model simply by the weight of its precision. Hence the heteroclite forms part of an analytical sequence that includes it—like John Wilkins's utopian language—and creates an equivalence between the classifications of the animals, the ordering of a library, and Wilkins's conjecture. The "common locus" sought by Foucault, which also implies meaning, is not found in these classifications because they function as metaphors "textualized" by the Borgian narrative, which is where these classifications disclose their analogies through their own mechanisms. It is at this point that we find in operation the Borgian parody of culture. A reconstruction of its arbitrary mechanisms returns us to the point of departure, to the name, no less utopian, that is equivalent to all names. In the area of culture this Borgian practice plays the dual role of displacing from culture its stable meaning and recovering from it its forms and models. It moves, therefore, toward the construction of a no less dramatized origin of language and its primordial functions, which are analogical and revealing.

This brings us to the central point of Foucault's analysis, to his criticism of utopias and to the distinction he makes between utopias and heterotopias. Contrary to what he states, utopias are not comforting; instead, they introduce a critical and dissolving activity within the order of the signification that language projects. They do not imply an improbable place and time but a virtual language, one that reformulates the norms and subverts the codes. Their cities are a map that questions our own, and their gardens and provinces reshape the natural and cultural order. In this regard we can think of Fourier and of the recurring utopian idea in Borges, as well as of the utopian schemes that are characteristic of our culture.

This is why utopias are, par excellence, heterotopias. Their grammar is a scandal of intelligence because it implies the design of contradiction, the radicalism that reunites words and things in the deconstruction of culture and history, opening the space of other constructions that question us. Finally, the "mythical homeland" to which Foucault consigns the Borgian text, China as a "privileged site," is nothing but a purely textual place, a conjectural encyclopedia displaced from its original purpose by a typical Spanish-American mechanism. This fact does not question Foucault's intuition or his remarkable purpose—his rich reconstruction of the archaeology of knowledge within diverse cultural orders—but simply places the Borgian mechanisms within the "archaeology" of Spanish-American discourse.

Both Julio Cortázar and Carlos Fuentes have referred to the absence of a critical, historical, and social dimension in Borges's work, and Mario Benedetti has reflected on the "unique case of Borges, a writer who is exceptionally gifted in terms of intellectual speculation but definitely ill equipped when it comes to capturing reality."[21] However, the production of his writing reveals mechanisms that are central to the elaboration of our cultural realities. There is clearly another area, more obvious, thematic, and declarative, in which Jorge Luis Borges, the intellectual and the citizen, pays tribute to the ideology of a specific subculture of Buenos Aires, the caricature of which emerges in the antidemocratic sallies of a paradoxically loquacious Borges. It is also likely that, in the end, his work dissolves its own recodifying dynamics in a no-man's land it has chosen for itself. This seems to be the suggestion of his last utopia, "Utopia of a Tired Man,"[22] in which the only perfection is that of oblivion and death. Nevertheless, the complexity of his work reveals us in the universalized sphere of our own cultural production and enables us to recover the sense of the imagination and critical practice that shape and constitute us.

Notes

1. Néstor Ibarra, "Jorge Luis Borges," *Lettres Françaises* 4, no. 14 (Buenos Aires, 1944): 9.

2. María Luisa Bastos illustrates the Argentine response to Borges's work in her book *Borges ante la crítica argentina, 1923–1960* (Buenos Aires: Ediciones Hispamérica, 1974). Emir Rodríguez Monegal has written a book on the most polemical phase of this debate: *El juicio de los parricidas: La nueva generación argentina y sus maestros* (Buenos Aires: Ed. Decaulión, 1956).

3. Humberto M. Rasi, "The Final Creole: Borges' View of Argentine History," *TriQuarterly* 25 (Fall 1972): 149.

4. Emir Rodríguez Monegal, *Narradores de esta América* (Montevideo: Alfa, 1962), p. 20.

5. Carlos Fuentes, *La nueva novela hispanoamericana* (Mexico City: Joaquín Mortiz, 1969), p. 26.

6. Ibid.

7. Jorge Luis Borges, *Other Inquisitions: 1937–1952*, translated by Ruth L. C. Simms (Austin: University of Texas Press, 1964), pp. 171–187.

8. Ibid., p. 185.

9. In a penetrating reading of Borges's writings, Walter Mignolo and Jorge Aguilar Mora have pointed out that writing "is not a representation of the world but a world in itself (as textual practice) and cannot but produce itself in the constant movement of decodification (reading) and recodification (writing)," ("Borges, el libro y la escritura," *Caravelle*, no. 17 [Toulouse, 1971]: 187–194).

10. Carter Wheelock arrives at the following conclusion with regard to the implicit debate between agnosticism and literary perception in Borges:

What we find in Borges—what fills his essays and is implicit, often patent in his fiction—is the esthetic equivalent and symbol of his philosophical position. As is well known, his philosophy consists largely in an agnostic affirmation that truth, although it may be known, is not recognizable. . . . Borges does not deny that literature should express truth; he denies that truth is available through expression. So he rejects expression in favor of suggestion, which he calls allusion.

"The Committed Side of Borges," *Modern Fiction Studies* 19, no. 3: 373–379.

11. Jorge Luis Borges, *Discusión* (Buenos Aires: Emecé, 1957), p. 161.

12. Jaime Alazraki has compiled the principal French and American critical readings of Borges in a book titled *Jorge Luis Borges* (Madrid: Taurus, Serie el escritor y la crítica, 1976).

13. Julio Cortázar has referred in the following terms to the lesson provided by Borges:

> At that time in Argentina we were subjected to a number of writers who still used the heavy and involved style of Spanish and French Romanticism. Suddenly there appeared a young man, a young Argentine who wrote, I would say, in a lapidary style, as though each word was a faceted and cut crystal, carefully thought out, before it was included in a phrase, as one who sets a very complicated jewel with many parts. This, which was above all a formal lesson, a lesson in the economy, precision, and rigor of means, has been, I think, the greatest lesson that Borges has given me. Borges taught me to eliminate all the flowery phrases, the repetitions, ellipses, useless exclamation marks, and the habit which is still found in much bad literature and which consists of saying in one page what can be said in one line.

("Julio Cortázar en la Universidad Central de Venezuela," *Escritura*, no. 1 [Caracas, January–June, 1976]: 162).

14. James E. Irby, "Borges and the Idea of Utopia," *Books Abroad* 45, no. 3 (Oklahoma, 1971): 411–419.

15. Jorge Luis Borges, *Other Inquisitions*, pp. 101–105.

16. Ibid., p. 103.

17. Michel Foucault, *The Order of Things: An Archaeology of the Human Sciences* (New York: Pantheon Books, 1970), pp. xvii–xix.

18. Ibid., p. xix.

19. Jorge Luis Borges, *Other Inquisitions*, p. 104.

20. Ibid.

21. Mario Benedetti, "Dos testimonios sobre Borges," in *Letras del continente mestizo*, 2d ed. (Montevideo: Arca, 1967), p. 73.

22. Jorge Luis Borges, *The Book of Sand*, translated by Norman Thomas di Giovanni (New York: E. P. Dutton, 1977), pp. 89–96.

4. *Pedro Páramo*

The first line of this novel by Juan Rulfo* establishes its filiation: "I came to Comala because I was told that my father, a certain Pedro Páramo, was living here." The search for the father identifies, first of all, the space of the journey: the hero sets out to face an unknown world as well as his own masks. This search, therefore, implies self-contemplation, that is, the formulas of the monologue; before going in search of Ulysses, Telemachus hears the voice of a god urging him to undertake the journey. For the Greeks this voice was symbolically an image of inner reflection. The irruption of self-awareness and the exhortation to action required the mask of a god because this was a ritual act. In Joyce's *Ulysses*, Stephen Dedalus also carries on an incessant monologue, despite the parody and parable of this ancient theme in that novel. The encounters on the journey—the journey of the son in search of his father and of the father in search of his family—end, in the realm of a myth, in a mutual return: Ulysses disguises himself when he arrives at his house, at the center of his own self, where he is awaited by Penelope, his wife in history, his own soul in the myth. The house is thus the sacred territory; but in the connotations of this myth the house is also the individual, which is why it must be conquered. In the desacralized time of the modern twenty-four hour routine portrayed by Joyce, Bloom enters his house and also finds his wife, piously vulgar, an allegory of the earth in which man will perhaps attempt his resurrection.

The Greek tradition does not allude to the notion of a lost paradise, as the Judeo-Western tradition does. The loss of paradise reunites the fathers, Adam and Jehovah, and the Christian tradition retains this primordial image, based on which the son is held to be guilty of the sins of his father. Guilt is extended in the son through

*Juan Rulfo, *Pedro Páramo*, translated by Lysander Kemp (New York: Grove Press, 1959). Originally published in 1955.

the very act of his birth, through the "original sin." This metaphysical separation also arouses a sense of guilt rooted in the intuition of an alienated life. Man is guilty of having been born, says Segismundo, another metaphysical searcher for a father linked with the State and its justification.

The search for the father is thus a metaphor and a hyperbole that conjugated several possibilities of reality. Its scheme evokes myth; its steps imply a rite: seeking the father, the hero searches and finds —or loses—his place in that reality.

In Rulfo's novel, Juan Preciado searches for his father, whom he does not know, in a village, Comala, about which he also knows very little. Abundio, the mule driver whom Juan Preciado meets at the start of the novel and who also proves to be Pedro Páramo's son, leads him to Comala. Juan Preciado finds the village deserted and discovers that Pedro Páramo is dead. In a monologue addressed to his mother he says, "You made a mistake, you didn't give me the right directions. You told me where this was and that was, and here I am in a dead village, looking for somebody who doesn't even exist." In Comala he finds Eduviges Dyada, who gives him lodging. Abundio continues his journey, but Juan Preciado stays because, in his words, "that's what I came to do."

Juan Preciado's search for his father also represents the discovery of a place that is his father's extension, his shadow, the equivalent also of the ancient paradise that is being sought. Desperate, Juan Preciado will later want to flee, to find a road out of Comala, but this road is as unknown to him as the one that brought him there. It is too late. In this novel the conquest of the patriarchal paradise is also the loss of that paradise; the son will die, merging with the place that takes his life and also his death, because here the world is another world. This novel reverses the metaphor of the search. The father does not exist; death, and even the world, do not exist. Juan Preciado wanders aimlessly among the voices and dies overcome by the terror of that unreality.

Giving the impression of being somehow more real than mere ghosts or apparitions, the voices and visions of this novel are presences. Eduviges Dyada reveals that Abundio died many years ago, but another shadow discloses that Eduviges has also been dead for years. The characters are dead people summoned by the presence of Juan Preciado, and they speak in another region made of life and death. None of them talk about their death or about the region of the dead while Juan Preciado appears to be alive. It is only after he relates his own death and is buried next to another corpse that this region is mentioned. *Pedro Páramo* is not a realistic novel, but neither is it a fantastic novel. The other world it presents, based solely on its own presence, has a clear-cut coherence in its very ambiguity. Unlike other novels set in similar regions—some German Romantic novels, for instance—the purpose of this novel in introducing the world of the dead is not to provoke terror, although this terror is insinuated. Rulfo presents his dead characters from close up; we know they are dead even when they speak or act.

But why is paradise populated by the dead in this novel? By having reversed the theme of searching for the father and then discovering that the father has died, paradise also disappears and is dealt with from the perspective of its reversal. And the other side of paradise is, of course, hell. Like Telemachus, Juan Preciado searches for his father, and like Moses, he seeks the promised land, but he discovers that he has descended into hell, the hell of paradise, in other words, the paradise of this earth.

Comala is another hell because the father died in this village and because he killed it while he was still alive. Pedro Páramo destroyed the village through the violence he exerted as its landowner. The blind power he accumulated brought physical and moral destruction to it and its submissive inhabitants. The dead in this hell are condemned to remain there forever. Here the dead prolong the suffering of their lives, their innocence, or their guilt. But theirs is not a religious suffering. The dead of Comala do not regret that they are not in some Christian heaven, they regret their own lives. Hell is, therefore, life itself, a life that determines the other side, death. Life is thus judged and made present from the side of death. A dark rebelliousness suggests the taut coherence of this world based on the popular conception of Catholic ideology.

Time and space are linked in this hell. When Juan Preciado finds Damiana Cisneros, she tells him:

> "I hear the dogs howling and I let them howl, because I know there aren't any dogs here any more. And on windy days you can hear the wind shaking the leaves, but you already know there aren't any trees. There must have been trees here once, or where would the leaves have come from?"

This coherence is the logic that joins the past world and the present; but Damiana Cisneros, like the leaves, is also dead. Hence this novel sustains its unusual logic on the presence, on the instant of appearing and disappearing, of its characters. Interestingly, this presence is almost never revealed through description. We know almost nothing about Abundio, and about a woman whom Juan Preciado sees crossing the street we are told only that she was "wrapped up in a rebozo" and that "her voice was a living human voice . . . she had teeth in her mouth, and a tongue that moved when she talked, and eyes like the eyes of everybody else on earth." This succinct description almost redundantly underscores the presence of this woman. The narrator tells us the following about Eduviges Dyada, another character:

> I listened, but I also looked at her closely. I thought she must have suffered a lot in her life. Her face was so pale, you would think there wasn't any blood in her body, and her hands were all wrinkled and withered up. You couldn't see her eyes. She had on an old white dress with a lot of lace, and a medal of the Virgin on a piece of twine, with the words *Refuge of Sinners*.

The narrator's description of Eduviges is the most detailed description given. On the other hand, we are told nothing about Damiana Cisneros. This suggests that the presence of the characters is supported almost entirely by the language, by the enunciation. The presence of Damiana Cisneros is typical, it is based solely on dialogue. When Juan Preciado asks her if she is dead or alive, she disappears; "Suddenly I found myself alone in those empty streets," he says.

On the other hand, the representation of space is constant and precise. The increasing heat, the incessant rain, and the arid desolation bring out the heavy, merciless oppression of this space. When seen from the perspective of death, the dark rebelliousness of life is somehow related with the victorious terror of black space, an infernal space that from the side of death seizes the time of the living.

When Juan Preciado finds Eduviges Dyada, she tells him: "But everything's different now, with the village so poor, and nobody ever comes here." The presence of Juan Preciado summons and slowly reveals the presence of this world, while he himself is thrust into and abandoned in this hell. At one point Juan Preciado looks for a way out:

> Empty wagons, shattering the silence of the streets. Vanishing down the dark roads of the night. And the shadows. And the echo of the shadows.
> I thought of going back. I knew that up there was the gap I had come through, like an open wound in the blackness of the mountains.

Here even the shadows are a mirage, another ghost, and we sense a hidden terror. But the return road is now just a trail defined as "an open wound," and the gap in the mountains is "up there." Hell, then, is down here, and the character is trapped.

The scene that follows this passage is one of the most ambiguous and intense of the novel. The incident concerns Juan Preciado's encounter with a couple who invite him into their house.

> I went in. It was a house with half of the roof fallen in, roof-tiles scattered over the floor, the roof on the floor. And in the other half a man and a woman.
> "Are you dead?" I asked them.
> The woman laughed. The man looked at me solemnly.
> "He's drunk," he said.
> "No, he's just frightened," the woman said.
> There was an oil lamp, a crude bed, and a chair with the woman's clothes on it. Because she was as naked as when God sent her into the world. So was he.

This couple are husband and wife, but they are also brother and sister. It is difficult not to associate them with the first couple condemned to lament their guilt in hell. Adam and Eve live at the center of this hell. Juan asks the woman:

> "How do you leave here?"
> "To go where?"
> "Anywhere."
> "There's lots of roads. One of them goes to Contla, and another comes in from there. Then there's another one that goes straight over the sierra. The one you can see from here . . ."
> —and she pointed out of the gap in the tiles where the roof was broken—"I don't know where it goes. That one over there goes to the Media Luna. And there's still another, that goes farther than any of them."
> "Perhaps that's the one I came in on."

From among these roads there is one, which the woman points to through the gap in the roof, that is higher than the rest, and another that runs through the land and leads to Comala. Although referring perhaps more directly to an "in" and "out" than to an "up" and "down," this image of the roads again suggests the space of hell. The woman relates her sin:

> "There isn't one of us living here who's in the grace of God. We can't even raise our eyes without feeling them burn with shame. And shame doesn't cure anything. At least that's what the bishop said when he came by here a while back for the confirmations. I went up to him and confessed everything.
> 'That can't be pardoned,' he said.
> 'I'm filled with shame.'

'That isn't the remedy.'
'Marry us!'
'Leave him!'
"I wanted to tell him that life had brought us together, had captured us and tied us to each other. We were so alone here that we were the only ones. And the village had to be populated somehow. Perhaps when he came back we'd have someone for him to confirm.
'Leave him. That's the only thing you can do.'
'But how will we live?'
'Like human beings.'"

This justification also brings to mind the first couple, just as the bishop's final condemnatory words evoke the biblical sentence of expulsion.

Juan later discovers that this woman is also a corpse, and he dies horror-stricken: "I remember seeing something like a cloud of foam, and wishing myself in the foam, and losing myself in the cloud. That was the last thing I saw." Thus, caught in the center of hell, along with the first condemned couple, Juan Preciado is absorbed by this hell, where several reversals are conjugated. After his death, Juan Preciado becomes aware of the reversal of his journey. "They said that Pedro Páramo was my father, and I came to look for him. That was the illusion that brought me here," he says. And he adds: "My mother . . . lived the happiest part of her life here in this village, but she couldn't come back here to die. That's why she sent me in her place." The void left by the search for the father is redoubled in this sequence. Dorotea, who is buried with Juan, tells him that she once had two dreams. In the first one she dreamed she had a son, but in the second dream she realized this had never been true. All her life she had searched for a son whom she had seen only in her dreams. She tells Juan: "They buried me in your grave, and I fit very well into the hollow of your arms. Only it occurs to me that I ought to be embracing you, not the other way around." Dorotea's and Juan Preciado's lives are joined in death because, in an erratic but analogical way, their searches cruelly coincide. This tomb is shared by a son who searches for his father and by a mother who searches for her son. The dialogue between Juan and Dorotea evokes the story of Pedro Páramo's wife, Susana San Juan, who is also obsessively linked to her father's death. From here on the world of the dead disappears in the novel because Juan Preciado, the living person who convoked it, is also dead. The story of Pedro Páramo, a reconstruction and a total presence from the side of death, is the prior story of hell. The death of the son is the axis between an "after" (which in the novel is a "before"—the arrival of the son) and a "before" (which in the novel is an "after"—the story of Pedro Páramo); the double-sided operation of the text that convokes, from its temporal spectrum, the time of the reader.

The time of Pedro Páramo's story, which was a flashback in the fragmentary construction of the novel while Juan Preciado was alive, returns as a present time. Hence when the son disappears in this novel the present ceases to exist or becomes something else, a past made present by the narrative: the voice of death. The reunion of father and son, then, occurs in death, because death transforms the past into a present time.

"For me, Juan Preciado, Heaven is right here where I am," Dorotea says, signifying the accounts of her "bad" dream (she thought she had a son) and her "good" dream (she realized she did not have him), accounts which are joined in the accusing consciousness of death. Dorotea's words also indicate the paradoxical unity of paradise and hell, or of the reversed paradise that Comala is. It is not possible to refer to the divine without referring to its shadow, the demonic, and vice versa. The divine aspect of this landscape is, precisely, a void, a world avoided as a way of rejection, a world covered by the complex web of innocence and guilt, of suffering and temporality. From the perspective of hell, death is not a final passing, because here its solitude is also another form of life. "And your soul? Where do you think it's gone?" Juan asks. And Dorotea answers, "It must be wandering around up there on earth, like all those others, looking for people to pray for it. I think it hates me for the bad things I did, but that doesn't worry me anymore. I'm rid of all the pain it used to give me."

This parable of death is extended to a point where death becomes so impregnated with life that the body, which has been abandoned in its solitude, does not even need a soul. The soul has left because the body refuses to feel remorse. In this novel death is perceived as a total protest, as a will subversively fixed in the life of a body that does not want to be lost, that lingers on even at the expense of the soul.

Pedro (rock) Páramo (wasteland) also symbolizes the death and damage caused by power. The exercise of power, which is the first level of the story, is the starting point from which this novel penetrates and destroys other levels of the reality it wants to question. As an absolute father, Pedro Páramo decides to "fold his arm" and watch Comala die. His death links the end of this novel with its beginning by what is also something of a parable: Pedro Páramo is assassinated by Abundio, the mule driver who leads Juan Preciado to Comala. The account of this assassination is very elusive—Abundio's wife has died and in a state of drunken anger he approaches Pedro Páramo asking for help to bury her—because the author does not want to make explicit that Abundio is also Pedro Páramo's son. At the story level this is not a symbolic patricide, but perhaps it is symbolic at the level of the dark relationships that the novel probes within the theme of the search for the father or for the son. It does not seem purely coincidental that Pedro Páramo is killed by one of his own sons. (Miguel Páramo, the only son who bears his father's surname, is killed by his own horse; and the name and the horse bring to mind, in yet another reversal, the story of another Michael, the archangel.) The hand of the son raised against his omnipotent father is the gesture that evokes, or simply confirms, the paradise in that hell.

The word *paradise* is used only once in the novel, in the episode of Pedro Páramo's death. Wounded, Pedro Páramo "could see the paradise trees swaying as they dropped their leaves. 'Everybody chooses the same path. Everybody goes away,'" he says to himself. "His ruined lands stretched out in front of him, empty." And finally: "After a few steps he fell down, pleading within but not speaking a single word. He struck a feeble blow against the ground and then crumbled to pieces as if he were a heap of stones." His death is double. He crumbles like the rock (father) he is, and the village crumbles with him. The "paradise" withers, and the garden is abandoned, as it was abandoned by the first couple.

Octavio Paz has written the following about this novel:

Whereas Malcolm Lowry's theme is the expulsion from Paradise, the theme of Juan Rulfo's novel *Pedro Páramo* is the return to Paradise. Hence the hero is a dead man: it is only after death that we can return to the Eden where we were born. But Rulfo's main character returns to a garden that has burned to a cinder, to a lunar landscape. The theme of return becomes that of an implacable judgment: Juan Preciado's journey home is a new version of the wanderings of a soul in Purgatory. The title is a (unconscious) symbol: Pedro, Peter, the founder, the rock, the origin, the guardian, the keeper of the keys of Paradise, has died. Páramo (the Spanish word for wasteland) is his garden of long ago, now a desert plain, thirst and drought, the parched whispers of shadows and an eternal failure of communication. Our Lord's garden:

Pedro's wasteland. (Octavio Paz, *Alternating Current*, translated
by Helen R. Lane [New York: Viking Press, 1973])

These comments by Paz are brief and incisive. The only objection
might be to the statement that "only after death can we return to the
Eden where we were born." This placing oneself within the Christian myth rather than within the novel, which denies the logic of
that myth precisely by reversing it, suggests that the religious dimension is central to this novel, and, in effect, that dimension is
there, but it is also reversed. On the other hand, maybe the hero
is not dead in the beginning, and it is only after his death that he is
replaced in the novel by his father. In my judgment, the fundamental
aspect of this novel is the death of the father in an infernal space as a
way of questioning the original guilt.

Paradise has become hell here on this earth, and the blame lies not
with the son but with the father and the multiple order he symbolizes. The son lives in the land transformed by the father into a paradise and a hell, and he rebels against this hierarchy, a hierarchy that
the novel itself refuses to uphold, proposing its own representation
and its own exorcism.

It is not arbitrary, therefore, to think that the religious act in this
novel is the assassination of the father, the extension of the search to
confirm his death, the fusion of two times in the son, although this
search and this assassination—two sides of the same act—also impose the dimension of death. At the extreme end of the hyperbole,
Pedro Páramo, the supreme and omnipotent father, is perhaps a fusion of God and the devil, just as Comala is a fusion of heaven and
hell. Perhaps the son wants to destroy both in order to redeem himself in the pursuit of innocence.

5. *Hopscotch*

Hopscotch,* Carlos Fuentes has stated, is to prose in Spanish what *Ulysses* is to prose in English. This comparison is possible because *Hopscotch*, first published in 1963, summarizes the new or current tradition of modernity in the Latin-American novel, a tradition that in the opinion of Octavio Paz is one of renewal. *Hopscotch* starts from the crisis of the novelistic genre as a representational system and from the baroque transgression of its Latin-American axis. Its foundation is another novel, one that begins when this book is closed.

The various readings demanded by *Hopscotch* are a game between the narrators, the characters, and the reader, or more accurately, this work is the repeated beginning of a game rather than its development or conclusion. Cortázar thus prolongs the reading, because this novel questions literature, the reader, and itself. The repeated beginning of the game implies its regeneration. *Hopscotch* is like the fluttering of a verbal phoenix.

At a certain point, the characters disclose that they are also readers of the novel. Through their reading in the texts of Morelli, these characters read themselves:

> "It isn't the first time that he's referred to the erosion of language," Étienne said. "I could mention several places where characters lose confidence in themselves to the degree in which they feel they've been drawn through their thought and speech, and they're afraid the sketch may be deceptive."

In another passage Morelli states that the character he wants for his novel is the reader.

The characters are thus readers and the reader is a character because the narrator wants to identify his searches with ours in an es-

*Julio Cortázar, *Hopscotch*, translated by Gregory Rabassa (New York: Pantheon Books, 1966). Originally published as *Rayuela* (1963).

thetics of defectiveness. Oliveira, addressor and addressee of the writing, constructs (from a first and third person point of view and from an insistent present) a past time in order to reconstruct himself in the fact of writing as reading. In the same way that he reads the world, Oliveira reads himself. But this yearning, this erratic and solitary drama, is an exploration of memory in a present time that gives way to the past and soon forces him to abandon this convocation from the perspective of the "I." He is forced to drop the point of view of the addressor because, groping about in the void that he at the same time wants to populate, he betrays himself in a mirror; under the different masks there is but a single face. To avoid this betrayal of a self-evident and perhaps false image, the addressor becomes the addressee, leaving the ambiguous pretext of the colloquy to the empty "you" personified by La Maga and making himself speak in terms of the image in the mirror, now in the third person.

The obvious verbal impregnation between the paragraphs in which Oliveira is addressor and those in which he is addressee again implies a continuous regeneration of the writing. Oliveira seems to carry on his multiple monologue in this third person, even in the dialogues with his friends of the Club, and La Maga's dialogues are just brief interruptions in Oliveira's verbalism. La Maga's letter to Rocamadour (that little paper boat floating throughout the book) is also sustained by Oliveira's reading, as are Morelli's texts. Likewise, the hyperbolic, loquacious dialogue between Oliveira, Traveler, and Talita is dictated by a sort of raised voice, by a reading aloud, in a broader space that Oliveira himself establishes. All this serves to mask the only narrator of the novel, Oliveira, who writes in the pluridimensional present of the novel after his personal story has ended and begins now as narrative.

Since the reader is also a character, the reading itself will be paradoxical. To start, Cortázar notes that there are "female-readers" and "male-readers." The former are interested in a passive reading, while the latter prefer to make the text through their reading. The former are the traditional readers of the traditional closed novel, while the latter are the new readers, the characters sought by the open novel. The reading of this novel is paradoxical because it imposes at the same time its narrative sequences—it is a novel after all—and the speculations of its literary and existential debates. Fiction is posed as debate, and this debate, in turn, is posed as figure. These levels thus function as signs. In their simultaneity, the ideas, episodes, and figures are transformed into the signs of a character (Oliveira), a spiritual situation (the search for an independent and common unity in which the experience of a narrator becomes the paradigm of the choices of every man), and an age, because through its conflicts and disruptions this novelistic adventure underscores the insertion of language in history.

The steps by which the reader becomes a character of *Hopscotch* are initiatory because the novel is always on its first page; it is constantly beginning again, continuously questioning itself. In this case, to read is to travel, to play at the game of reading, to invent a rite.

The "Table of Instructions" of this reading mechanism invites us "to choose" one of two possibilities: to read the book in a normal fashion, stopping with chapter 56, at the close of which there are three little stars that indicate the end, or to begin with chapter 73 and follow the sequence indicated at the end of each chapter. This second reading sequence imitates the game of hopscotch because in the reading we are jumping from chapter to chapter, from square to square, playing in the gridded figure of the novel. The dash in front of the number at the end of each chapter is obviously a minus sign; the reading is thus also a subtraction.

If we choose the first reading sequence we find that the novel is divided into three parts. The first part, "From the other side," refers to Paris, and the second part, "From this side," is set in Buenos Aires. Here the novel "ends." The third part is entitled "From diverse sides: expendable chapters," and in the "Table of Instructions" Cortázar suggests that the reader can ignore it without feeling remorse. Let us assume that a reader, as a character, decides to consider expendable these "expendable chapters." On the "last" page of his reading this reader will find Oliveira balancing himself on the edge of a high window and looking down into the courtyard of a psychiatric clinic at Traveler and Talita (all three of them work in this asylum, which is their ironic context). The two figures below look at him and talk to him from the hopscotch:

> Talita had stopped in square three without realizing it, and Traveler had one foot in six . . . and there was some meeting after all, even though it might only last just for that terribly sweet instant in which the best thing without any doubt at all would be to lean over just a little bit farther out and let himself go, paff the end.

The last game in Oliveira's search begins and ends in the precarious square formed by the frame of the window of a room in which he has locked himself, declaring what amounts to both a comic and metaphysical war. *Hopscotch*—which acknowledges the labyrinth of the game in order to reunite "heaven" and "earth" as squares of a single figure—is both an innocent and deadly game. Its innocence stems from the possibility of playing the game in a committed manner starting from an intellectual questioning, which is what Oliveira represents, because he is also a typical character who feels he must come to grips with the hell of western contradictions and attempt to resolve them within the contradictions themselves. That is why in this first ending Oliveira sits in the window and acts out his personal drama through the farcical context of his potential suicide, dramatized by his reflective and humorous detachment from his own quests and his paralyzing analysis of them. This window is his square in a game of hopscotch that makes him its victim. For Oliveira, the uniting of heaven and earth, man and woman, La Maga and himself, the other side and this side, truth and appearance, in short, the uniting of our multiple contradictions, is a game that can only be final, a suicide, directly or symbolically.

> The best thing without any doubt at all would be to lean over just a little bit farther out and let himself go, paff the end.

At the level of the narrative, Cortázar's "paff" may be suggesting, in the same farcical vein tapped by Oliveira, the character's suicide or his grandstanding play. Perhaps Oliveira has let himself fall toward the ground, where his double, Traveler, and La Maga's double, Talita, (doubles by contradiction rather than by similarity, in other words, doubles by analogical opposition) stand in their squares trying to calm him. The phrase "paff the end" can suggest this suicide, but it can also suggest that, paff, the novel or the first reading has ended. Cortázar refers to the novel as a "metaphysical slap," as a slap to the reader, of course. Hence this "paff" is also the slap the narrator gives the reader, brother and accomplice in the end, to seal their pact.

The slapped reader has two choices. He can put down the book or take a chance with the third part, the "expendable chapters." In terms of this first reading of the novel, which follows the normal sequence, these chapters are another reading. The novel thus contains one and a half readings. In this third part the reader meets Morelli, who invites him to criticize what he has read, and recovers Oliveira. In these chapters a prior time in Paris is prolonged and a later time in Buenos Aires fades, suggesting another resurrection of Oliveira, who in fact starts the writing from this point.

In the second reading sequence suggested for this novel the reader must contend with more complex levels: the expendable chapters are included in the narration. The first reading is more novelistic, while the second is more critical, but between them they constitute the birth and transfiguration of the novel, its formulation and its sacrifice. *Hopscotch* is a metaphor because it joins two realities in a single figure; it becomes, in fact, a metaphor of itself.

The first chapter of this second reading introduces us to the deconstruction and construction sought by the novel. These operations mutually provoke and recognize each other in the same space. Oliveira is the speaker in the following passage:

> How often I wonder whether this is only writing, in an age in which we run towards deception through infallible equations and conformity machines. But to ask one's self if we will know how to find the other side of habit or if it is better to let one's self be borne along by its happy cybernetics, is that not literature again? Rebellion, conformity, anguish, earthly sustenance, all the dichotomies . . . what a hammock of words, what purse-size dialectics with pajama storms and living-room cataclysms. The very fact that one asks one's self about the possible choice vitiates and muddies up what can be chosen . . . Everything is writing, that is to say, a fable. But what good can we get from the truth that pacifies an honest property owner? Our possible truth must be an *invention*, that is to say, scripture, literature, picture, sculpture, agriculture, pisciculture, all the tures of this world. Values, tures, sainthood, a ture, society, a ture, love, pure ture, beauty, a ture of tures . . . Why surrender to the Great Habit? . . . We burn within our work, fabulous mortal honor, high challenge of the phoenix . . . within, maybe that is the choice, maybe words envelop it the way a napkin does a loaf of bread and maybe the fragrance is inside, the flour puffing up, the yes without the no, or the no without the yes, the day within Mani, without Ormuz or Ariman, once and for all and in peace and enough.

This confession is also the multiple beginning of the novel, in other words, a genuine program. Here language evolves in a debate on thought, art, society and culture in a collage of our time assimilated verbally in such a way that the possibility of choice can begin to shape a character and form a new perception. This is the approach of a chronicle. Whatever the anecdote or the narrative pretext, the narrator follows the same point of view that establishes a cross section in that undifferentiated landscape in relation to which the anecdote is questioned. This is why the narrator speaks of "the principle of indetermination, so important in literature" and why he says about Morelli that "[he] wanted his book to be a crystal ball in which the micro- and macrocosm would come together in an annihilating vision." Indetermination as an esthetics implies the rejection of any prior determination and the free advance of the narration in this macrocosm occupied by a microcosm, and vice versa. This porous and erratic space is also indeterminate because it is not resolved, because it does not require solutions. Hence Oliveira speaks of "that which is defective," of that lack of awareness which is also, in the instances when he does not abuse the landscape of that chaos, another possibility of knowledge.

Returning to the lengthy passage quoted above, we find written beauty being questioned and threatened by the two areas into which the narrator has divided this chaos: "infallible equations" and "conformity machines." Between these two realities, it states, "we run towards deception." The threat to writing is also a threat to the adventure that the character has begun. The deception is encountered in technology and in the established routine of everyday life and its orders, as well as in literature, because of the hoax which is at the bottom of everything discursive. However, to question literature is also to lay bare the third area, the area of chance in which the character places himself in order to confront the simple dualities of our time, the "purse-size dialectics" to which he refers. What remains of all this is the passion of the work, the conflagration in a chosen city, a conflagration invented by language to destroy all dichotomies. Beauty, the ultimate value, requires this critical survey in order to return to it as a possibility. The entire novel is this survey and this possibility.

Cortázar turns time and again to the subject of "the Great Habit," repeatedly satirizing the everyday routine, the established orders, and conformity. This repetition can also be paradoxical. The characters are aware of this reiteration, but this does not stop them from criticizing "futurism" for the umpteenth time or from talking about "form and substance." Could it be that Oliveira is afraid that he himself may derive from one of the established orders, be it called the family, work, or history? His open rebelliousness, a form of his will to search, the scheme of his will to unity, is perhaps related to the liberations sought by Surrealism, but above all it is related to the individual and anguished rebellions of the second postwar period. "I don't like technology any more than you, it's just that I feel the world has changed in the last twenty years. Any guy who's past forty has to realize it," Oliveira says, yielding a datable debate. Oliveira's filiation is curiously visible in his nonconformist insistence, in his loquacious need to challenge the established order, which is why his discourse is paradoxical. His tautological lumping of habits and technologies in order to reject them indicates that his relations with them involve more than a simple rejection. His satirical attitude toward a brother who chastens him and toward old people, bosses, or simple women, etc., also indicates the irritated presence of a defense mechanism in Oliveira, who is also the product of a traditional Buenos Aires full of aunts from whom he has fled.

Nonconformity is essential to *Hopscotch* as the reflection of a central rebellion, in spite of the reiterations that link it to the patterns of the novel of the artist as hero. In addition, this rich debate signals the context in which Oliveira defines his response: the possibilities of chance.

"Would I find La Maga?," Oliveira asks himself. He wonders because this possibility is left to chance, to a frustrated chance, now that writing reconstructs the past. Oliveira's encounters with La Maga were chance encounters; he would happen to see her on a bridge, at places staged for passing encounters, in a no-man's land. On such occasions:

> She would smile and show no surprise, convinced as she was, the same as I, that casual meetings are apt to be just the opposite, and that people who make dates are the same kind who need lines on their writing paper, or who always squeeze up from the bottom on a tube of toothpaste. . . .
> But now she would not be on the bridge. . . . In any case, I went out onto the bridge and there was no Maga. . . . We each knew where the other lived . . . but we never looked each other up at home. We preferred meeting on the bridge, at a sidewalk café, at an art movie, or crouched over a cat in some Latin Quarter courtyard. We did not go around looking for each other, but we knew that we would meet just the same.

Chance is thus the sign of these encounters and also their order, because chance underscores the mutual freedom of the characters, their will to nonconformity, the magic of the world in the instant of the encounter, the love contained in the rite. This is why Oliveira says:

> even now, Maga, I wondered if this roundabout route made any sense, since it would have been easier to reach the Rue des Lombards by the Pont Saint-Michel and the Pont au Changes. But if you had been there that night, as so many other times, then I would have known that the roundabout made sense, while now, on the other hand, I debase my failure by calling it a roundabout.

Chance gains meaning in communication, but it awkwardly loses it in solitude. This response through chance to the established routine also requires gratuitousness and insignificance, giving a value to what is useless:

I took advantage of such moments to think about useless things, a practice I had begun some years before in a hospital and which all seemed richer and more necessary every time since. . . . The game consisted in bringing back only the insignificant, the un-noticed, the forgotten. . . . It was about that time I realized that searching was my symbol, the emblem of those who go out at night with nothing in mind, the motives of a destroyer of compasses.

"The disorder in which we lived . . . seemed to me like some sort of necessary discipline," Oliveira also says, bringing to mind Rim-baud's sacred disorder, evoked in another part of the novel as a sign or mirror. Like Rimbaud, Oliveira also leaves a written testimony of his season in hell, because he seeks unity in the resolution of contra-dictions and dichotomies. The only difference is that Rimbaud's po-etic rebellion, which demands subversion, has become in the novel a discursive rebellion demanding criticism, which is why Oliveira in-sists on a caricature of himself:

. . . it occurred to me like a sort of mental belch that this whole ABC of my life was a painful bit of stupidity, because it was based solely on a dialectical pattern, on the choice of what could be called nonconduct rather than conduct, on faddish indecency instead of social decency.

Oliveira recognizes the fragmentation of his own marginal image. The dualisms he struggles against persist in him to the point of de-termining his response (chance) starting from the problematic con-text of society (the established order). La Maga, "always fumbling and distracted," is Oliveira's opposite, a pole that in revealing itself also reveals him in his polarity; in other words, it reveals that he also is a term of a duality. "Knowing that . . . it was always easier to think than to be, that in my case the *ergo* of the expression was no *ergo* or anything at all like it," Oliveira says, because he plays at being La Maga's pole.

And I felt antagonism for all these things when I was with La Maga, for we loved each other in a sort of dialectic of magnet and iron filings, attack and defense, handball and wall. . . .
    It grieved me to recognize that with artificial blows, with Manichaean beams of light, or desiccated, stupid dichotomies I could not make my way up the steps of the Gare de Montpar-nasse where La Maga had dragged me to visit Rocamadour. Why couldn't I accept what was happening without trying to explain

it, without bringing up ideas of order and disorder, of freedom and Rocamadour?

Here love reveals the other dichotomies, straining them and making them more poignant. Love thus becomes one more struggle, an inevitable frustration. "Maybe one had to fall into the depths of stupidity in order to make the key fit the lock to the latrine or the Garden of Gethsemane," Oliveira says, announcing at the outset his own course between liberation from those dichotomies and the drama of that liberation. "I would have to get so much closer to myself, to let everything that separates me from the center drop away," he says. The anxiety for an "axis" that he senses in this exorcism, the search for a center of gravity, is also the yearning for a dreamed paradise, for an identity within the surrounding plurality. This is also the dream that Morelli announces for the literature that really matters.

The adventure of destroying the self in order to reconstruct it, the old scheme of "sainthood," also demands the rejection of a world corrupted by definitions, by dualistic simplifications:

> . . . black or white, radical or conservative, homo- or hetero
> sexual, the San Lorenzo team or the Boca Juniors, meat or vege-
> tables, business or poetry.

And the method for this destruction seems to be "the road of tolerance, intelligent doubt, sentimental vacillation." On one hand Oliveira sees the paradigm of "the struggle for struggle's sake," of "the handsome saints, the perfect escapists," and on the other hand he realizes that "if lucidity ends up in inaction, wouldn't it become suspect? Wouldn't it be covering up a particularly diabolical type of blindness?" Caught between these extremes, between the lines of the dualism that again confronts him, Oliveira strikes out on his own, marching toward his thunderous failure—the discursive scheme of his figure requires likewise its own parody—when the square in the game of hopscotch, which attempts to reconcile the extremes of the figure, turns out to be the window of a vaudevillian asylum. After this failure, resurrection insinuates itself slowly and gravely, crepuscular in some way. The last pages of Oliveira's story are also closer to the first page, because we should not forget that he writes the novel to read himself in the various masks of writing.

The path, the search for unity, is developed here in reverse. Between the "latrine" and the "Garden of Gethsemane" Oliveira states he is falling into the depths of stupidity, in the traditional line of knowledge that promises wisdom in suffering, the path towards the end of night, confession as the exorcism, etc. A quotation from

Lezama Lima says: "Analyzing this conclusion once more, from a Pascalian point of view: true belief is somewhere in between superstition and libertinism." Morelli also notes a quotation from Pauwels and Bergier suggesting "that binary reasoning might be replaced with an analogical consciousness which would assume the shapes and assimilate the inconceivable rhythms of those profound structures." We are also told that:

> It was curious that Morelli enthusiastically embraced the most recent working hypotheses of the physical and biological sciences, he presented himself as convinced that the old dualism had become cracked in the face of the evidence of a common reduction of matter and spirit to notions of energy.

Superstition and libertinism combined are thus Oliveira's analogical method for making stupidity a signifier capable of overcoming the dualisms already questioned in the doubts about the Cartesian schemes.

Oliveira begins by speaking of truth as invention, of beauty that is a truth threatened by the delusion of seeing itself. His adventure is the victim of this delusion when he is overcome by the threat of the unresolved dualisms and loses La Maga; in other words, he loses Paris, where to extend one's hand was to establish the reading of the world, where the bridges invented chance as communion. Oliveira returns to Buenos Aires, where he meets Traveler and his wife, Talita. Traveler, who has never been away from Buenos Aires, is also Oliveira's double, but he is an antagonistic double, a caricatured pole; and Talita is also a lighter double of La Maga. Oliveira forces in vain the relationship with his two friends, seeking to repeat in this world of allegories, where conversations always seem to be referring to an empty space, the truth he lived in Paris, that no-man's land that was a place of encounters. Oliveira's adventure has become a laughable, farcical posturing in Buenos Aires. A loquacious joker, this circle reveals him now in the pilgrimage of the artist through culture, in his sacrifice in a metaphysical rebellion, recovered also in the structure of the novel that returns him to the initial moment of the writing.

That is why this novel, concerned with beauty as the ultimate value and with truth as total communication and with unity of narrator and reader, at this level also becomes a moral novel. Its persistent assault against the established routine, against the "Great Habit," has to do with its ethical rebellion, with its will to break away. In the first of the two epigraphs to the book, "Abbot Martini" speaks of "this collection of maxims, counsels, and precepts," of a "universal morals," and of the "spiritual and temporal happiness of men of all ages"; and in the second one humorist César Bruto says, "I start gettin nutty ideas like I was thinkin about what was forein and diffrent . . . [and] I jes hope what I been writin down hear do somebody some good so he take a good look at how he livin and he dont be sorry when it too late." These epigraphs suggest the ethical concern of the novel, no matter how much Cortázar, forced to take a position of detachment by his fear of established literature, resorts to humor, just as he resorts to variations of phonetic writing as another form of detachment.

Oliveira is seen by Morelli as "the nonconformist": "This man moves within the lowest and the highest of frequencies, deliberately disdaining those in between, that is to say, the current band of the human spiritual mass." As we have already seen, the nonconformist Oliveira responds through chance; chance is his style, his lack of measure and his way of measuring. This is why we sense also an opposition between Oliveira and Morelli, who is more systematic. Oliveira's enormous frustration stems not only from his opposition to La Maga and from his tautological intellectualism, but from the broken line of a search that never becomes elective—although it claims to be so at the level of creation—because it lacks a center of gravity and a free perspective in relation to the rhetoric of culture. Hence every event is determined for him simply by chance, even when this chance enables him to see beauty in the world or leads him to the parodies of humor. And from that fertile gratuitousness he can disintegrate infinitely the established reality, as well as the reality that is yet to be discovered, and even himself. Oliveira thus gives the impression of being a hollow character. He places himself in all points of view, and the naïve abuse of his own image makes him imagine different masks, but it limits any transformation. Perhaps we can assume that Oliveira reconstructs himself after the episode in the hospital window, that his contradiction is also an insertion into history, into a traditional feeling of experience, into the will to transcend, and that he is a farcical figure of the culture of the 1950s, of the Latin-American adventure in that particular context. In any case, the fall is the allegorical theme of the novel, and resurrection is its return to the source in the ritual of writing, in the leap to form.

The wisdom of Morelli, whose accident (chance) would seem rather to be part of his own games, matches against that disintegration the possibility of subtracting through language a reality that is in itself excessive, because artistic form subtracts that accumulative verbalism. Of course, Morelli's secret hedonism is also a kind of

skepticism, if for no other reason than that his age or his margination doom him inevitably to culture. Morelli is a theoretician of new
departures because he is also a theoretician of decomposition, of a
multiple crisis. In the center of that crisis this mask is a skeptical
project.

The pervasive presence of chance, which is the nucleus of the
character, also appears to be the mechanism of the novel itself. This
is why *Hopscotch* constantly breaks it geometry, its field; its formalization is fragmented by the underlying presence of chance events
that do not seem to be part of any sequence. In *Hopscotch*, therefore,
the form is a rebeginning while the writing is fluctuating and accumulative. In any case, the disintegration that chance fosters in the
character and the diversity of volumes it fosters in the form are also
at the center of the problems posed by *Hopscotch*, which poses these
problems not in order to solve them, but in order to destroy itself
by destroying them, revealing them in that reformulation, and re-
emerging in its beauty and depth through the many books that it becomes, through the slap that wants to change the reader by rebelling
him in its rebellion.

6. Morelli on the Threshold

Hopscotch * is many books in one, and one of these many books concerns Morelli, the author, or better still, the persona whose questioning of literature is also the convocation of another literature that implies this novel itself, along with its critical foundation and poetic open-endedness.

In "chapter" 22, Horacio Oliveira witnesses an accident in which a man is struck by a car on a Paris street. This man, who Horacio and Étienne visit in the hospital, turns out to be Morelli, a writer who the speakers of *Hopscotch* have read at length and who, as the central image of a marginal literature, rejects through the demands of his reformulating work the established literary currents. The speculation of the speakers of this novel, their need of a new formal system for a more radical poetic option, is generated in this questioning.[1]

Morelli's activity redoubles the formulation of the novel itself. In it, this apocryphal author lives the richness of a convergence of transgressions. The characters read his notes, they read the same novel that writes him, and thus witness the nucleus of a critical operation whose sign is the possibility of another novel, of another reader.

Several authors, several personae, Morelli is first of all the kind of writer one would like to glimpse on the threshold of his workshop. This nostalgic movement, which comes to us from the biography of the literary renewal that developed in the 1920s, is linked to another movement; Morelli is also the tacit writer who acts behind every major work, presupposing the fervor and abyss of a language of which we see the final product, rather than the vertiginous origin.

Through Morelli this origin is established in *Hopscotch* in its daz-

*Julio Cortázar, *Hopscotch*, translated by Gregory Rabassa (New York: Pantheon Books, 1966). Originally published as *Rayuela* (1963).

zling plurality, showing itself in the excess of its critical drama, implying the energy of its broad formal modification. But Morelli is even more. He is the mythical author, or the author as myth, of a literature that at times is able to reveal, in the self-referencing of its questioning, its ludic and critical reason, its interrogating fiction.[2]

It is not mere coincidence that the center of change in *Hopscotch*, the possibility of a verbal liberation that occupies and foretells itself—a center around which, in fact, our own literature has revolved, revealing to us its diverse matter in the testing of its transgressions—is the space that provokes Morelli. Provoked by this space of change, Morelli's game and drama, in other words, the formal discontinuity and the critical response, develop in turn the debate of the poetics of a novel that reconstructs itself starting from its negation as a novel.

Pierre Menard, the infinite author of the *Quixote*, might have been the paradigm of a literature that, with Borges and his poetics of "extenuation," we know reiterates itself in an *ars combinatoria* that makes us parties to the fiction of his myth. One generation later Morelli is perhaps another paradigm, because with Cortázar we have gained a literature that reconstructs itself and is liberated in the other figure it initiates, in the changed reader.[3]

A mythical author, or, the myth of the author, Morelli is thus a blank space, the generating center of the other novel that lives behind this one—because in writing *Hopscotch* Cortázar not only acted critically, in the vortex of his disruption, questioning the naturalistic tradition of his genre, but also questioned his own departure, his own tradition of change, establishing at the center of this redoubling of his writing the subtracted or despoiled space that Morelli and the Morellianas deduce. We could say that Cortázar attempts to establish the blank space of Mallarmé within the antirationalistic and nondualistic exploration of surrealism, but this formula might be incomplete, because, by being a generator of analogies, Morelli's blank space acts in the face of the profuse reality of the contemporary culture and situation, attempting a broad series of negations in its need to reevaluate the norms in a world that devalues all norms. Consequently, Morelli redirects those "forces . . . that advance in quest of their rights to the city" and also suggests the "punishment for having remembered the kingdom." A convergence of poetry and criticism, his sign is mediation.

Metaphorically, the speakers in *Hopscotch* also read in Morelli their own author, in the sense that Cortázar invents in Morelli the literature that invents him. This metaphorical level is not accidental. Whereas the three stages of dialectic thought imply a rationalistic and successive scheme, the three levels of "metaphoric thought" postulate a poetical and instantaneous conversion. Analogical language, which Borges attributed in "The Aleph" to mystics, pertains in fact to formal structures; the instant that coalesces the three sides of the "metaphor" or the various levels of the "figure" is no longer successive but simultaneous. The three "sides" of *Hopscotch*, which is a metaphor, are thus only one, which is why this reading by "leaps," like the game of hopscotch, renders better the multiplicity of that coalesced instant. The keenness of a speculative energy functions as the other side of the same imaginary form. As it shapes itself, the novel not only creates its critical dimension but also prolongs the communication of a poetic knowledge that can no longer be reduced to finalist categories or even to enlightening postulates, as some of the critics have wanted to believe. This poetic knowledge again legitimizes the notion of a reality whose center has been promised to us. Not by chance, the purpose of Morelli is to name once again, to recognize "the name of the day." This is the paradisiacal yearning of the novel: the search for the "Adamic language," for a language revealing the world and stating us, recovering in its genuine speech a common destiny.[4]

The speakers seek in Morelli, as they do in Zen, this central speaker, but Morelli in turn writes "as if he himself, in a desperate and moving attempt, had pictured the teacher who was to enlighten him." *Hopscotch* imagines itself in the novel written by Morelli; the readers reconstruct themselves in the options of *Hopscotch*. Mediation—the initiations of the despoilment—sets in motion that search for an axial need, which literature reconvokes here starting from the *roman comique*, from the agony of questioning and the morals of nonconformity, from a defectiveness measured by reference to a surmised fulfillment.

In the initiation of the hopscotch, in this game of stages devised to conjugate in a single liberating movement the "earth" and "heaven" of an inherited code that must be changed, in this ironic and obsessive game, the novel jumps through Morelli's square—or Morelli's square infers the possibility of destroying the rules in order to rewrite them. The importance of the novel in Morelli, of the Morelli space in *Hopscotch*, is the seditious task of modifying through the new game of forms the density of a culture—the contemporary dark forest—that deceives through its partial solutions, and of taking the step that follows the restraint of the "blank page" and the lack of restraint of the *vases communicants*.

Among the many books contained in *Hopscotch*, the Morellianas are, then, the reading of one of them, the access toward its center, although clearly their reverberations can only be followed in the edifice itself of the novel.

The notion of change generated by *Hopscotch* begins with a poetic diction, which is resolved in an open prosody, and exchanges the traditional canons of "composition" for the aleatory possibility of "figures" in an analogical system. In the transformations of this system, which seek to modify the "purpose" itself of the genre, Morelli's book undoubtedly has a convocating role, not only because it links us to a debate that transcends the situation of our literature, but also because it commits our reading of the literary "prospects," establishing in that verbal profusion the standard of a radicalized demand with which we have won the right to a new freedom in the circulation of reading.

This Morellian reading thus proceeds from *Hopscotch* and returns to it. It is a spectrum of that novel, one of the several possibilities of choosing pages, convergencies, or places presented by every text that interacts with the center of a change. This also proves the plurality of a work whose reading, at the beginning of our creative maturity, prior to Lezama Lima's *Paradiso* and shortly after the Borgian library, begins another cycle of transformations in our literature. The other texts with a bearing on Cortázar's poetic narrative, *La vuelta al día en ochenta mundos* and *Ultimo round*, comment, I believe, on this modification starting from Cortázar's workshop, another spectrum of Morelli's workshop. Their tone is different, but their intent is similar; they refer other phases of critique (the questioning response) and of a celebration (the play of meaning) and their convergence in fervor and irony.

Hopscotch does not seek its center in a new "literary theory" but in a poetics of exclusions and integrations fulfilled in the renewed entity of a questioning language that alters the notion of what stands for real. This action—and the word *action* is reiterated for a reason— begins as a displacement, because this poetics (critique and the open desire for a revealing language) subverts our conventions by confronting them with the irruption of a full presence. This demand enables us, at the same time, to see Cortázar in the light of the poetic convention he nurtures and liberates.

On the other hand, the text "Algunos aspectos del cuento," a memorable talk given by Cortázar in Havana, helps us recover the tacit level found throughout these pages: that a literature of change establishes its own tradition, and that this movement begins with an acute consciousness of formal freedom, starting from which a short story or a novel first gain their specificity. It is after this fulfillment that Morelli speaks, on the threshold of another.

Notes

1. Chapter 99 of *Hopscotch*, in which the characters discuss Morelli's ideas and projects after reading the Morelliana in chapter 112, is the key to understanding the importance of this author in the speculative debate lived by the novel's speakers. Cortázar's ideas, potentiated in a paradigm of his own radicalism in Morelli, are discussed by his own characters, which implies that they have read or are reading the novel itself as the author writes it. In this game of mirages and redoublings the novel *comments* on itself.

2. A new exchange in this hall of mirrors emerges from the possibility that Morelli himself may be the "author" of *Hopscotch*, its metaphor. Morelli is writing a novel and when Oliveira and Etienne visit him in the hospital he asks them to take back to his apartment a quinternion ("number 52 and put it in its place between 51 and 53,") which we immediately suspect involves *Hopscotch* in a self-reference. Morelli indicates also that the character he is interested in is the reader. And, in fact, the characters are readers of his work. A paradigm of the change itself that Cortázar is setting in motion, both authors coincide in a direct reference to *Hopscotch*, to attempt the novel as a subtraction, which is what the numbers at the end of each chapter indicate.

3. *Menard/Morelli*. "Pierre Menard, Author of the Quixote," implies that literature has already been written, that the great authors already exist, and that the only thing which remains is to gloss these books and thus be those authors. This is a central idea in Borges; the themes are repeated, it is unnecessary to forge new metaphors. Morelli, on the other hand, wants to destroy literature and reinvent the use of the word, to rescue the mediating and analogical power of language and to modify not an abstract man, but a concrete reader. Morelli is marked by the modern critical foundation (Baudelaire, Mallarmé), but also by the great period of the crisis of naturalism (surrealism, Joyce, Pound) and lives the beginning of a literary reformulation, the utopia of a primordial language able to identify the certainty and celebration in poetry. But to systematize his creed would be to lose sight of its center, the speculation about change, revolving in search of a new language.

4. *"Metaphoric thought."* I am referring, obviously, to the classic scheme of the metaphor—two terms that provoke a third term—and not to the phrase called "metaphoric," which is a more or less fortunate comparison from which Cortázar wants to eliminate the inevitable link *as*, a link that in Lezama Lima, however, sets in motion the delta of complementary phrases which soon free themselves from their grammatical generator and become autonomous. On "the demon of analogy," see Cortázar's essay "Para una poética" (*La Torre*, no. 7 [Puerto Rico, July–September 1954]), which indicates

some of the author's possible sources on this subject, especially the anthropological studies by Lévy-Brühl. See also the remarkable essay by Octavio Paz, "La nueva analogía" (*Los signos en rotación* [Madrid: Alianza Editorial, 1971]); along with the fundamental essays by José Lezama Lima in *Introducción a los vasos órficos* (Barcelona: Barral Editores, 1970).

7. Reading *Paradiso*

(Parts I–III translated by Susan Jean Pels)

I

Any interpretation of *Paradiso** can only be approximative, because this novel cannot easily be reduced to a process or a structure. But perhaps Lezama Lima himself proposes a suitable coherency: the expansion of language, which replaces the conventions of reality. Still, an analysis of the novel must in any case be provisional because this expansion comprehends a complex hierarchy that, beyond or in a reappraisal of literature, organizes a world view whose components are a symbiosis of cultures, a synthesis of Greek and Christian conceptions, and even of Oriental aspects, which acquire form as *poetics*.

Paradiso situates the personal experience of a formative process—in order to elucidate it as poetics—within a reality unified as if by verbal enchantment. In other words, the entire novel becomes the debate and discovery of a means leading to the finding and formulation of a conception of reality based on poetry. The coherency of poetic apprenticeship is what is most secret and also most visible in the book, because while this coherency establishes the novel's *form*, it also establishes the text's progress toward an integrative poetics that comprehends complex levels. On the one hand, it traces the family chronicle (the hierarchy of nobility as a form of human relations and the nucleus of the home as an *axis mundi* defining José Cemí); on the other hand, it follows Cemí's personal literary destiny (based on a metaphorical debate over the complexities of Eros); and, as a consequence of these two processes, the search leads to the peculiar synthesis of the culture in which Cemí lives (also as a form of nature) and the resultant formulation of that synthesis as a poetics, an understanding of reality through words.

*José Lezama Lima, *Paradiso*, translated by Gregory Rabassa (New York: Farrar, Straus, & Giroux, 1974).

These *vases communicants* constitute the internal process of the novel, its historical and symbolic coherency. Lezama's Baroque incorporates zones of all cultures in order to expand the mechanism of the image, and at times this incorporation is only illustrative or comparative (that is, an expansion of the space of the image). But often the incorporation is also allegorical or symbolic because this Baroque is not merely "literary" or literally textual (as Góngora's laborious, gratuitous Baroque probably was); rather, it is a symbolic Baroque. In other words, Lezama creates a "superreality" with a baroque figure, but this figure is not only a signifier but also a new meaning, and, as such, it supposes allegorical expansion and symbolic implication. It should be kept in mind that he speaks in the novel of "the creation of the law of extension by the Tree of Life," which is the reproductive principle of his language as "nature," as a figure and as a symbol.

II

This process of the conquest of reality by poetry is a cycle, a universal epic, that begins in the first image of the novel (the sick child) and concludes in the last image (the poet who recognizes the voices, the hesychastic rhythm, the poetry of totality). These images are intimately related within the poetization of the story. The disease is perhaps an allegory of birth itself, an image of man severed from divinity by his very human nature (although in Lezama there is no explicit metaphysical guilt that would directly suggest the Christian concept of original sin); the final image, that of the man who transforms the world in poetry, also suggests a profound allegory of the word as the recovery of innocence, as the foundation of paradise in verbal creation, as the link in temporality, elucidating experience as a form of created Nature.

In a conversation with Alvarez Bravo (*Orbita de Lezama Lima*, Havana, UNEAC, 1966), Lezama explains that for him poetry conceives of man's end not in death but in resurrection. It is precisely this Christian principle that is found in the profound unity of *Paradiso*. The final image recalls the first one, and also the death of Oppiano Licario, through whom it symbolically incorporates the previous deaths of Cemí's father and of his uncle Alberto. Licario (Icarus, the adventurer of the word as time and as resurrection) was the strange and solitary witness to these deaths, perhaps a kind of image projected by Cemí himself. In this projection of the allegory, Cemí can witness the deaths of father and his uncle, both of which occurred at night, leaving no trace in his memory. They must, there-

fore, be recalled for him by Licario, the enigmatic witness who finally surrenders his enigma in the multiple resurrection symbolized
by José Cemí as the advance sentinel and the craftsman of rhythm
and of poetry.

But let us return to the first image. The child Cemí, who has
asthma, is covered with sores, and the servants are in despair because they do not know how to ease his attack, how to assume the
ritual responsibility placed on them by the situation, because the
boy's father and mother are not at home.

> No comment was passed among them, as if they did not
> want to face up to this situation that was beyond them. Their
> thoughts were focused mainly on the Colonel's return and the
> attitude he would take toward them. Since the strange connec-
> tion that might exist between their watching and the spreading
> of the welts was ambiguous, it unnerved them to think that per-
> haps the connection was quite close and it might appear to be
> their fault.

There are three servants to take care of the child—Baldovina, Truni,
and Zoar. Truni, Lezama notes, is also called Trinidad, and she "defined the ritual and the rite: Zoar as God the Father, Baldovina as the
daughter, and Truni as the Holy Ghost." This is one of the configurations reiterated in the novel: the triad as a group of complemen-
taries. The image also suggests another constant in the book: the
successive displacements. In this fundamental episode, the parents
have been displaced and Cemí falls ill in the presence of the servants, figures who also replace the figures of the Trinity. Moreover,
in Lezama's mechanism, Cemí himself is displaced by the trin-
itarian figure, since the author speaks of "the daughter" and not the
son (Cemí), who here is a fourth term of the figure. José Cemí is undoubtedly an alter ego of the author, and his name may represent a
radical declaration in this mechanism of displacement, since when
Licario meets Cemí for the first time—a meeting that establishes
his destiny as a figure in the novel—he recognizes him by the ini-
tials J.C. Is this then a parallel between Cemí's poetic destiny and
the destiny of Christ the Son? Whatever the answer to that question,
the resonant significance of this episode lies in the rituals practiced
by Truni and Zoar in their attempts to cure the child. When Cemí
awakens he tells Baldovina, "Now these crosses are going to stay
etched on me and no one will want to touch me because of Truni's
kisses." And Baldovina says to him, "What you've got is the king's
evil, which spreads out like streaks, like the red blotches of a royal
poinciana tree. Like a little circlet of seaweed that first floats over

your skin and then gets inside your body." These images of kisses, of crosses etched on the body, of blotches like internalized forms, are images that the author recapitulates in the episode as expansions of Cemí's own figure.

Thus illness becomes a visible metaphor that on the one hand allegorizes the advent of human nature and on the other hand initiates the specific destiny of one character; and this initiation recognizes the proximity of death ("the Colonel and his wife agreed that it was, purely and simply, a miracle that the boy was still alive") and especially the symmetry that will exist between Cemí's troubled, asthmatic breathing and the discovery of breathing as the integrative rhythm of poetry.

Cemí's illness also generates strange resonances in relation to his father and decisive adjustments in relation to his mother. In chapter 6 José Eugenio Cemí decides to teach his five-year-old son how to swim:

> "I don't think you can learn how to swim by yourself," he said. "So I'm going to teach you today. Now, you jump into the water and hold onto this finger." He held up his forefinger, created for the exercise of authority, strong, like a midget who was an important personage in the Tower of London. The forefinger curled like an anchor and then straightened up like a reed that jumps its moorings but then comes back to root itself in the sand once more.

The child jumps into the water and holds onto his father's finger as the boat moves along.

> José Cemí clutched his father's forefinger with his whole hand, feeling the resistance of the water as it tightened like a stone against his panting chest. "You're not afraid any more, now you can learn by yourself," he said. The Colonel withdrew his finger just as a small whirlpool formed.

The child's body then disappears beneath the water and the father, frightened dives in to rescue him.

The following episodes show the father vaguely troubled by his son's asthma because he wants the officers to see his children as strong and forthright when they wander through Morro Castle. The father—Lezama calls him the Chief—points out a dark, gaping hole in the building and tries to frighten his children by telling them how in colonial times they used to throw prisoners in there; later Cemí will find out that they throw garbage down the hole, attracting voracious sharks in the water below, and the image becomes an obsessive nightmare. The father also has his daughter Violante swim in a pool and the girl runs the risk of drowning; again the father rescues a child from the water, and again the image of the pool and its infernal center becomes a obsession in Cemí's dreams. Cemí's illness worries the father "incessantly," and he decides to attempt a cure, which the novel portrays with relentless terror—he fills the bathtub with crushed ice and submerges the small invalid. "The scene had something of an ancient sacrifice about it. Except that the Colonel did not know to which deity he was making the offering. And the mother, shut up in the farthest room, began to weep and pray." The child counters this confused obsession of his father with a pious and silent reply—he pretends not to be frightened, conceals his dread, and tries to console his father when desperation at wresting the son from this illness leads him to torpor and repentance. The father thus tries to free Cemí from one part of his nature, the asthma that Cemí already accepts as an initial and definitive part of his destiny.

In this account—which does not stress the rich psychic vibrations of the episodes—we must keep in mind above all the references to the father's finger and to the repeated rescue from the water. In a nightmare Cemí sees his own arm covered with sweat:

> Sweat passed along his arm again, and again he experienced the separation from his father's finger. . . . Then a broad fish swam up. . . . The fish eyed the forsaken finger and laughed. Then it took the finger into its mouth and began to afford it protection. Towing him by the finger, it brought him to a patch of floating moss where the carefully calculated rhythm of his new breathing began. Then he no longer saw salvation in the fish, but instead his mother's face.

His mother's face, as a protective solution that prolongs Cemí's new breath, also appears, overcoming the terror of the episodes with his father, resolving them in a model of profound protection. The father's finger seems to repeat, in the symbolic pattern of the beginnings of Cemí's life, that other finger of the Father giving shape to Adam. Actually, the father casts his son into the waters of life, only in this case the son is destined by an illness that confuses the creator, making him despair and dive into the river to save his son and also, curiously, one of his daughters. The gaping hole, through which they throw prisoners and garbage, and which ends in the sea full of sharks, also indicates the obscure and vaguely tenebrous vision of the origins, suggested by the anecdotes, but which Cemí incorporates, eliminating that funereal implication, bringing the origins an integrated harmony; and this discovery of harmonious meaning is explained in dreams, the allegorical region of poetic understanding.

It is in dream that the anecdote is recomposed and organized into a symbol; the father's finger is withdrawn from the water, and immediately Cemí's finger finds its own harmonious solution. The fish that recognizes and protects this solitary finger seems to be the figure of Christianity leading him to a new place where his breathing is a "carefully calculated rhythm," that is, the anticipation of poetry, of that rhythm of breathing that is the rhythm of the created universe. The fish finally changes into the mother and then the harmony of integration is closed; the presence of the mother, the order she generates as a transparency of Nature, is also the solution to the origins, because this illness is now part of an origin guilty in its separation from God, but as the emblem of an irrevocable destiny. Because of this the father's death, too, will transmute into an absence that must be sought in the manifestation of poetry itself.

The last scene of this sequence of relations with the father has the Colonel showing his son two contrasting engravings in an open book:

> The father pointed at two small, square pictures on the right and left pages, with two captions: The Student and The Grindstone. The first was the usual picture seen in study halls, a midnight scholar resting his elbows on a table covered with open books, ribbons marking the pace of his reading. . . . In The Grindstone, the man's shirt is puffed up by a gust of rain, an unstarched handkerchief wrapped around his jaw as if he had the mumps, and the wheel is densely cloaked in sparks, the rosettes of a rain of stars on a full-moon night. His curiosity ran faster than the time it took him to distinguish between the two pictures, and when José Cemí's forefinger stopped on the picture of the grindstone, he heard his father say: "Student." Thus a warped accommodation of gesture and voice caused him to believe that the student was the grindstone and the grindstone the student.

The father has shown him these opposing emblems in order to suggest, pedagogically, a preference for the student, and so he asks, "When you're older, do you want to be a student?" "What's a student?" But Cemí has inverted the images and responds with metaphors that allude to the grindstone and surprise the father, who "was startled at his son's rare gift of metaphor, his prophetic and symbolic way of understanding a profession."

Prophetic and symbolic because for Cemí, with his maturing destiny, the opposition between the two images is false; he integrates them through language, thus displacing his father's finger with his own.

III

Octavio Paz wrote that Lezama Lima's baroque is a verbal world that is fixed, like a stalactite, and this is quite true; time fixed in a glance, a stalactite fixed in poetic adventure are also recurrent images in *Paradiso*. And the image is the mechanism that amplifies language, based on a syntax that develops in turn a geometric expansion; and the very peculiar punctuation detaches, sometimes obsessively, the zones of this verbal forest. These are tense, unwieldy sentences that intersect each other, that are integrated into the broad framework of detailed evocation.

These baroque reconstructions in the widened space of the phrase correspond also to an oral tendency, but to oral speech as atmosphere, if it can be so called. Lezama's is not a spoken language, not even in the dialogues, but a writing, which veils the warm reverberations of the game of speech. This speech as atmosphere prompts Lezama to avail himself of descriptions of oral language as another image, as an extension of written language; the novel is full of metaphorical descriptions of speech, evocations of orality that also generate that atmosphere. For example:

> Then the Colonel would turn up, and she would become the target of a volley of questions to which she would respond, nervously distracted, with a counterpoint of curtsies, starts, and lies, so that while the Colonel baritoned his laughter, Baldovina tried to make herself invisible bit by bit; and when he spoke to her again, his voice had to penetrate a forest so dark and with so many obstacles that he would be forced to amplify it with echo upon echo until he seemed to be summoning the whole household. And Baldovina, who was only a household fragment, would be reached by such a small particle of his voice that he would now have to reinforce it with a more peremptory tone to carry the force of a command.

Thus the voice is the living pattern that unifies the space of an event in evocation. The voice is also the correlate of a character, his active definition. The unsuccessful organist Mr. Squabs, for example, defines his destiny in his language; he has to move to a new climate because of an affliction of the larynx and "This move had innocently darkened his destiny, one which he believed to be rich with artistic gift, bringing him to a dense terseness." Florita, his wife, "baritoned, as if accompanying her husband the organist," and also spoke "broadening her vowels." We read of workers who, "devouring the syllables like a ghost who makes a clock run slow, were amusing themselves." Señora Augusta is also described by her language; she says: "I have a lisp, and I've had it ever since I was a small child, when with my little sister I used to make fun of the sibilant sounds made by a funny cook we had." Uncle Luis is "talkative, although with a rich flow of palatals transformed into explosive syllables, incorrectly dividing syllables and swallowing the ends of words"; this character is the center of a detailed description by speech: "If you pronounce the word *horloge* correctly, I'll give you mine, because I intend to buy another."

Lezama also describes the "baritonal density" of a phrase; he says that the use of the diminutive indicates that the speaker is taking the side of the listener and that "reproduction exists by look and shout . . . because a shout can reproduce itself by the conjugation of different things"; he also speaks of "the sexual slowness of conjugation" in a character whose syllables "walked in the smoke like spirals that he would recover with the corner of his eye." And he writes of "syllabification," "monosyllables," "the open hollow of a shout," or someone who speaks "slowly and syllabically," "raking her words with little bubbles of sticky saliva," "muttering syllabic divisions or exploding palatals toward the ceiling." All of this suggests the poetry or the eroticism of oral speech, which is the pattern of time and of the spoken nature of a multiple dialogue with reality. Therefore two bodies embracing and caressing are described as "syllabifying with fruition."

But language can also be the metaphor of a relationship, such as that of José Cemí and Alberto Olaya.

> Alberto did not cast a glance, as on the previous occasion, and as he went up the steps to his apartment, the match dancing now with muscular energy, he said, "It bothers me when I look up and find two legs in front of me." José Eugenio had caught the round impact of the phrase, but Alberto Olaya was already going into his apartment, leaving the syllables bodiless, bringing the body around to collect the syllables.

And immediately afterwards we are told that José Eugenio "felt the syllables again, spoken next to him, but without clearly perceiving his shadowy bulk, his existence resting on an age-old boredom. And yet the phrase, walking like a centipede, tail like a serpent's head, head with the indentations and outcroppings of a key, of a clue to a puzzle, would give him the labyrinths and bays of other years that

Chronos would offer him. The key to his first-born and genetrix happiness, a shadow of death to slip along his street"; which connects this metaphor of speech with José Eugenio's marriage, that is, with the birth of Cemí.

But language is essentially the central character of the novel, its pursuit and its conquest formulated as a poetics. Therefore Cemí's experience is developed as a process that comes to constitute the other absolute language of poetry. In chapter 7 we read an episode that clarifies one of the focal points of this process. Demetrio says to Cemí: "Come close so you can hear what your Uncle Alberto wrote, and you'll get acquainted with him and his special ebullience. This is the first time you'll hear language made into nature, with all its artifices of allusion and loving pedantry." This experience of language become nature is but another allegorical anticipation of Cemí's own style, because Alberto's letter is written with a metaphorical, imagistic passion, Lezama's absolute love of the word. The episode also reveals that Cemí's childhood and adolescent experience is a series of initiations into the process of learning that take on the aura of an almost religious destiny opening the way for the advent of Cemí the poet:

When his grandmother and his mother withdrew as Demetrio began to read the letter, Cemí felt as if he had suddenly risen up into a chamber where what was said would follow an inexorable path to his ears. When he first drew his chair closer to Demetrio's, he thought he was going to hear a secret. As he listened to the succession of the names of submarine tribes, his memory not only brought forth his class in secondary school where he studied fish, but the words themselves rose up, lured up out of their own territory, artificially grouped, and their joyous movement was invisible and ineffable as it penetrated his dark channels. Listening to that verbal parade, he had the same feeling as when he sat on the wall of the Malecón and watched fishermen pulling in their catch, the fish twisting as death overcame them outside their natural habitat. In the letter those verbal fish had been hauled out twisting too, but it was a twisting of jubilation as they formed a new chorus, an army of oceanids singing as it disappeared in the mist. When he drew up his chair and was then the only one in the room listening, since his Uncle Alberto was pretending not to hear, he felt the words taking on substance and he also felt a soft wind on his cheeks shaking those words and giving them movement, how the breeze blew the peplums in Panathenaic processions, as meanings oscillated, were lost, and then reappeared as a mast in the midst of the waves, full of invisible alveoli formed by fish bites.

Cemí moves from the discovery of language in Uncle Alberto's letter to another poetic initiation, this time connected with the sense of orderly adventure which will shape the first discovery—the beautiful encounter with his mother after the disturbances in Upsalón. Experience as a totality, which is the breath and substratum of the novel, is manifested here by the mother, along with the announcement of poetry as the configurating order that harmonizes reality. She tells him:

"Waiting for you to come home, I was thinking about your father and thinking about you, saying my rosary and asking myself: What will I tell my son when he comes back from that danger? The passing of each rosary bead was a prayer for a secret will to go with you all through your life, and for you always to have a determination that would bring you to seek what can be seen and what is hidden. A determination that would never destroy, but that would look for the hidden in the visible, and find in the secret what will rise up for the light to give it form."

Rialta admonishes him not to reject danger, but always to try what is most difficult, danger as epiphany:

"When man throughout his days has tested what is most difficult, he knows that he has lived in danger, and even though its existence has been silent, even though the succession of its waves has been peaceful, he knows that a day has been assigned to him in which he will be transfigured, and he will not see the fish inside the current but the fish in the starry basket of eternity."

This moral of poetry appears dictated by the mother and inscribed on the portals of the most difficult adventure that Cemí must undertake—to pass through erotic hell in order to transfigure it, too, into a moral of creation, into epiphany. The "light" (a recurrent image in the novel) configures what is secret, Rialta observes, and the poetic risk demanded by this configuration is connected to the perpetual instant which marks the identity of creator and created. As in Uncle Alberto's letter, as in the poetic conduct of Oppiano Licario (who pursues "the hare of the instant") at the end of the novel, in this second poetic opening the mother has recourse to the instantaneous, perpetuating image of the fish in poetry and in light. And later on she connects this prefiguration of Cemí's poetic destiny with his father's death:

> "For me the event, as I told you, your father's death, left me with no answer, but I've always dreamed, and those dreams will always be the root of my being alive, that it would be the profound cause of your testimony, of your seeking difficulty as transfiguration, of your answer. Some doubters will think that I never said these words, that you invented them, but when you give the answer and the testimony, you and I will know that I did say them and that I will say them as long as I live and that you will continue saying them after I have died."

The response to the father's death is also the transfiguration of the mother's response, and so poetry is the testimony of this root whose absence acclaims it not as invention but as truth. Poetry is truth, because invention is woven by a verbal presence that reveals an original absence. Thus, for Cemí, the memory of his father will have become visible in his mother's voice through the invocation "look for danger in what is most difficult," and this transfigured search is the truth and the order of poetry as a destiny.

And this entire process takes shape in the formulation of the novel as a poetics when Oppiano Licario meets Cemí at the end. For Licario, a phrase evokes reality because language, magically, precedes and configures it; reality is an extension of the phrase. Here language is nature because the process of learning through initiations has been completed; Licario, the verbal parable of Cemí himself, alter ego of the poetic enigma, dies integrated into the rhythm conquered by Cemí's destiny.

Emir Rodríguez Monegal (*Mundo Nuevo*, No. 24) has established the necessity of an anagogic reading of this novel that, according to Dante's classification in *Il Convivio* (*The Banquet*) corresponds to "the definitive and spiritual meaning of the text." This reading is undoubtedly fundamental in the case of *Paradiso*, and this search for the sublime, in a radically spiritual literature such as Lezama's, is based on that adventure of the poetization of the world, of the poet as the destiny that reveals nature, of man seen as the image of a creation understood within a primordial and total reality. This implicit religiosity orders the extraordinary verbal world of *Paradiso*.

IV

The contrapuntal play of metaphors, which produces the freedom of the analogies, also creates the web of the image. The image is prolonged, in turn, in the hyperbole channeled by the modeling form. "Actually, when a likeness is most elaborated and most approximates a Form, the image is the design of its progression," Lezama has written in an essay entitled "The Possible Images" (*Orbita de Lezama Lima*), and just as in his works "the body upon taking itself as body takes possession of an image," the novel is the body of a materialized Form, a sequence of images revealing a manifested unity and also its other side, the primordial unity. In his conversation with Alvarez Bravo, Lezama stated: "The oblique experience is as if a man, without knowing it of course, by flipping the switch in his bedroom were to produce a cascade in Ontario." This experience is, therefore, the prolongation of poetry, the open method by which to integrate similarities through the word.

The image represents a path of poetic knowledge:

As they passed by a tomb in which the body of St. Flora was reproduced in wax, Doña Augusta said to her grandson: "That's a saint there, a real dead saint." . . . That it wasn't an image, but a very ordinary wax mold made with no excess of realism, added to the confusion, and Cemí, six years old, could not perceive the objects he was discovering as he lacked the framework that might have helped him to form analogies and group dissimilar objects around nuclei to be distributed and newly arranged.

As a child Cemí still does not recognize the possibility of analogical knowledge afforded by the image, but he is already aware of a sense of form or of the style of one of the formulations of his world:

The tale at which Cemí had surprised his grandmother, talking about the day her father had been exhumed, disappeared in a sudden whirlwind of invisible dust. The yellowish delicacy of St. Flora's wax, which he already felt to embody the extended, violated shadow of death, began to change into the smile of Doña Augusta and Rialta. His imagination would resurrect that smile whenever an introduction to the world of magic was needed. The smile that he observed on his grandmother and his mother was not a reaction to pleasant or comic motivations. It was the artifice of an upright goodness governed by delicacy and will, seeming to dissipate errant and sinister spirits. Cemí's approach to other people depended on whether they could produce an imitation of one of those smiles where ancestral artificiality finally poured out goodness and confidence, as if we could penetrate the eyes of animals that watch a train pass, inserting ourselves be-

tween an illuminated world entirely free of causality in the
golden region of a serene portent.

This passage reveals a private heaven within the family, in other
words, the archetypical forms by which reality will later be appropriated; but it also reveals a hierarchy of poetic knowledge. Cemí is
still not able to define the analogies in the image because he is just
beginning to discover objects. These analogies are based on the
dissimilarities that, integrated as similarities by a new order, are
transformed into images. This is the highest poetic knowledge, the
occupation of the world by the word, the discovery of reality as a
modeling of the form. Cemí already recognizes the first levels of this
progression: sentiment and imagination. The early sense of death,
which is one of the fundamental experiences and the intimate
mechanism that poetry transfigures into an absent origin, emerges
here from the awareness of an object, the wax figure of St. Flora, and
is also linked to the prefiguration of family separations, but this feeling is appropriated by the imagination and is elicited by the noble
resource of the smiles of his mother and grandmother, "serene portent." So although in this incident knowledge is not yielded by the
image, it is yielded by a familiar and archetypical formula, by the
context of the nobility that the family projects. In recapitulating this
episode Lezama construes Cemí's initial experience as image, in
other words, as knowledge, because although in the novel we witness a process of initiation in the struggle to conquer a poetics, the
description of this process is a recapitulation that starts from the image, from the knowledge sought throughout the story. This is true
because in Cemí's story, in the poetic process, the total image is a
search made with images; in other words, the Form must be made
flesh in the form, the Word in the words.
    It is within this verbalized world that we recognize the base or the
context of the poetic adventure. In the above passage Cemí uncovers
these bases in the idea of the family as a form of spiritual nobility, as
a sense of the maternal wisdom, as the inexhaustible flexibility of a
creole culture. This rootedness in the family is also a rootedness in
the land, in secureness and kindness. We have already noted the
mother's disclosure of the intimate connection between the death of
the father and the poetic destiny of their son in its dimension as response and testimony. This rich and complex creole nobility is,
then, the foundation on which Cemí's adventure will rise beyond
sentiment and imagination towards the spiritual knowledge channeled by the image through the prism of contemplation.
    The image is the signifier of complex significations, a formulation

comprised of the freest dissimilarities that in the metaphor burst forth as analogies, creating beyond their terms a new domain. When Cemí's father and mother are married, they are the terms of an image that is just beginning. "José Eugenio Cemí and Rialta, dazzled by the gravity of the symbols, exchanged rings as if the life of one fell upon that of the other through the eternity of the circle. They felt in the proliferation of faces of family and friends a convergence into the unity of image that had begun." In these convergencies the image is the force that succeeds in transposing the space and time of the situation, creating a hyperbole that summarizes the situation in the "eternity of the circle." And like this figure, which has no beginning and no end, the image rescues reality for the idea of absolute poetry.

The image is thus a metamorphosis of time and space: "when the cornucopia of things to come has a tendency to upset itself on top of the stifled moment"; "like the parade of a Chinese military band placed between eternity and nothingness"; "in the living room, every piece of furniture seemed to be stretching, emerging from the dawn." Hyperbole prolongs the object through comparison, and this mechanism is infinite because it can provoke images by discovering analogies through the "poetically unconditioned," through a "hyper-telic method" (see conversation with Alvarez Bravo), in a visualization that the word conjures outside its own organized figure. This freedom of conjuring opposing terms and prolonging them in a unity is never gratuitous, however, because with these new relations the image embodies a formal process, a path of knowledge that always refers to the calm but inflexible development of a poetics.

Severo Sarduy has written that Lezama's metaphorical mechanism is actuated by a sort of "unfolding": "Free from the dead weight of verisimilitude, from all exercise of realism—including its worst variant: magical realism—and given to the demon of correspondencies, the Lezamean metaphor reaches a distance from its terms and a hyperbolic freedom that is obtained in Spanish (I disregard other languages: ours is by nature baroque) only by Góngora. In Lezama the distance between signifier and signified, the gap opened between the phases of the metaphor, the scope of the *how*—of the language, since the metaphor implies it in all its *figures* of speech—is at its greatest" (*Mundo Nuevo*, No. 24). This "unfolding," this distance between the subject and its complements is so wide that the decisive part of the metaphorical phrase is frequently not the subject but the predicate adjective. It is even possible to lose from sight the real determining object because it is often absorbed by a proliferation of comparisons which submerge it in another, purely verbal reality. This displacement proceeds without interruption; it is a progression of wonder. The reader, who is being displaced from the subjects or objects toward the terms of comparison, perceives he is being pushed toward the unknown limits of the figure that is being proposed, toward a region in which the pervasive atmosphere is one of wonder. And while the object is being integrated as the element of a broader figure in this baroque space, the reader also reaches the point of integrating himself as the element of another form, of a current that is unpredictable in its creationist, aleatory movement. The reader thus experiences reading as a naked experience, ascending, along with language, to the luminous realm that sparks these expansions of the image. The act of reading becomes an eroticism of this tactile light, which lingers resolutely in its painstaking discovery of the world.

The breakthrough incited by the contemplative activity of the image and the depth of knowledge achieved through the progression of wonder is revealed in the game of jacks, a truly labyrinthian ritual that evokes the image. Cemí and his two sisters are playing jacks. Their mother, who had been watching them, also joins the game.

> They had reached that point of choral ecstasy that children achieve so easily. Their time, the time of those around them, and the time of the external situation all coincided in a kind of temporal abandonment, where camphor or poppy seeds, in a silent and nocturnal vegetal growth, prepare an oval and crystalline identity, and where the isolation of a group provokes a communication that is like a universal mirror.

This universal mirror may also be an image of the novel itself, since it views language as the germinative growth of a supernature. The interesting point about this episode is that the game, magically and because the mother joins it, reveals the process by which an image is formed:

> The square formed by Rialta and her three children changed into a circle. . . . A rapid animism was transmuting the tiles, and their inorganic world was being transfused into the receptive cosmos of the image. . . . To the four jacks players, the tiles were an oscillating crystal that broke up silently after coming together silently, never losing its tremor, making way for fragments of military cloth, feeling harsh hobnails, freshly polished buttons. The fragments disappeared, reappearing at once, joined to new and larger pieces, the buttons falling into their sequence. The collar of the tunic was precisely starched, waiting for the face that would complete it.

The hallucinating, giddying game reconstructs the figure of the dead father.

> Penetrating that vision, seemingly released by the flash that pre-
> ceded it, the four inside the illuminated circle experienced a sen-
> sation that was cut short as it opened up inside for an instant,
> and then the fragments and the totality coincided in the blink of
> a vision cut by a sword. Rialta nestled her head in her arms and
> let go the anguish that had accumulated that day; she wept until
> she was sated.

Thus the ritual game is also the labyrinth that reconstructs an image. The image conjugates the episode as a desired form, as wonder.
The mechanism—the game—and its process—the conjured vision—are summed up in that instant, which coincides with the totality; and this procedure is also the ritual of the universal mirror
that the novel itself represents. In these episodes the extraordinary
aspect of the contemplative discovery rests, it seems to me, in its
gratuitousness, in its representation of the occult, which in this
novel destroys the banal notion of everyday life. Here everything, including the most petty detail, occurs at the incandescent edge of
contemplation, where every detail stands out in relief. This is why
the labyrinth expands when a door is opened or when two objects
fortuitously coincide in a show window. These coincidences create a
new space, a different order that discovers the enigma of seeing in
the enigma of the object.

The last passage also discloses the part played by Cemí's family
throughout his poetic adventure. The mother is the starting point,
the manifested form of an unmanifested, unconquered form linked
to the father; and the home is the permanent background, the fertile
soil of this adventure.

In *Paradiso* the home is the *axis mundi*, the image par excellence,
the central fire. It is not an excluding image, however. It is an incorporating image starting from which the world is an unknown house
waiting to be inhabited. It is not simply a matter of chance that the
last pages of the novel narrate the nocturnal adventure of Cemí entering a three-floor, lighted house in whose center he will find himself. In addition, the home is transformed in the evoked, oozing oralness, thus preserving in its spatial anchor the flavor of a time that
has already been lived.

The family context is the common background of the transformations and also the constant mirror against which the characters are
defined. In defining Cemí's friends—Fronesis and Foción—Lezama

feels that he must define their family "mirrors," in other words, their personal labyrinths. This family context is defined, in addition, by the creole virtues that predominate within it. In this sense Uncle Alberto is probably the most animated character of this virtuous setting:

> All the lordliness of the Cuban bourgeoisie showed in him, the disdain, the domination of their surroundings, in which they came and went at will, accompanied by certain propitious deities that seemed to wave their hands, calling to approach without fear. It pleased his deities to have given him those gifts and a gracious, pleasant manner, which usually responded by shooting a precise arrow at the hare of the instant.

And also:

> For the family dynasty of the Cemís and the Olayas, the small diabolic dose of Alberto was more than enough. The family watched over and cared for that little devil cat as if he were the end result of a classical and robust development, characterized by smiling good sense and allied to the river of time in which that ark floated with alliances intertwined at the roots. Except for certain small features, Uncle Alberto formed an inaccessible and invisible part of this lustrous family tapestry, as if to receive the caress of the generations.

Courtliness is one of those high creole virtues, a form that establishes the standard of nobility in the life of the family and in society.

"Discipline should be accompanied by the grace that the image bestows, for to cut off from oneself the possibility of memory is an act which only mystics can support, living in the ecstasy of Paradise's plentitude," Lezema writes in this novel, stressing in this passage the potentiality of the image, an expanding nucleus of the past reconstructed by the desire to effect a formal process capable of convoking that plentitude.

In the last scene of the book, in which Cemí advances into the night to possess the enigma of poetry, he moves through a series of images: "This transition from amusement park into forest was invisibly assimilated by Cemí, for his hallucinated state kept the range of the image's possibility on its feet." He enters the lighted house where Oppiano Licario's sister gives him the poem that Oppiano had written about Cemí: "Reason and memory by chance / will see the dove attain / faith in the super-natural"; the discovery, therefore, of poetry as unity.

V

If courtliness is an eroticism of family nobility because it conjugates grace and wisdom, friendship is the opening of a world that conceives Eros as the conjugation of opposites, as a center from which nature, reality, is occupied, in the sense of the *occupatio* of the Stoics. As part of the process leading toward an integrating poetics, *Paradiso*'s astonishing eroticism is an uninterrupted debate, an exorcism of its other side: homosexuality. This debate brings together Foción, Fronesis, and Cemí, the three polemicists involved in the verbalization of an Eros that is about to be formulated. In his madness, Foción, who bears a *Neronian* sign, loses the possibility of defining his own eroticism at the level of poetic transmutations. The opposite is true of Fronesis, of *Goethean* sign, and especially of Cemí, who will make of Eros another analogical mechanism for discovering similarities. Thus, this conflictive debate will again be resolved in its poetic prolongation, a true guiding thread in this erotic labyrinth.

This debate is developed in chapter 9, which begins by describing a skirmish between rioting students and the police. The description suggests a battle between the Achaeans and Trojans. Cemí is confused by the turmoil, but suddenly "he felt a hand take his and pull him along from column to column every time there was a pause in the shooting." Like a warrior rescued by a god from the battlefield of Ilium, Cemí is rescued by Fronesis, whom he does not recognize until they have both reached safety. The Greek plot underlying this episode is also the plot of their friendship, and this incident brings together the three friends for the first time. A sort of introduction, this episode leads to another introduction, to Cemí's mother's words about his destiny and the epiphany of danger in the search for what is most difficult. This tortuous, labyrinthine search by means of Eros brings out the family history of the friends in order to disclose the reformulation of a deep-rooted eroticism. Although it would take too long to summarize this debate, it does not involve excluding viewpoints but, rather, different perspectives of homosexuality that eventually conjugate a central point of view; the origin conceived as an androgynous beginning and the end seen as liberation from sin. Toward the end of the chapter Cemí has a magical vision of an enormous phallus leading a strange procession. This image anticipates one of the final images of the novel, when Cemí has entered the "lucifugous house":

The emblemata of the mosaics were executed in red cinnabar, the lance was transparent like a diamond, a steel gray shaped the sword stuck in the ground like a phallus, and every trefoil showed a key, as if nature and super-nature had been united in something meant to penetrate, to jump from one region to another, in order to reach the castle and interrupt the feast of the hermetic troubadours. A garland tied Eros and Thanatos together, the submersion into the vulva was the resurrection in the Vale of Glory.

The lengthy debate on homosexuality can be understood starting from this type of metaphorization. The androgynous substratum of creation on which the dialoguers insist would thus be the source of the transformation, the matrix that prolongs the similarities, converting nature and supernature into transparent similarity. This duplication of nature through eroticism is also related to the recurring image of the tree of life, which in the novel is allegorically related with the phallus. This explains why the episode (chapter 11) in which Cemí listens to Foción's protracted monologue on the anality of the god Anubis and on how the embryo is prior to all sexual dualism (Mercury) is followed by a decisive passage on poetry and its practice. It should be noted that this type of construction is the basis of the narrative structure of the novel: one episode summons another in a successive hyperbolic transformation. The section on the practice of poetry in chapter 11—which transforms the exacerbated speech of an inebriated Foción—presents the poetic views of Cemí, who now conjugates in a new space the objects around him:

That immense populated area, from the alabaster Minerva to the Cuban smokers' engravings, was matched by the two bronze statuettes, the angel and the baccante, on each side of the Pueblan cup. At first with terror, and then with everyday joy, he viewed the coincidence of his navel, his omphalos, with the center of a universal phallic dolmen. Those groupings with an expressed dimension and with a directional waft were thought created, were animals of durable images that drew his body toward the earth so that he could ride them.

It seems to me, therefore, that the complex debate on homosexuality tends to exorcise an erotic point of view at this poetic level: eroticism is the ground on which objects coincide in order to create new objects, new images that expand our vision. The materialization of imagination, the invisible becoming visible, seems to require in this poetic system an eroticism capable of conjugating the poet with creation, with the Form, through an identity prior to sexual dualism; in other words, poetry is born from a totalizing eroticism, from an erotic inception defined by an unrestrained freedom to plot the conjugation of opposites in the essential similarity of reality. Nevertheless, this integrating eroticism, this germinative center, is also an asceticism, because its analogical freedom is guided by the intimate and irreversible march of a destiny whose labyrinths must evoke the "paradisiacal solution" announced by Foción.

The encounter of the *omphalos* and the universal phallic dolmen—axial symbolism—is also the encounter of the word and nature, the mutual creation of the poet and of the universe created by God. Poetry should find the axis of its condition in an intimately religious context, where it acquires its creative dimension, its principal justification. Poised between the descent into Hades (Foción) and the return to the light (Fronesis), Cemí sublimates eroticism through his discovery of the gnostic space, of officiating poetry, of the word as a religious act that leads to the axial encounter.

VI

Poetry has its origin in Eros, which generates its drive toward an incorporating knowledge, and that is why language is a supernature in the new space of its expansion:

> The door to the classroom closed, Cemí looked it up and down as if it were an inebriated Polyphemus who had come out to stop him from dealing with those questions in the Goethean tradition of "precise perceptive fantasy," which was almost the way in which the *intelligere* embraced its Eros, a lustful fanaticism of knowledge that was the shade from the tree of life, not in the antipodes of the tree of knowledge, but in the shade that joins the silent heaven of the Taoists to the Word that fertilizes the city as the supernatural.

The path leading to the unity of poetry is one of apprenticeship, a configuration and integration of different discoveries. Lezama gives us the following insight into the process of poetic formation:

> Like Fronesis, he had been led by the impassioned reading of Plato to polarize his culture. Those great rhapsodies in the *Phaedrus* and the *Phaedo* brought him to that mixture of exaltation and lament which constitutes love and death in the flash of their conjoinment. The hallucinated fervor for unity laid out, perhaps unsurpassably, in the *Parmenides* brought him to the mysticism of the relationship between creator and creature and to a conviction of the existence of a universal marrow which

controls series and exceptions. In the *Charmides* he would discover the seduction of the relationships between wisdom and
memory. "We know only what we remember" was the Delphic
conclusion of that culture. . . . And the unforgettable months of
his adolescence, spent with the *Timaeus*, which taught him
Pythagoreanism, and the apparent respite offered by the *Sym-
posium*, spawning the myths of primitive androgny and the
search for the image in reproduction and in the sexual comple-
mentaries of the Topos Ouranos and the Aphrodite Ourania.

A revitalization of the past and a search for the unknown are also
dimensions of the poetry conceived by Cemí and formulated as poetics by Lezama Lima. The above passage assembles the substratum of
a poetry activated by love-death, mystical and guiding unity, wisdom
and memory, Pythagorism and symbolism, the image sought in the
original androgyny. The discovery of the image that conjugates these
levels is also the discovery of the gnostic space. The practice of poetry is the materialization of the word, an entering into the gnostic
space, "which expresses, which knows, which has a density that
contracts to bring forth"; "gnostic space, tree, man, city, spatial
groupages in which man is the median point between nature and the
supernatural." In this poetic convocation, seeing plays a decisive
role. It discloses the alliance with incarnations in time, and this is
the instant of epiphany.

This way of seeing is outlined in the section of chapter 11 that describes the exercise of poetry in Cemí. The coincidence of a cup between two bronze statuettes evokes a baroque space. The coincidence of objects in a unitary space that prolongs them into an image
is a poetic allegory, an exercise of Lezama's poetic system. In this
instance it involves creating "cities invented by those groupings"
that allegorize the words in this episode.

He was able to establish that those groupings had temporal roots,
had nothing to do with spatial groupings, which are always a still
life; for the viewer, the flow of time converted those spatial
cities into figures, through which time, as it passed back and
forth like the labor of the tides on the coral reefs, produced a
kind of eternal change of the figures, which by being situated in
the distance were a permanent embryo. The essence of time,
which is the ungraspable, by its own movement that expresses
all distance, achieves the reconstruction of those Tibetan cities
which enjoy all mirages, the quartz doe of the contemplative
way, but into which we are not able to penetrate, for man, everything external producing an irradiation which reduces him to a

diamond essence lacking walls. The man knows that he cannot penetrate into those cities, but in him there is a disquieting fascination with those images, which are the only reality that comes toward us, that bites us, a leech that bites without a mouth, that by a contemplative method sustains the image, like most of Egyptian painting, and wounds us precisely with what it lacks.

In this passage Lezama has described its limits in the labryinth it ventures to discover, as well as the proximity or the final convocation that its unitary adventure is able to call forth in its void, in its absence. Thus, "the image in the distance is always contemplative," because it summons the Form in its form, because it repeats as supernature that which exists in the form of created nature. The image provokes an axial relationship, the union of the *omphalos* and the universal dolmen. Poetry is a religious act, the Tibetan city, the gnostic space that evinces the Unity. In an article entitled "Para llegar a Lezama Lima," Julio Cortázar discusses the passages that are central to the poetics of this book. He states that in this novel words are converted into objects and then objects are transformed into words. This is precisely what is involved in the gnostic process, the path from a temporal vision to a baroque space. In addition, this vision is animated by a "lingering of nature," in the presence of which an observant lingering, "which is itself nature," implies the discovery of rhythm, in other words, the prolongation of the look in the framework of the "hyperbolic memory" (see the dialogue between José Cemí and his grandmother).

Guided by these discoveries, chapter 12 appears to be an allegory of the poetics that Cemí is beginning to formulate. This chapter, which consists of literary exercises written perhaps by Cemí himself, interposes the following four sequences, which will later be conjugated: the story of a Roman general, that of a child and a vase, that of a nighttime stroller, and the curious story of the music critic who prolongs a timeless, grotesque life. The final shuffling of these stories allegorizes the theme of time. Through the intervention of his wife, the music critic appears to be outwitting time by prolonging an artificial life, but in the end his story is a grotesque absurdity. He dies, and the Roman warrior surprisingly appears in his glass casket.

Instead of a music critic surrendered to sleep to conquer time, the face of a Roman general who moaned, immobilized as the possibility of dying in the whirlwind of battle was obliterated for him. . . . Now the critic can perceive the drops of the temporal, but not as other mortals do, for death, not sleep, begins now to really give him the eternal, in which time cannot be conquered, beginning with the non-existence of that sin which is time.

In the final scene of this chapter, two centurions are rolling dice in the ruins of a Christian temple that had previously been an academy of pagan philosophers. A Greek bust falls and interrupts the game, changing the marks on the two dice to a four:

> The two dice achieved a four, one alongside the other, as if the two surfaces had joined their waters. The four remained under the ruined cupola in the center of the crossing of the nave and transept. The two centurions covered themselves with a single cape, from the neck there arose something like the head of a large turtle, and trying not to stumble, they strode off with the pace of a forced march.

This scene suggests a symbolic synthesis of the four stories developed in this chapter, perhaps in a religious framework, because four is the number of the Ineffable Name, "the fountain of nature that always flows, God." Thus, and although this chapter undoubtedly contains much richer allegories, Cemí is shown developing an exercise of poetry that is resolved in the symbol.

The presence of Oppiano Licario dominates the remaining chapters, and through him poetry is postulated as the final image of *Paradiso*. As we already mentioned, Oppiano is also an allegory of Cemí himself, a projection of him toward the past, toward the decisive moments of his life at which he was not present (the death of his father and of his uncle Alberto), and therefore his encounter with this fulgent Icarus represents the closing of an open cycle, the encounter that links a past and a destiny in the relating of a *Bildungsroman*.

Oppiano and Cemí meet on a bus marked by the sign of the decapitated head of a bull, a multiple image of power. Oppiano's conversation with several girls on the bus could also apply to the rich process of Cemí's discovery of poetry:

> Every instant brings a fish out of water and the only thing I'm interested in is catching it . . . if not for an occasion, whirlwinds of coincidence frozen into sculpture, how would we be able to show wisdom? Life is a web of indeterminate situations, each coincidence is something that wants to speak at our side, if we interpret it, we incorporate a form, we control a transparency. . . . The only thing that can interest me is the coincidence of my ego in the diversity of situations. If I let those coincidences pass, I'll

feel myself dying when I interpret them, I'm the maker of a miracle, I've dominated the unformed act of nature.

Here poetry is defining life, prolonging it by the coincidence through which the "I" incorporates nature, sculpturing the instant. From a compelling vision, poetry now becomes the breath of imagination, a new axis of the world:

That ancestor (his father) had endowed Licario from birth with a powerful *res extensa* which could be watched from his childhood on. The cogitative had begun to burst out, to divide or to perform subtle breathing exercises in the expanding zone. . . . The *occupation* of extension through the cogitative was so perfect that in it cause and effect reworked incessantly in alternating currents producing the new absolute order of the cognitive being. It broke with Cartesian mathematical progression. In the analogy, two ends of the progression developed a third progression, or a march to encompass the third unknown point. At the first two ends, much nostalgia for the expansive substance continued to persist. The discovery of the third unknown point at the moment of recovery, was what visualized and slowly extracted from the extension the analogy of the first two movables. Cognitive being attained its sphere always in relation to the third, errant, unknown movable, before that moment given by the disguised mutations of ancestral evocation. . . . Thus, where that spatial ordering of the two points of analogy intersects with the temporal, movable unknown, Licario situated what he called *Poetic Syllogistics*. . . . Licario nourished himself, in his cogitative extensibility, on those two currents: an ascent of the germ until the act of participation, which is knowledge of death, and later in the poetic awakening of a cosmos that reverted from the act to the germ through the mysterious labyrinth of the cognitive image.

Licario is, therefore, the allegorical realization of Cemí, the mirror that projects him. His definition through poetry, his destiny occupied by poetry is also an anticipation of his disciple, who will incorporate his dead teacher in the center of this verbal ritual. Licario is the key that opens the flaming house from which Cemí will emerge toward a new beginning, toward the recognition of rhythm, that is to say, toward the unity of his own experience in poetry, in *Paradiso*. The analogy of the terms in a progression that develops the third term of the adventure, creating the image, is also the germinative and nuclear eroticism, and this syllogistics is also an asceticism, a mysticism of total poetry (or a poetry of totality, as Octavio Paz prefers) as an enchanted vision of the world. In the end it is David, not Oedipus, who in his praise reproduces the Creator, the verbal supernature, the unified paradise, the garland which links Eros and Thanatos. This fabulous novel thus formulates a poetics as a multiple adventure, as an amazing metaphor of the world.

8. *One Hundred Years of Solitude*

In addition to its obvious quality, part of the great success of *One Hundred Years of Solitude** can be attributed to the fact that it is a lengthy tribute to the reader. This novel demands and obtains the best from each reader; it tests the reader's availability and then assaults and transforms it by transgressing verisimilitude, exciting the imagination, motivating the sensibilities, demanding a sense of humor, and evoking compassion. It also demands that a historical parallel be established with its scheme, with the century of Latin-American events whose vast possibilities of pain and happiness end in death and destruction, that is, in the closing of one period and in the proximity of a different time, because the world and time of this novel are both closed, they have ended. The history of Macondo is another version of the Latin-American past, but it is in the novel itself—between the foundings and the apocalypse—that these births and destructions have their own scheme, motivation, and subtle dialectics.

These relationships between different worlds and times form the central structure of this novel. This structure includes at least four sequences of worlds and times: (1) the mythical world and time of the founders; (2) the historical world and time ushered in by Aureliano Buendía and his wars; (3) the cyclical time of the old age and death of the initial characters and their world changed by the insertion of Macondo into a vaster reality; and (4) the deterioration of Macondo, *axis mundi*, by the depleting effect of the exchange of its reality of the external world and time, which is tantamount also to the extinction of the family line, the axis of Macondo. Let us examine these relationships in some detail.

*Gabriel García Márquez, *One Hundred Years of Solitude*, translated by Gregory Rabassa (New York and Evanston: Harper & Row, 1970). Originally published as *Cien años de soledad* (1967).

The mythical world and time of Macondo's foundation implies a search for a lost paradise. Hoping to reach the sea, José Arcadio Buendía, patriarch and founder, has undertaken, together with various other families, an exodus through the jungle. During the painful march through the swamps, he dreams that "right there a noisy city with houses having mirror walls rose up. He asked what city it was and they answered him with a name that he had never heard, that had no meaning at all, but that had a supernatural echo in his dream: Macondo. On the following day he convinced his men that they would never find the sea. He ordered them to cut down the trees to make a clearing beside the river, at the coolest spot on the bank, and there they founded the village."

This search, which can be seen as a search for a paradise, is not necessarily equivalent to a religious undertaking. It suggests above all the drive toward the rediscovery of the world, the need to conquer that world through a primordial identity, the dream of reestablishing an original reality. Thus, the journey and the founding are placed in the context of ritual. José Arcadio Buendía decides to leave his village after he kills Prudencio Aguilar to destroy the rumors of Buendía's unconsummated marriage. Already in the motivation of this journey, in this self-imposed expulsion, a ritual begins to form. This episode takes on even greater significance from the fact that Ursula, José Arcadio's wife, is his cousin; they are equivalent to the primordial couple. For this reason of kinship she tries to insist on not consummating the marriage, horrified by the curse of giving birth to a child with a pig's tail. The sin and punishment of an amorous relationship that is also a blood relationship thus appear at the beginning of this journey. The son is born without the feared pig's tail, but José Arcadio Buendía has killed a man in order to kill a rumor, and his guilty conscience drives him to undertake the journey, to expel himself from the village. The sense of humor with which Gabriel García Márquez relates these incidents and the way he expands them through hyperbole should not prevent our recognizing in them the roots and rituals of an archetypal fantasy: the guilt of love, the expulsion, the search for another world, the pursuit of another innocence. Paradise is mentioned twice in these first pages: "The men of the expedition felt overwhelmed by their most ancient memories in that paradise of dampness and silence, going back to before original sin . . ." and "[they] dismantled their houses and packed up, along with their wives and children, to head toward the land that no one had promised them."

A dream reveals to José Arcadio Buendía that he has found the site for his city. He sees a city whose walls are mirrors, another emblematic image. Later he comes to believe he has understood the dream when he sees a block of ice for the first time, but these mirrors will also become a mirage in the destruction that occurs at the end of the novel.

In this primordial zone the world is organized archetypically: objects emerge for the first time; José Arcadio Buendía discovers through his own calculations that the world is round; death is still unknown ("The world was so recent that many things lacked names, and in order to indicate them it was necessary to point"); Macondo appears to be an island; and Colonel Aureliano Buendía reports that the region is surrounded by water. This isolated world is sustained by the fantasy of José Arcadio Buendía and by the presence of Melquíades, the magician, a sort of internal author of the work, a hyperbole of the author himself. An unrestrained desire for knowledge leads José Arcadio Buendía to experiment constantly with magnets, magnifying lenses, and maps. This quest is another mythical dream: the need for science, for knowledge. The plague of insomnia is therefore also a parable, inasmuch as it reveals this experience of the world. Realizing "the infinite possibilities of a loss of memory," José Arcadio Buendía marks everything with its name, and "thus they went on living in a reality that was slipping away, momentarily captured by words, but which would escape irremediably when they forgot the values of the written letters." The reality threatened by a loss of memory suggests allegorically that the plague of insomnia will rescue it through knowledge and will make it tangible and alive. The past begins to be constructed starting from this conquest of reality.

José Arcadio Buendía announces the end of the mythical time when he states that "it's Monday" on a Tuesday and continues to affirm this even on Friday. He says: ". . . but suddenly I realized that it's still Monday, like yesterday. Look at the sky, look at the walls, look at the begonias. Today is Monday too." And later: "On Friday, before anyone arose, he watched the appearance of nature again until he did not have the slightest doubt but that it was Monday." From the point of view of the other characters it is in fact not Monday, but in a mythical world time is not linear. Consequently, José Arcadio Buendía is taken for mad and tied to a chestnut tree, where he dies. But actually he does not die. Tied to the tree of life, the enormous patriarch is still the founder, the Father. Melquíades, a sort of serpent who invites his audience to eat of the fruits of science, also dies without dying. He is rejuvenated in the sacred zone of that world, the room of the successive alchemists in which Melquíades has written the history of Macondo and of the Buendías, his prophesies, which are the novel itself. Ursula, the mother, while being per-

haps the most pragmatic character in this world, is also an archetypal character. With the exception of her initial march through the
swamps, she is the only character who does not experience any
transformation apart from that of aging. As the Mother, she is a mirror that reflects the events occurring around her.

After this mythical time, Colonel Aureliano Buendía's wars indicate that Macondo has become part of a more concrete, historical
time. Time becomes historical as Macondo's second generation witnesses the expansion of its world. This historical time reveals its political dichotomies and its elements of social injustice in the banana
company's transformation of the village through its methods of
extortion. Macondo's world is infiltrated by a conflictive, outside
world. In the mythical world time was a norm, and the narrator says,
"time put everything in its place." In the world transformed by history, on the other hand, time is equivalent to chaos, and the narrator
states, "time finally confused everything."

The ludicrous thirty-two armed uprisings instigated and lost by
Colonel Aureliano Buendía, the contradictory fortunes of rebellion
and politics, and the eventual destruction of Aureliano, who is bewildered by the hidden factors of power, suggest in the novel the
madness threatening this history, as well as its deep confusion and
its destructive thrust. The thirst for justice becomes in the end, a
blind slaughter. Pure rebellion, the total war declared by the Colonel, is thus condemned to the absurd destruction of itself and of the
world it jeopardizes. When Aureliano, who has been condemned to
death, returns to Macondo, he is startled to see how the town had
aged in one year.

As this historical time draws to a close, time becomes a spiral and
cyclically recovers the world. In this world the notion of time is governed by the recollections of the characters: old age recalls a bygone
time. When Aureliano Segundo asks Ursula if what he has read in
the history left by Melquíades is true, "she answered him that it
was, that many years ago the gypsies had brought magic lamps and
flying mats to Macondo. 'What's happening,' she sighed, 'is that the
world is slowly coming to an end and those things don't come here
any more.'" In her old age Ursula decides to educate Aureliano
Segundo's son to become Pope:

> No one would be better able than she to shape the virtuous man
> who would restore the prestige of the family, a man who would
> never have heard talk of war, fighting cocks, bad women, or wild
> undertakings, four calamities that, according to what Ursula
> thought, had determined the downfall of their line.

This cyclical time suggested by the repetition of the family line is something akin to a game of mirrors. The kinship ties in this novel are intertwined by the reiterative game of names and by the two personality types: "While the Aurelianos were withdrawn, but with lucid minds, the José Arcadios were impulsive and enterprising, but they were marked with a tragic sign." The only cases impossible to classify are those of José Arcadio Segundo and Aureliano Segundo, identical twins who confuse even the family, but it is precisely through this hyperbolic identity that they reveal the spiral reiteration running through their family history. When José Arcadio Segundo announces that he is setting out for the coast to search for a Spanish galleon that had gone aground many years earlier, Ursula shouts: "I know all of this by heart. It's as if time had turned around and we were back at the beginning." The grandchildren repeat the actions of their grandfather by making another effort to reach the outside world. Aureliano Triste plans to build a railroad and draws a sketch on the table: "Looking at the sketch that Aureliano Triste drew on the table and that was a direct descendent of the plans with which José Arcadio Buendía had illustrated his project for solar warfare, Ursula confirmed her impression that time was going in a circle."

At the vortex of this spinning time, Ursula can now judge the history of her family; she becomes aware of the full presence of her descendants and understands them for the first time. She realizes Aureliano had fought all his wars out of "pure and sinful pride" and because he was incapable of loving. In the "lucidity of her old age" she discovers that Amaranta was not a hard woman but "the most tender woman who had ever existed." In this time she also realizes "that her clumsiness was not the first victory of decrepitude and darkness but a sentence passed by time. She thought previously, when God did not make the same traps out of the months and years that the Turks used when they measured a yard of percale, things were different." She wants then to allow herself "an instant of rebellion" as a protest for "over a century of conformity."

"Shit!" she shouted.

Amaranta, who was starting to put the clothes into the trunk, thought that she had been bitten by a scorpion.

"Where is it?" she asked in alarm.

"What?"

"The bug!" Amaranta said.

Ursula put her finger on her heart.

"Here," she said.

Thus, judging a depleted time, the Mother points to herself as the center of the enormous failure of a century destroyed by conformity.

This cyclical time, like the mythical time before it, brings out the recurring theme of the symbols, of the objects that become archetypes: the Colonel makes little gold fish that he then melts and pounds again into little fish, and Amaranta laboriously weaves her own shroud. This entire time, then, is filled with echoes, it is infiltrated by previous times and worlds. "It's as though the world was going in circles," Ursula says, because time repeats itself.

The death of the characters returns the mythical world to a reality complicated by experience. Death, like love, war, solitude, and the other factors affecting the life of the characters, is also transfigured in this novel through hyperbole. Thus the narrator always transfers us to another reference, to a new possibility of its thematization. In this zone in which the novel turns on itself, the possibilities of death also suggest the allegorical context that suddenly summarizes the life of a character. Raveling and unraveling time through the little gold fish he manufactures, before he dies Colonel Aureliano Buendía hears the shouting of the children and the music of the circus:

> He saw a woman dressed in gold sitting on the head of an elephant. He saw a sad dromedary. He saw a bear dressed like a Dutch girl keeping time to the music with a soup spoon and a pan. He saw the clowns doing cartwheels at the end of the parade and once more he saw the face of his miserable solitude when everything had passed by and there was nothing but the bright expanse of the street and the air full of flying ants with a few onlookers peering into the precipice of uncertainty. Then he went to the chestnut tree, thinking about the circus, and while he urinated he tried to keep on thinking about the circus, but he could no longer find the memory. He pulled his head in between his shoulders like a baby chick and remained motionless with his forehead against the trunk of the chestnut tree.

Aureliano sees in the circus the parable of his own life. As the fanfare ends he recognizes his solitude in the emptiness of the street. He derisively urinates on the tree of life, where the presence of his father can still be felt, and dies leaning against the tree. The flowers that rain from the sky when the founder dies and the thread of blood and gunpowder at José Arcadio's death are also signifiers of these characters. In the shadow of her own death, Amaranta reconstructs the entire presence of her life "in the unbounded comprehension of solitude." Death itself has told her that she will die when she finishes weaving her shroud. Thus, she weaves her complicated life in order to die.

Caught in this spiral of time, the world begins to deteriorate when the family line, which is its axis, goes into a rapid decline. The expectant fullness of the mythical world and the fabulous confusion of the historical world are replaced by a decaying reality, by a decline leading to total destruction. Hinting at this destruction, the narrator announces that the axle had become worn; Macondo is the *axis mundi*, but the line of the Buendías is also an axis, and so is the constructed and reconstructed house, especially Melquíades's room, rooted in its mythical time, where time does not flow and where the grandchildren discover that "it's always March and always Monday."

Macondo ages with the war and is rejuvenated by the banana boom, but its history demands destruction. The shifting realities and the comings and goings of its characters slowly bring about its decay. The flood, which is a parable originated by the exploitation of the banana company, leaves a solitary and lost town from which the young people attempt to flee. Macondo now lives a farcical, insidious past,

> a past whose annihilation had not taken place because it was
> still in a process of annihilation, consuming itself from within,
> ending at every moment but never ending its ending. . . . In that
> Macondo, forgotten even by the birds, where the dust and the
> heat had become so strong that it was difficult to breathe, se-
> cluded by solitude and love and by the solitude of love in a house
> where it was almost impossible to sleep because of the noise of
> the red ants, Aureliano and Amaranta Ursula were the only
> happy beings, and the most happy on the face of the earth.

The last descendants of the line of the Buendías love each other with the courage their ancestors failed to show, but they also bring about the end. They do not realize that they are aunt and nephew, and their child is born with a pig's tail. Amaranta Ursula dies in childbirth, and Aureliano sees his son transformed into "a dry and bloated bag of skin" dragged away by the ants. Then he recalls the epigraph on the parchments left by Melquíades: "*The first of the line is tied to a tree and the last is being eaten by the ants.*" Studying the parchments again, he realizes that "Melquíades had not put events in the conventional time, but had concentrated a century of daily episodes in such a way that they coexisted in one instant." Reading the parchments, he discovers in them his own fate, his imminent death. A wind destroys Macondo, "the city of mirrors (or mirages)." In reading the parchments, in reading the novel itself, this character reads himself. The ancient metaphor of the "book of life" thus closes the world and time.

García Márquez has explained that *One Hundred Years of Solitude* is the story of a family trying to avoid the birth of a son with a pig's tail. He has stated that this is the unity of the novel, but aside from being an internal motivation, it would appear that this fear is just another thread in the plot. The unity of the novel, its coherence, is actually found in its structure, in its formulation. The stories of the various characters are interwoven by the author's skillful manipulation of a structure based on temporal discontinuity.

According to García Márquez, this novel was initially developed following a chronological sequence, but he soon realized that it was impossible to write a linear history of Macondo and the Buendías. The key to this structure is found in the sentence that attributes to Melquíades the arrangement of events to coexist in one instant (discontinuous time), rather than in the order of man's conventional, chronological time. The daily episodes of an entire century thus unfold at the same time, because the time of this novel is sustained by the time of reading: the reader constructs the temporality of the novel as he relinguishes his chronological notions of time. Hence the presence of the future in the present time of the narrative, a present time embedded in a weightless past, since the perspective of this writing requires the discourse of the chronicle. The temporal discontinuities, the leaps in time that juggle this century of episodes, are underscored by the profuse use of formulas such as "every year," "many years later," "long hours," "several years," "in a few years," "several centuries later," "for several weeks," and so on, formulas that never clearly state a temporal measurement but that insinuate it by broadening the reverberations of time, insuring a continuity that in fact is essentially temporal. In addition, these formulas evoke the narrative tone of legends and thus introduce a convention of verisimilitude at the very core of the fantasy. In this novel the play of reality and fantasy is never dual; the narrative presence of the temporal compels "fantasy" to be a part of "reality," to be a spontaneous possibility of it.

Fantasy and reality constantly shift back and forth within the only web they form, underscoring the various worlds of the characters. For Ursula, for example, reality is immediate: "The concert of so many different birds became so disturbing that Ursula would plug her ears with beeswax so as not to lose her sense of reality." José Arcadio Buendía, on the other hand, "fascinated by an immediate reality that came to be more fantastic than the vast universe of his imagination," reveals another side of the changing possibilities of reality and fantasy. The men and women that Ursula brings to Macondo carry with them "pure and simple earthly accessories put on sale without any fuss by peddlers of everyday reality," in contrast to the disrupting magic of the gypsies. The plague of insomnia, a fantastic parable, threatens to disintegrate language, on which the characters base their knowledge of reality, and in his dreams José Arcadio Buendía sees himself walking through infinite rooms and "he would find Prudencio Aguilar in the room of reality. But one night . . . Prudencio Aguilar touched his shoulder in an intermediate room and he stayed there forever, thinking that it was the real room," a parable of his death.

It is more frequent, however, to find the immediate reality being extended in fantasy, which is its echo, its own vision. The mechanism of this extension is hyperbole. Fantastic elements are routinely introduced directly into the narrative. For example:

> This time, along with many other artifices, they brought a flying carpet. But they did not offer it as a fundamental contribution to the development of transport, rather as an object of recreation. The people at once dug up their last gold pieces to take advantage of a quick flight over the houses of the village . . .

and:

> She was in the crowd that was witnessing the sad spectacle of the man who had been turned into a snake for having disobeyed his parents.

This method of evoking the realm of the fantastic, which is a primary clue to the reading of this novel, is based on humor and on a sense of amazement and of the dramatic, as illustrated by the rain of flowers at José Arcadio Buendía's burial, the ascension of Remedios the Beauty, and many similar episodes. But the fantastic element functions as a reverberation of the referent, especially when an anecdote is distorted by hyperbole. Humor and fantasy are thus provoked in the contrasts, in the intimate oppositions, in the spontaneous exaggerations, and in the use of accumulation and giantism, which García Márquez, a Rabelaisian in the end, prolongs. This hyperbolic mechanism is visible, for example, in all the episodes of amorous initiation. The relations of José Arcadio with Pilar Ternera and the gypsy girl and of Aureliano with a prostitute disclose this mechanism. When he returns to Macondo tattooed from head to foot, José Arcadio, who raffles his virile member among a group of prostitutes, is himself a hyperbole. The same is true of Aureliano Segundo, an outrageous reveler, who fills the house with guests, "invincible worldly carousers," and whose eating contest with The Elephant is typical of this Rabelaisian tone. Aureliano's wars are dramatized by hyperbole, and Amaranta's conduct turns this use of hyperbole inward. The fantastic element is therefore such a clear transparency of reality that García Márquez has not had to resort to objective and accumulate details to represent it. Instead, the hyperbolic mechanism freely sustains the sense of amazement in the chronicle itself. This accounts for the profuse use of adjectives; qualities here are always clearly superlative.

But even the zestfulness of the fantastic element as a prolonging reference eventually feels the drama of cyclical time and of the end time, because on the other side of the hyperbole, at the end of the exaggerated and fervent exercise of fantasy, lies the white circle of solitude and the terror of the curse. The solitude of these one hundred years of events lives in all the protagonists as a condition fixed in the spiral of their history. Solitude is one of the traits of the Buendías, and it is also a precarious form of union: "they took refuge in solitude"; "more than mother and son, they were accomplices in solitude." Melquíades returns from death "because he could not bear the solitude"; Remedios the Beauty matures in solitude; Fernanda is humanized by it; and Aureliano goes astray in the solitude of his immense power. Solitude is also the mirror that recovers a life in the passing instant of a recurring time. In this instant "solitude had selected the memories" for Amaranta, who thinks about Rebeca, unyielding in the intransigence by which she conquered "the privileges of solitude." Colonel Aureliano Buendía also capitulates, reaching "an honorable pact with solitude." Ursula reviews the history of her family from the perspective of solitude as a clairvoyant awareness. The last characters are "secluded by solitude and love and by the solitude of love." In the end we are told that the "races condemned to one hundred years of solitude do not have a second opportunity on earth." Solitude is thus a many-sided condemnation pervading everything from the smallest habits (Ursula looks through the window following "a habit of her solitude") to the most significant moments and even to the summing up of an entire life. In a moment of lucidity in which she sees her life flash before her, Ursula senses her guilt in having lived "over a century of conformity." In the human condition, the novel seems to be saying, conformity condemns us to solitude, to the absence of communion. Conformity reduces existence to the endless daily occurrences in which man is always the object of a world that determines him and in which he succumbs without full consciousness, without being able to fight back.

This conformity and its unchallenged bastion, solitude, are also bound together by an ancient taboo, by an absurd and fanatical curse: the son born with a pig's tail. This fear is spread, above all, by Ursula. It inhibits love and reveals feelings of guilt. Her children are born without the dreaded tail, but Ursula sees the curse in every potential evil. When she discovers the unabashed nakedness of her son José Arcadio, she fears that the curse may have been manifested in this manner, and when Colonel Aureliano Buendía becomes a banal tyrant, she threatens him with death: "It's the same thing I would have done if you had been born with the tail of a pig," she says. However, the curse comes true only for the one couple that freely love each other. The end of the family line betrays the sin at the origin and the guilt in love, part also of the character of this century condemned by its own alienation. Man, who lost paradise and reconquers it by inventing an archetypal world, loses it again in the solitude that transpires in the proximity of punishment and death. The curse of the son born of sin points therefore to a region of explicit guilt and implied rebellion. It reveals the irreversible condemnation of an age, a family line, and a history. These one hundred years of solitude find in the dialectics of several worlds and time the exorcism by which this novel makes them beautiful and terrible and also claims a different time, a time of innocence.

9. *The Autumn of the Patriarch*: Text and Culture

The complexity of *The Autumn of the Patriarch** has not gone un-
noticed by its readers, several of whom have sought to account for its
power of persuasion,[1] but this complexity still requires further me-
thodical analyses capable of following the debate on Latin-American
history and culture rekindled by Gabriel García Márquez through
his writing. The notable international success of García Márquez's
novels should not make us believe, however, as has easily occurred
in the case of Borges, that the values of a work are measured by its
international dissemination. These values are revealed, instead, in
the capacity of the work to reshape the notions and perceptions of
our own literary tradition and cultural space. The extraordinary dimension of García Márquez's writings emerges not only from his
widely recognized mastery of storytelling, but also from the fruitful
participation of his works in the reformulation of a Latin-American
literature capable of resolving its peculiarity and its universality, capable of accounting through fiction for the experience and consciousness of the culture that generates it. Czech novelist Milan Kundera
has stated that "to speak of the end of the novel is a local preoccupation of West European writers, notably the French. It's absurd to talk
about it to a writer from my part of Europe, or from Latin America.
How can one possibly mumble about the death of the novel and have
on one's bookshelf *One Hundred Years of Solitude* by Gabriel García
Márquez?"[2] To go just a bit further, we would add that in his works
García Márquez also gives account of the constitutive process of
the Latin-American cultural consciousness by having articulated
through them one form of its privileged realization. The following

*Gabriel García Márquez, *The Autumn of the Patriarch*, translated by Gregory Rabassa (New York: Avon Books, 1977). Originally published as *El otoño
del patriarca* (1975).

notes seek to illustrate this debate from the perspective of a semi-ological approach to the literary text within the sphere of culture.[3]

The Code of Politics

The Autumn of the Patriarch is, in effect, a novel about a Latin-American dictator, but it is also a novel about the Latin-American people who suffer this paradigmatic tyrant. Just as the nameless patriarch of the novel is the sum of all the dictators of a space centered in the Caribbean, but including the city of Comodoro Rivadavia, and also of the name, facts, and products (coca, rubber, tobacco) of several Latin-American countries, so too the collective narrator of the novel is a sum of popular voices. The history of Latin America is thus reconstructed in the dialogue between this collective narrator and that nameless power. This process of communication, generated in the production of a writing, functions first of all as a political code, in other words, as the information modeled by the deciphering of power.

The political code implies recognition of the norms that shape the historical consensus. But here this consensus involves a distortion: history has been usurped by the dictatorial power. Political tyranny—with its violence, arbitrariness, and indulgence—replaces history, and the discourse of history is then in fact only a discourse of power. In the process of its production by a collective consciousness, this discourse models its own deciphering of the distortion, but not before recording—and the novel illustrating—the unmistakable functioning of the code of repressive power.

This code provides ample proof of its absolute domination. Its coherency is systematic and implies an underlying model of political and economic oppression, but its unrestrained expansion is no less systematic in the exercise of a terrifying hyperbole of power. These hyperbolic repercussions are magnified at the level of popular culture, where the arbitrariness of the absolute dictator and his outlandish popular image merge in the carnivalization of power fostered by the text.

In the first place, then, the political code emerges from the harsh evidence of our colonial and dependent condition. One of the sources of this dictatorial power is the colonial phase of our history; the other is its imperialistic phase. Patricio Aragonés states it clearly: "everyone says that you're president of nobody and that you're not on the throne because of your big guns but because the English sat you there and the gringos kept you there with the pair of balls on

their battleship." Dependency is a vicious circle, a state of permanent crisis:

> we had used up our last resources, bled by the age-old necessity of
> accepting loans in order to pay the interest on the foreign debt
> ever since the wars of independence and then other loans to pay
> the interest on back interest, always in return for something gen-
> eral sir, first the quinine and tobacco monopolies for the English,
> then the rubber and cocoa monopoly for the Dutch, then the con-
> cession for the upland railroad and river navigation to the Ger-
> mans, and everything for the gringos through the secret
> agreements.

The text extends this process of denationalization in the hyperbole of the Caribbean Sea transferred to the Arizona desert, but the
internal consequences of this power structure are equally verifiable.
The first of these is repression, and here repression reveals the antinational, surrogate function of the dictatorship:

> [they] begged us in the name of the nation to rush into the street
> shouting out with the gringos to stop the implementation of the
> theft, they incited us to sack and burn the stores and mansions of
> foreigners, they offered us ready cash to go out and protest under
> the protection of the troops who were solidly behind the people in
> opposition to the act of aggression, but no one went out general
> sir, because nobody had forgotten that one other time they had
> told us the same thing on their word of honor as soldiers and still
> they shot them down in a massacre under the pretext that agita-
> tors had infiltrated and opened fire against the troops.

Violence is, of course, the political practice of this barbarous power:

> they're going to fall on you like a pack of dogs to collect from you
> in one case for the killings at Santa María del Altar, in another for
> the prisoners thrown into the moat of the harbor fort to be eaten
> by crocodiles, in another for the people you skin alive and send
> their hides to their families as a lesson.

As always, this violence is institutionalized in a force inherent to
repressive governments:

> he made him absolute master of a secret empire within his own
> private empire, an invisible service of repression and extermina-
> tion that not only lacked an official identity but was even difficult
> to conceive of in its real existence, because no one was responsible
> for its acts, nor did it have a name or a location in the world, and

yet it was a fearsome truth that had been imposed by terror over other organs of repression of the state.

Just as this systematic model of power shapes the political code, other sources form the dictator's ferocious, pathetic, and delirious repertoire. These sources are the facts and stories about Latin-American dictators—and also about Franco—that have been documented or are spread as opinions, jokes, or versions. At this level, seminal in its own right, the text finds a means of access to the popular version of the dictatorship, that is to say, to the interpretation of power in terms of the popular culture. So that even though we may discover features that seem to evoke a specific dictator and situations that appear to be based on the experiences of certain other tyrants, the decisive element in the configuration of this character is the fact that through this proliferating and ubiquitous figure the text generates the carnivalized mythology of power.[4] The political code is thus transformed into a different code, that of popular culture.

Within the context of colonial domination, and focusing on the monumental figure of the dictator as a hyperbole of power, the text is produced as the totalized space of a reading of history. Here history is tantamount to politics; the total historical experience, from the discovery of America by the colonial enterprise of Columbus to the geographical plunder of imperialism, is rendered by the text as a travesty. The text demands the occupation of this historical space as an overall model denouncing the profound disruption of the Latin-American political experience. This is why it unfolds in a recurrent time—in which the act of the colonial origin is also the anticipation of a no less colonial future—rather than in a chronological time. Beginning with pre-Colombian times and continuing through the decades of financial imperialism, the code of power has been the same. Its figure is thus not a single person but, instead, all our dictators. The following image conjugates the historical moments:

> [he] opened the window that looked out onto the sea so that perhaps he might discover some new light to shed on the mix-up they had told him about, and he saw the usual battleship, anchored in the shadowy sea, he saw the three caravels.

History is viewed as anachronism and anticipation; its origin and its present time occur simultaneously in the spectacle of the text, in the scene of a writing that is tantamount to the space of consciousness.

The functioning of the political code does not stop there, however. Its connotative power is certainly much greater and involves other, less explicit, levels of the text. Turning again to the nameless patriarch, for example, the very fact of his namelessness implies the possession of all names, not only because he derives from our most visible tyrants, but because he transcends history through his encompassing historicity. We know that occasional protests and rebellions are silenced, and we also know that the tyrant is a figure agonizing in his loneliness and old age, but here power is not only the government or its authoritarian form, it is something more sordid and fundamental: the distortion of all communal norms, the perpetual model of domination. Thus the archetypal dimension of the patriarch occupies history and distorts it. Viewed from the perspective of the collective narrative, of popular legend, his figure acquires a mythologizing dimension; it is projected back to the origin and is the representation of power. Hence it also occupies language, imposing between words and things a conditioning that is simultaneously arbitrary and systematic.

"Bendición Alvarado didn't bring me into the world to pay heed to basins but to command, and after all I am who I am, and not you, so give thanks to God that this was only a game," the patriarch warns. At times, a religious substratum is clearly visible as an ironic referent in the novel. This is not intended to indicate that the omnipotent patriarch has also expropriated the repertoires of faith, but to illustrate in this textual caricature of it the comic license that total power attributes to itself. The point to be noted in this case, however, is the brazen tautology of the "I." "I am who I am"; that is to say, the loss of a name is the subject's gain inasmuch as his individuation is not contained in a name but in the representation of his archetypal person totalized by power. "*I am not you*"; in other words, you have a name, and that name, like your person, belongs to the absolute power. As distorted by this dictatorial power, politics implies the abolition of the "other," the shattering of the "you." Later, in the delirium of his old age, we read that

> one night [the patriarch] had written my name is Zacarías, he
> read it again under the fleeting light of the beacon, he read it
> over and over and the name repeated so many times ended by
> seeming remote and alien to him, God damn it, he said to himself, tearing up the strip of paper, I'm me, he said to himself.

The dictatorship is likewise a pronominal distortion. The patriarch, who does not require a name of his own, has occupied a grammatical category with his person and refuses to make a distinction between it and himself, revealing the evil root of his appropriation of all names. In effect, the patriarch is defined not only in the hyperboles of the collective narrative, but also in the successive nominal repertoires that, through description, enumeration, and the associative and conjunctive text itself, pour out a sort of holocaust of names, images that consume themselves in the great devouring space of power. This power thus appears to be infinite. All names are attributable to it in the unending description of its attributes, in the sinister resurrection of its profound arbitrariness, and in the total occupation of our history. This operation contains within it, however, the end of absolute power, because the narrative turns back on itself from its reconstructive present, from its common voice, from the day of the delirious dictator's death.

When the ferocious Sáenz de la Barra establishes an even more implacable system of repression within the dictatorship, power itself reveals the tyrant's impunity: "you aren't the government, general, you are the power." But is he? The patriarch has been equally ferocious, but for some reason he feels that his notion of power has been carried to an extreme by this henchman. For the henchman total repression "was the only power possible in the lethargy of death which in other times had been his Sunday market paradise." In other words, power is cyclical, it establishes itself as a natural order, and its own excesses must insure its restoration, its continuity. Sáenz de la Barra's rationality is a literal power that lacks continuity: an evasion of power. The patriarch's arbitrariness, on the other hand, is rooted in a power naturalized by his manipulation of that "Sunday marketplace."

No name: all attributes. The names of the world write the properties of the omnipotent dictator, thus modeling the nature of his usurping power. This is, then, a constructive process that gives rise to myth in language. The movement of language generates the mythological construction of the patriarch as the representation of power. His origins, feats, loves, deaths, and resurrections are sustained by a mythologizing discursive process in which the names substantiate his archetypal figure.[5]

Power is thus established as a natural order, but it is perceived as a naturalized disorder. The political code of a distorting absolutism implies, in the end, a modeling of reality, and this modeling occurs within the sphere of culture, whose own popular order adopts, assimilates, and responds to the perpetuated violence. The model of politics thus competes closely with the model of culture, attempting to subject, manipulate, and incorporate it.

This is why the political code of tyranny replaces ideologies—the religious conceptions, for example—and itself expands as an undeclared ideology. Its legitimization is an act of force and terror, but it also includes the arbitrariness of its domination: it is self-sufficient as an occupying power. Its normative practice induces a reduction of history and regulates the consensus. Its judgments imply an unrestricted appraisal and hierarchization deriving from the use and abuse of power, and, for this same reason, it represents the subjugating occupation of the life of an entire people. Proceeding as a natural power, the political code of tyranny seeks to appear as the expression of a culture when in fact it operates as its negation. But in this tension it reveals, precisely, its most intense conflict, because the questioning of the dictatorship from the juncture of popular culture is a debate between a reality humanized by a model of consensus and a distortion imposed by an authoritarian model. Thus, even though a people may live the naturalized disorder of the dictatorship as an ideological order, it is in the workings of its own culture model that this order is finally dismantled and defeated. In other words, culture as a way of knowing resolves and counters the ignorance promoted by the political distortion,[6] which brings us to the code of culture.

The Code of Popular Culture

We know that traditional political regimes attempt to reinforce the basic forms of social life, the relations of production, and the divisions among social groups. We know also that culture is part of the dynamics of history, contributing to the perpetuation or transformation of society.[7] Within this dynamics *The Autumn of the Patriarch* acts in the productive and critical sense that characterizes the popular culture that sustains it. Through its semantic operations in a specific cultural field, this literary text functions at the same time as a *text of culture*. From the point of view of semiology, this text represents a "condensed program" of Spanish-American culture.[8]

If, as Lotman contends, culture is the aggregate of information and also the means for organizing and preserving it—which implies a social conflict hinging on the "struggle for information"—then *popular culture* represents a specific form of the functioning of this information based on the communication that the collective speaker emits and receives, a process that models the historic experience in the collective memory.[9]

These forms of communication are a repertoire signifying a process of signification. They also imply a system of displacements, reductions, parodies, and, in general, a carnivalizing practice—through the masquerade, the feast, laughter, etc.—that celebrates the perpetuity of the people and emerges as a natural occupation of the public space, as Bakhtin has amply documented.[10] The dissolving power of that energy responds in this way to the malaise of history and liberates in consciousness a place of identity. Indeed, in our cultural reality the depredations perpetrated by the internal domination to which we have been subjected are a long history of violence against the sources of our Latin-American culture, whose popular formations have often been distorted and almost always eroded. Nevertheless, struggling against a tradition of ethnocentric violence, it has confronted, adapted, and revised its own versions of its conflictive and still unresolved origin. This, then, is the dimension of popular culture that we find in *The Autumn of the Patriarch* as a code receiving, processing, and generating the writing of the spectacle of power. The semantic forms of popular culture are elaborated and resolved as an articulating syntax in writing. In other words, the carnivalization of the text gives an account of the conflictive interaction of a history formulated as communication.

At the first death of the patriarch, which is the death of his double, Patricio Aragonés, the funeral ceremony soon becomes an outpouring of jubilation, which the patriarch observes "horrified with the idea of being quartered and devoured by dogs and vultures amidst the delirious howls and the roar of fireworks celebrating the carnival of my death." The carnival expresses the joy of popular liberation, but it also predominates in the production of the text itself through the circular point of view of an account that begins with the still questioned, but consummated, death of the dictator. But along with the carnivalized popular culture that contaminates the totalized account of the text, there is also a populist exercise of power acting as the natural form of its imposition. This is the false carnival of power, in other words, the manipulation of disorder as an order seeking to dominate the popular culture. This can be observed in the following passage:

> and still he governed as if he knew he was predestined never to die, for at that time it did not look like a presidential palace but rather a marketplace . . . because no one knew who was who or by whom in that palace with open doors in the grand disorder of which it was impossible to locate the government. The man of the house not only participated in that marketplace disaster but he had set it up himself and ruled over it.

On its own, writing places in the account of the speakers the summary judgment of dictatorial power given by popular culture. The same process is reflected in the following sequence:

> everything had been a farce, your excellency, a carnival apparatus that he himself had put together without really thinking about it

when he decided that the corpse of his mother should be displayed for public veneration on a catafalque of ice long before anyone thought about the merits of her sainthood and only to contradict the evil tongues that said you were rotting away before you died, a circus trick which he had fallen into himself without knowing it ever since they came to him with the news general sir that his mother Bendición Alvarado was performing miracles and he had ordered her body carried in a magnificent procession into the most unknown corners of his vast statueless country.

In each case the text carnivalizes the information, but at the same time it distinguishes the tensions that are popular in origin from the manipulations of power. In this incident the despot reveals his frustrated project of replacing the popular version of the religious order. The farce reveals the comic paradox of the manipulation: "they had paid eighty pesos to a gypsy woman who pretended to give birth in the middle of the street to a two-headed monster as punishment for having said that the miracles had been set up by the government." This feigned childbirth, an event from the lore of the public square, is manipulated in this instance by the established power, but it is clearly false, so that for the public it becomes a dual spectacle.

The spectacle of power develops in the text as a conflictive production, rather than simply as a polar production, and it is only in the textual totalization of this polyvalent writing, as we shall later see, that it is finally resolved as an inclusive and continuous integration. The popular view of the patriarch, even within culture, implies an ambivalent movement: the gathering of information discloses this movement, but the sense of the movement is discerned only when the information is processed. The patriarch is not always perceived as monstrous—as he is to our consciousness as readers—while he is still a source of information that must be assumed, processed, and modeled; and the text does not shy away from this first evidence, which it resolves in the end. The text includes this evidence ("it's him, she exclaimed with surprise, hurray for the stud, she shouted, hurray, shouted the men, the women, the children") because it discloses the deep fear and impotence felt by the people in the presence of power. The same thing occurs in a later incident: "long live the stud, they shouted, blessed be the one who comes in the name of truth, they shouted." Here the religious allusion is given an ironic twist by the text. Thus the patriarch's death, which begins the liberation of consciousness, creates a certain perplexity:

and yet we didn't believe it now that it was true, and not because we really didn't believe it but because we no longer wanted it to be true, we had ended up not understanding what would become of us without him, what would become of our lives after him.

Some readers have almost resented the fascination exerted by the patriarch, but this is part of the ambivalence of the information gathered in the text and it is resolved in the integrating judgment suggested by the collective narrator.[11] This, then, is a work about information. From the perspective of social life information is emitted and recognized in the terms of a precarious and oppressed condition; from the standpoint of the uses of power it seeks to impose itself as the natural order of alienation; but from the point of view of the accounts of popular culture it is processed and elaborated as knowledge and response. Writing brings out these distinctions, formalizing their occurrence as a spectacle and carnivalizing their textual proliferation. Within this communicative network a reading of history is progressively being shaped as a promise of culture.[12]

Whereas for the Americans the country is a "nigger whorehouse," for the patriarch it is a "brothel of idolators." But the tyrant's opinion of the people is also paradoxical:

> he was left with the undeserved burden of truth . . . in this nation which I didn't choose willingly but which was given me as an established fact in the way you have seen it which is as it has always been since time immemorial with this feeling of unreality, with this smell of shit, with this unhistoried people who don't believe in anything except life.

From the point of view of the people this criticism is a virtue. Stripped of history, the only possibility left to the people is to reaffirm their own existence, and, therefore, the awareness of their fulfillment is based on the deciphering of that history. Naturally, the energy of the popular culture is what sustains the life of a community, and within it the scars of underdevelopment are clearly the product of the erosion suffered by that culture. In this novel the code of popular culture encourages a productive conversion: transferred to a textual practice, this practice sustains the fulfillment achieved. This conversion acts through systematic humor, crushing irony, numbing sarcasm, and hyperbolic paradox, thus creating the current of earthy, unrestricted, and reducing humor that also pervades the creative joy of *One Hundred Years of Solitude*, although in *The Autumn of the Patriarch* humor has an added analytical dimension, inasmuch as this novel is a reflection on a political tragedy approached from the perspective of cultural comedy. The humor is certainly Rabelaisian to some extent, but it is above all a characteristically Spanish-American popular humor that creates here a system of expansive communication based on its festive oralness. It is not surprising, then, that when Manuela Sánchez disappears, humor becomes a chorus of voices, popular songs, and a dance of writing: "they told him that she'd been seen in the madness of Papa Montero's wake, tricky, lowlife rumba bunch." Here the information is duplicated within its popular source, going toward and returning from the rhythm captured from a carnivalized culture.

In contrast with the sordid origins of power, the origins of the people are a carnivalization, as suggested by the festive reconstruction of Columbus's landing. Despite the interaction of the codes of political power and popular culture, the writing of the text and the discourse of culture is articulated by the general difference between them. From the pedestal of power the patriarch trusts in "the final argument that it didn't matter whether something back then was true or not, God damn it, it will be with time"; but from the reality of popular culture there is a more stable truth and a fuller certainty. The myth of the patriarch within the narrative is constructed, quite clearly, by the popular culture, but in this same act it openly carnivalizes him, transforming him into a parody of power that is no less terrible, certainly, but which at least is discernible in terms of a repertoire of its own. This is the point of view explored by writing as it releases the detailed store of information that is always processed by the cultural code.

The Mythological Code

The disjunctions of the political and cultural codes are resolved in the mythological code. This code accounts, of course, for the other two, but it also permits those significant internal tensions to be discerned in a symbolic field of forces that produce an ulterior consciousness.

It is here that the absence of information opens a cultural void, a loss of identity, in which the myth of the origin of power emerges:

> there was no one who doubted the legitimacy of his history, or
> anyone who could have disclosed or denied it because we
> couldn't even establish the identity of his body, there was no
> other nation except the one that had been made by him in his
> own image and likeness where space was changed and time corrected by the designs of his absolute will, reconstituted by him
> ever since the most uncertain origins of his memory.

This origin fuses history and cosmology as a fatalistic determinism: a model of the origin occupies reality and, therefore, replaces history.

Reality is divided into a *before* corresponding to primitive times ("the times of the Spaniards were like when God ruled more than the government, the evil times of the nation") and into an interminable *after* corresponding to the patriarch's power. The mythologizing construction disregards, of course, the chronology of events. The patriarch had witnessed the landing of Columbus, but he is also one of the generals of the wars of independence and a partner in the American invasion. He is an archetypal figure of power and therefore a model of its historical meaninglessness. The interminable parade of American ambassadors parodies the stability of this model. The origin is thus only a projection of the present, in other words, a draining of historical meaning and its occupation by power.

The free scope of this model permits the manipulation of mythology by the established power, which seeks to incorporate the repertoires of popular culture. This free scope is disclosed in an unrestricted delirium of power that seeks to exert its will even on the natural order. It is here that the mythological code reveals its function. In the delirium of his love for Manuela Sánchez, the bewildered patriarch asks himself

> what was going on in the world because it's going on eight and everybody's asleep in this house of scoundrels, get up, you bastards, he shouted, the lights went on, they played reveille at three o'clock . . . and there was the noise of startled arms, of roses that opened when there was still two hours left until dew time . . . and [they] replaced the flowers that had spent the night in the vases with last night's flowers, and there was a troop of masons who were building emergency walls and they disoriented the sunflowers by pasting gilt paper suns on the windowpanes so that it would not be noticed that it was still nighttime in the sky and it was Sunday the twenty-fifth in the house . . . while he opened a way lighted by the day through the persistent adulators who proclaimed him the undoer of dawn, commander of time, and repository of light.

The comic license of the patriarch readily exposes a mythological code adapted to the hyperbolic demands of his will, although it is based on an inversion: the carnivalesque apparatus that his servants construct also reveals the will to reorder the natural order, to convert the repository of power into a manipulatable source of reality. Thus, whereas popular culture proceeds by a system of conversions, the mythology of power acts by a process of inversions.

The same process is at work in the episode of the eclipse, which the patriarch interprets as an example of his power, in the incident in which in the process of imposing martial law "he declared a state of plague by decree" and "Sundays were suppressed," or when "he stopped time by his orders on the abandoned streets." The mythological code operates beneath the hyperbole, illustrating a crazed will to power and also reconstructing its own cosmology as the reformulated origin.

This is why the people see in the dictator the signs of the beginning and also of the end of time; in other words, they convert to their own code the threats, derisiveness, and delirium of the tyrant. Thus when the patriarch makes his son a major general the omens begin again:

> That unprecedented decision was to be the prelude of a new epoch, the first announcement of the evil times in which the army cordoned off the street before dawn and made people close balcony windows and emptied the market with their rifle butts so that no one would see the fugitive passage of the flashy automobile with armored plates of steel.

Leticia Nazareno presides over the new, evil times by her abusive and, in the end, punished plunder of the public markets. Elsewhere we read that "even the most incredulous of us were hanging on that uncommonly large death which was to destroy the principles of Christianity and implant the origins of the third testament." Beneath the hyperbole we find once again the mythical rebirth of a new age, in this case with the shudder of the future.

Thus these inversions construct in the text the mythology that sustains *a world inside out*. In effect, starting with the mythological origin of power we perceive that the inversion has modeled the historical reality; the world is continually being formed through the cycles of power, but its model of distortion is an unavoidable determinism. The world is inside out at its very origin: violence and political oppression occupy its foundation and distort it. The mythology of the origin is, therefore, a loss of the origin.

This inside out reality has a corresponding "inside out" man, a dictator whose mythological dimension is "totalizing" but whose individuality is reductive. Thus, when he decides to go near the people, he leaves a series of catastrophes in his wake because his power is disruptive: "he was not aware of the string of domestic disasters that his jubilant appearances brought on."

This dimension also includes a physical caricature. His origin is uncertain, and his sex is a stigma, as the "camp follower" declares, "she let go of it with fright, go back to your mama and have her turn you in for another one, she told him, you're no good for anything."

The apology for his condition is brutally illustrated in his displaced orgasm. The agony of an inordinate old age is also indicative of this condition.

The exact dimensions of this mythological power, which death reveals in its final derision, are defined at the end of the text, when the tensions are resolved. The summary judgment is finally a speech of consciousness and the myth yields to the evidence: "he had learned of his incapacity for love in the enigma of the palm of his mute hands . . . and he had tried to compensate for that infamous fate with the burning cultivation of the solitary vice of power"; "he had known since his beginnings that they deceived him in order to please him, that they collected from him by fawning on him, that they recruited by force of arms the dense crowds along his route"; and "[he] discovered in the course of his uncountable years that a lie is more comfortable than doubt, more useful than love, more lasting than truth." The sweeping response of the text emerges in this final revelation:

> he was condemned not to know life except in reverse, condemned to decipher the seams and straighten the threads of the woof and the warp of the tapestry of illusions of reality without suspecting even too late that the only livable life was one of show, the one we saw from this side which wasn't his general sir, this poor people's side.

This response is grounded in the popular culture, in the full awareness of its liberation. The mythology of the inside out world dissolves at this point in a surge of consciousness that affirms the real social existence and rejects the confiscating and substitutive power. The patriarch now becomes

> a comic tyrant who never knew where the reverse side was and where the right of this life which we loved with an insatiable passion that you never dared even to imagine out of the fear of knowing what we knew only too well that it was arduous and ephemeral but there wasn't any other, general, because we knew who we were while he was left never knowing it forever.

The reaffirmation of an enduring popular and communal existence enhances these final pages with the almost epic breath with which writing conveys the birth of consciousness.

Having confronted from within the repertoires of popular culture and of power, the mythological code, which induces the hyperbolic expansions of the text, yields to the last evidence of the text, to the production of a consciousness deriving from the action of the speakers, an act that propitiates the judgment of all times in the dialogical scene of this writing. This final evidence takes us back to the beginning of the text, but only after confirming on the last page the popular jubilation over this final impeachment: "the good news that the uncountable time of eternity had come to an end." With the death of the "patriarch" an entire people arrive at the adulthood of recognition; with the destruction of a mythological model the inside out world collapses and the popular culture recognizes its creative social dimension; with the disappearance of the distorting power based on this model an age without history comes to an end and a new age is announced. The end is thus a new beginning because it returns us to the point of departure of this debate, to the collective narrator.

The Code of the Collective Narrator

The first page of the text opens on the "vast lair of power" and on the vultures that announce the patriarch's death. "Only then did we dare go in," the narrator says. A people deprived of a written history reconstruct their past starting from this first scene in their oral history. It is in their own narrative that they learn, face themselves, and discern. One of the triumphs of this novel is its construction on a scheme of alternating the speakers who give evidence; in other words, the account unfolds from the perspective of a collective narrator whose code is developed as the central productive system of the text. This code forms the circuit of communication, and through it the information transmitted gives account of its sources, indicating the instances of direct evidence and those of hearsay, inferential, and indirect knowledge that construct the semantic space of the communication. This is where historicity is produced in opposition to a history seized by power, in the debate that will liberate a shared consciousness.

The first death of the dictator also marks the first day of consciousness, the narrative of what has been seen unleashing the sum of what has been heard in order to reset the stage of what has been lived. Whereas the unwritten response of the people is to survive the dictatorship, to live longer than the tyrant, their wisdom lies in their capacity to discern, formulated in this case as the extensive process of relating. The collective narration is established, therefore, as the privileged space of knowing. Even in this elaboration of the text, which corresponds to a peculiar modeling of the Latin-American *text of culture*, García Márquez achieves a poetic result of remarkable persuasive power because the textual model he produces resolves the tradition of a formal debate that is characteristically our own, that of the founding text that constructs a narrative system in which literature reformulates culture. This tradition is encountered, among others, in the textual drama of the chronicles of the Indies (especially in the cultural text of Inca Garcilaso), in the discursive elaborations of Sarmiento, and in the reordering song of *Martín Fierro*.

> And among the camellias and butterflies we saw the berlin from stirring days, the wagon from the time of the plague, the coach from the year of the comet, the hearse from progress in order, the sleep-walking limousine of the first century of peace, all in good shape under the dusty cobwebs and all painted with the colors of the flag.

This museum of power confirms the false, silenced carnival. The accumulation of this collective evidence adds credence to the information about the patriarch's death, which is then put to its first test: "Only when we turned him over to look at his face did we realize that it was impossible to recognize him, even though his face had not been pecked away by vultures, because none of us had ever seen him." This crisis of information, then, demands verification:

> and even though his profile was on both sides of all coins, on postage stamps, on condom labels, on trusses and scapulars, and even though his engraved picture with the flag across his chest and the dragon of the fatherland was displayed at all times in all places, we knew that they were copies of copies of portraits that had already been considered unfaithful during the time of the comet, when our own parents knew who he was because they had heard tell from theirs, as they had from theirs before them, and from childhood we grew accustomed to believe that he was alive in the house of power.

The information is thus lost in the origins of the narrative, at the point where the mythologized dimension of the patriarch begins. But we can already sense that the perspective of the debate of the narrative is what will place all the cycles of information within the holocaust of power produced by this collective narrator.

In the realm of myth, the code of the collective narrator formalizes the communication, processing it in its own ambiguity:

> The second time he was found, chewed away by vultures in the same office, wearing the same clothes and in the same position, none of us was old enough to remember what had happened the

first time, but we knew that no evidence of his death was final, because there was always another truth behind the truth.

Whereas different versions and alternatives support the construction of a myth, the narration of a text that is being produced collectively requires thorough verification because the communication emitted returns from the addressee as certainty, and it is through this dialogue that the speakers take shape. This certainty is what organizes knowledge:

> None of us was old enough to have witnessed that death of Bendición Alvarado but the fame of the funeral ceremonies had come down to our times and we had trustworthy reports that he did not go back to being what he had been before for the rest of his life. . . .

This is why the myth reaches a crisis point when it is confronted with the evidence of an information that reduces it to its real measure:

> Shortly before nightfall, when we finished taking out the rotten husks of the cows and putting a little order into that fabulous disarray, we were still unable to tell if the corpse looked like its legendary image.

The collective narrator is, then, the *collective I* of the popular culture. Its work shapes a cyclical series of information: the messages are emitted by an addressor (us) to an addressee (us). The information is thus circular and shifts as it processes and formalizes the messages in new circles of incorporation. The place of the addressor is constantly occupied by a momentary "I" that is part of a plural narrator, to which he delivers his message before returning to the latent collective chorus. Writing is thus mobilized by opening a syntagmatic space that expands as an articulated and, at the same time, free montage. The different codes alternate, confront each other, and interact, connoting the polyphony of an extraordinary enriched writing capable of achieving a supple dynamics in its broadly designed rhythms. In the process of alternating the speakers who comprise the collective narrator, as the messages are reiterated they go through different codes and thus take on different connotations and tensions. It is also through this reiteration that the meanings emerge as forms of the expression, creating the spectacle of a text that reveals its own semantic unfolding as a completely free and, unquestionably, rigorous game. Therefore, the narrators' perception of the critical information they received and emit also goes through the carnivalization of the writing of speech, in other words, through the feast of the names of the world that write the fullness of consciousness.

Actor and author of the information, the collective narrator is, in the broadest sphere of the textual carnivalization, the executant of the transgressive word because the official law is dissolved by the conversions of the popular culture as it moves between the addressor and the addressee in the cycle of communication.[13] Dissolving laughter and critical consciousness are mutually generated in this manner.

In addition to the collective narrator, who begins and ends the novel, reinitiating the critical communication in both instances, the place of the narrator is occupied by the patriarch himself, by a second person that detaches itself from the narrative as a dialogue inserted in the rhythm of the account, and by the third person of the text, as the open space of the chronicle. This narrative encounter is also a kind of textual theatricality of the communication.

The point of view in this novel is structured around the following series of narrators within narrators: a third person, which sometimes reverberates as the other part of an "us" seen in a mirror and which must be viewed as the space of the reference objectified by the text; a first person plural, a "we" that sustains the greatest amount of information and unfolds in different speakers; a first person that is occupied, for example, by the patriarch himself and confronts the collective narrator as a decoded referent and, alternately, as a curt public speaker or a deranged private speaker agonizing in his speech; and finally, a circulating second person of the communication that updates the event and the account of it.[14] Where, then, does the narration originate? What sustains this theater of voices? The answer is, of course, the book, or rather, the Book. Because here, as in *One Hundred Years of Solitude*, the beginning and the ending are articulated in the enigma of the book as the space that by replacing reality gives back to it a revealing center. But this is yet another code.

The Code of Writing

If, as Barthes suggests, the code is a system of the commonplace,[15] then the code of the commonplace par excellence is writing resolved in the book, there where the enigma of language is reestablished as a material space, in a language that refers to itself, in the "pure book" proposed by Derrida.[16]

In *The Autumn of the Patriarch*, before this final remittal to the act of the book, there is still an intimate debate on oralness and writing. Writing, it is true, occurs as the oralness of an expansive narration sustained by the polyphonic duration of the phrase. But it is also true that the speakers from the popular culture have an oral notion of language: the communication recognizes this dialogical nature. And, nevertheless, in the production of the narrative we encounter a plural writing: the names of the world are recorded time and again from each code to substantiate a realm whose meaning has been distorted by authoritarianism. This writing is, therefore, total. It writes the world with the names of the world in order to remake it as the original space of certainty, the joy and enigma of language. This is also true in *One Hundred Years of Solitude*, but now it carries a different risk: to reestablish in a world inside out the systematic conversion of a different world, a world liberating names starting from the subversion of its historicity.

The debate between oralness and writing is resolved, therefore, in a liberating text, but it is dramatized in the experience of a cultural conflict. Lacking a history of themselves, the people are also faced with a corresponding lack of documentary writing:

> Although all trace of his origin had disappeared from the texts, it
> was thought that he was a man of the upland plains because of
> his immense appetite for power, the nature of his government,
> his mournful bearing, the inconceivable evil of a heart which had
> sold the sea to a foreign power and condemned us to live facing
> this limitless plain.

Phrases such as "it was thought," "it was conjectured," or "it was known" denote referred information. This oral information replaces the texts and contradicts the false image of the patriarch's grandeur given by the school texts. For the tyrant, writing is another repressive mechanism, and its use to protest his rule is forbidden. During one period of his rule the patriarch is illiterate, but he later learns to read, inspired by Leticia Nazareno. Even so, there is no difference between the written and oral law of his government, although writing the law exposes the dependent nature of his rule: "Previously, during the occupation by the marines, he would shut himself up in his office to decide the destiny of the nation with the commandant of the forces of the landing and sign all manner of laws and decrees with his thumbprint." This thumbprint, this body writing, exposes the colonial condition. And when the ancient patriarch becomes a shadow of his former power and begins to lose his memory of writing:

[he] tore the margins off ledgers and in his florid hand wrote on them the remaining residue of the last memories that preserved him from death, one night he had written my name is Zacarías, he read it again under the fleeting light of the beacon, he read it over and over and the name repeated so many times ended up seeming remote and alien to him, God damn it, he said to himself, tearing up the strip of paper, I'm me, he said to himself, and he wrote on another strip that he had turned a hundred.

This broken writing discloses the patriarch's increasing loss of control, even though his authority is still proclaimed by the bureaucratic writing of his newspapers in yet another distortion: "splashing about in the reading of his own news . . . he learned of historic phrases that his ministers of letters attributed to him." But he is not blind to the facts ("he checked the facts on paper against the tricky facts of real life"), and writing becomes the evidence of his final defeat, "until the last nostalgia trickled away through the fissures in his memory and all that remained was the image of her on the strip of paper where he had written Leticia Nazareno of my soul look what has become of me without you."

In this novel, writing is recorded writing and read writing. It is a spectacle that transmutes oralness, an inscription of the world in the restoring rhythm of the text. It is a discontinuous writing that resolves a configuration of critical and celebrative experience and whose material manifestation is a narrative of language itself. This also accounts for the importance of the "men of letters" in the novel.

The appearance of a

warrior from other lands and other times . . . a withdrawn young man, troubled by haughtiness . . . who wanted arms and assistance for a cause which is also yours, excellency, he wanted logistical support and political aid for a war without quarter which would wipe out once and for all every conservative regime from Alaska to Patagonia

incites the patriarch to declare that "he's got a fever in his quills." This censure of the young, romantic revolutionary is also applied to the writers:

he proclaimed a new amnesty for political prisoners and authorized the return of all exiles except men of letters, of course, them never, he said, they've got fever in their quills like thoroughbred roosters when they're moulting so that they're no good for anything except when they're good for something, he said, worse than politicians, worse than priests, just imagine, he said.

The first parallel is between the young revolutionary and the "committed" writer; the second is between the gamecock and the men of letters: they all participate, in effect, in a struggle. Everything else follows from this recognition of the impugning aspect of writing. To the antipopular authority this impugning quality is its most certain threat, its negation. This underlines the subversive capacity of a writing that denounces the very root of underdevelopment: the colonial condition.

In the same vein, at the Rubén Darío poetry recital the patriarch cannot but acknowledge the fascination of a poetry that evokes "the eternal splendor of an immortal nation larger and more glorious than all those he had dreamed of during the long deliriums of his fevers as a barefoot warrior." This nation is nothing other than the poetic language conquered by Darío, that "heavy minotaur" who leaves the patriarch "excited by the revelation of written beauty." The revealing and impugning power of writing is thus inscribed in the debate on the discernment of the language of critical consciousness. This debate generates, in turn, the political meaning, its production as a liberating practice, and this practice confronts the machinery of domination, the political oligarchy of authoritarianism and dependency, the mark of colonialism. This political meaning is illustrated also by the anticolonial rebellion of General Lautaro Muñoz, an event that exposes the extent of the antinational plunder. Writing takes us back to the beginning, to its history as denunciation. In other words, it returns us to its appeal to revolt, there where writing itself is a work of impugning meaning. Thus the book that transforms history into a revealing self-consciousness is also an evidence of that other rebelling world: the memories of its liberated potentiality.

We have witnessed, therefore, a complex textual process. The codes as well as the narrators act in the "totalized" elaboration of a history that models reality as a myth, usurping its meaning. In this way, the communication of the speakers accumulates the information that makes of the patriarch and of power the mythological figure of a Latin America occupied by dictatorial rule. The entire novel is the encompassing construction of this tragic determinism, and therein lies the strength of its bitter political denunciation. But at the same time we have confirmed throughout the novel the deconstruction of this mythology of absolute power. The death of the archetype of power is the perspective of the narrative, carnivalization and criticism are its practice, and in this process the codes and narrators have dislocated the codification of absolute power. This novel is the deconstructed construction of power: the myth and its deconstruction occur at the same time, and writing has produced a book of the history of the beginning as a history of the end, that is to say, the book of the subversion of language, its accession to meaning in the foundation, once again, of the liberating consciousness.

Notes

1. See Graciela Palau de Nemes, "Gabriel García Márquez, *El otoño del patriarca*," *Hispamérica* 11–12 (1976): 173–183; Angel Rama, *Los dictadores latinoamericanos* (Mexico City, 1976); Julio Ramón Ribeyro, "Algunas digresiones en torno a *El otoño del patriarca*," *Eco* 187 (May 1977): 101–106. Domingo Miliani has constructed an interesting typology of the dictator in a study titled "El dictador: Objeto narrativo en *Yo, el supremo*," *Revista de crítica literaria Latinoamericana* 3 (Lima, 1976): 55–67; and Jaime Mejía Duque, *El otoño del patriarca o la crisis de la desmesura* (Medellín, n.d.).

2. "Kundera on the Novel," *The New York Times Book Review*, 8 January 1978.

3. On the semiology of culture see Janvan der Eng and Mojmir Grygar, *Structure of Texts and Semiotics of Culture* (The Hague, 1973); Ecole de Tartu, *Travaux sur les systèmes des signes* (Brussels, 1976); Umberto Eco, *A Theory of Semiotics* (Bloomington, 1976).

4. Sarmiento's well-known comparison between Rosas the dictator and Rosas the *estanciero* in *Facundo*, as well as the populist and autocratic measures taken by Dr. Francia, seem to have generated some of the hyperbolic images in this novel. Graciela Palau de Nemes has advanced a revealing account of the historical sources of the text and has even documented the supposedly inordinate hyperboles in the novel: "The sale of the sea is a consummate hyperbole and an unmatched allegory of a dictatorship. It feeds on a perfidious historical reality: the schemes of the Dominican caudillos Pedro Santana and Buenaventura Báez, who between 1845 and 1878 were ready to sell their country to the highest bidder, whether Spain, France, England, or the United States. Santana annexed the county to Spain; Báez negotiated a loan with English bankers in 1869; Samana Bay, on the northeastern coast of the island, in the Atlantic, became a booty. During his provisional government (1866), General Cabral proposed sharing with the United States the sovereignty of the waters of the bay in exchange for its defense. Báez later proposed the annexation of the entire country to save himself from ruin. During the dictatorship of General Ulises Hereus (1822–1899), the bay and the peninsula of Samana continued to be the booty with which foreign powers were tempted; the foreign debt increased and payments steadily declined. Confronted with the threat of English intervention, the United States intervened and took over the collection of customhouse duties to insure the payment of the foreign debt, which was settled with another loan from the United States in 1907. Between 1916 and 1924, using as pretext the continuous civil disorders, the United States again intervened and Ameri-

can marines occupied the country. The era of Trujillo followed this occupation and the rest is contemporary history" (Graciela Palau de Nemes, "Gabriel García Márquez," p. 178).

5. "Ainsi, le mythe et le nom sont, par leur nature même, inmédiatement liés. D'une certaine façon, ils peuvent chacun être determinés par l'autre, l'un se ramène à l'autre: le mythe personnifie (il nomme), le nom est mythologique" (Y. M. Lotman and B. A. Uspenski, "Mythe-Nom-Culture," in Ecole de Tartu, *Travaux*, p. 23). The lack of a name leads him to demand and usurp all names: thus, the mythological inversion of the name.

6. Louis Althusser has shown that, from a critical point of view, as "conceptions of the world" ideologies constitute an illusion; however, under their imaginary representation of the world they also allude to reality. In *Pedro Páramo*, for example, the popular Catholic ideology is represented as truth, as a natural order. In *The Autumn of the Patriarch* we also find a deconstruction of the ideology imposed as a world view by an authoritarian political model. See Louis Althusser, "Idéologie et appareils idéologiques d'Etat," in *Positions* (Paris, 1976), pp. 67–125.

7. See Max Horkheimer, "Authority and the Family," in his book *Critical Theory: Selected Essays*, translated by Matthew J. O'Connell and others (New York: Herder and Herder, 1972).

8. "From the semiotic point of view culture may be regarded as a hierarchy of particular semiotic systems, as the sum of the text and the set of functions correlated with them, or as a certain mechanism that generates these texts. If we regard the collective as a more complexly organized individual, culture may be understood by analogy with the individual mechanism of memory as a certain collective mechanism for the storage and processing of information. The semiotic structure of culture and the semiotic structure of memory are functionally uniform phenomena situated on different levels: being in principle the fixation of past experience, it may also appear as a program and as instructions for the creation of new texts" (B. A. Uspenski et al., "The Semiotic study of Cultures," in Janvan der Eng and Mojmir Grygar, *Structure of Texts*, p. 17).

9. "At one time Tylor defined culture as the aggregate of tools, technological equipment, social institutions, faiths, customs, and languages. Today one could give a more general definition: the aggregate of all non-inherited information and the means for organizing and preserving it. From this emerge very diverse conclusions. Above all it substantiates the concept of mankind's need for culture. Information is not an optional indication of, but one of the basic conditions for man's existence. The battle for survival—both the biological and the social one—is a struggle for information" (Jurij Lotman, "Culture and Information," *Dispositio* 1 [1976]: 213–215).

10. Mikhail Bakhtin, *Rabelais and His World*, translated by Helene Iswolsky (Cambridge, Mass.: M.I.T. Press, 1968).

11. J. R. Ribeyro: "In short, I would have wanted García Márquez's dictator to be not only likeable, but also detestable." Angel Rama: "The ignominy or the perversion can only be measured from it [the reader's consciousness], and this should serve to temper the series of somnambulistic

narrative inventions by interposing a protective shield to the fascination they exert."

12. "Dans une perspective sémiotique, on peut représenter le processus historique comme un processus de communication durant lequel l'afflux d'information nouvelle ne cesse de conditioner des réactions-réponses chez un destinataire social (le socius). . . . Ainsi les événements reçoivent un sens: leur *texte est lu* par le socius" (B. A. Uspenski, "Historia sub specie semioticae," in Ecole de Tartu, *Travaux*, p. 141).

13. On the carnivalesque author-actor see Julia Kristeva, *El texto de la novela* (Barcelona, 1974).

14. On the functions of the point of view of the narrator see Percy Lubbock, *The Craft of Fiction* (New York, 1921); Wayne C. Booth, *The Rhetoric of Fiction* (Chicago, 1961); Ludomir Dolezel, "The Typology of the Narrator: Point of View in Fiction," in *To Honor Roman Jakobson* (The Hague, 1967).

15. Roland Barthes writes that the code is a supratextual organization of the order of the "déjà-vu, de déjà-lu, de déjà-fait." See his "Analyse textuelle de un conte de Edgar Poe," in Claude Chabrol, ed., *Sémiotique narrative et textuelle* (Paris, 1973), pp. 29–54.

16. Jacques Derrida, "Force et signification," in *L'écriture et la différence* (Paris, 1967).

II. THE SITE OF THE TEXT

10. The Site of the Text

1. *Pedro Páramo*

At each new reading *Pedro Páramo*** conveys to us again the effectiveness of its coherence as an enigma. A description of its parts would not disclose the structure of this work because its shifting unity occurs as a self-referring, specular space. The enigmatic nature of the structure suggests the internalization at work within it. Its technique and forms and its development of a syntax proceed by faint signals. Convention is typified and textualized to the point that we read in it the clues of a space entirely occupied by language but, at the same time, desolate and empty.

The space of this novel is sustained by the most classic form of nominating. A language of designation and a dialogic language distribute the story, the account, in the causal, reconstructive surface. But this space is also empty: its metaphors are the desert (devastation as opposed to fertility) and hell (what is below as opposed to what is above). The space is therefore double: causal language in the story but also language that immediately vanishes because its reference does not exist and is a mere convention, the lunarlike vista of a world that has disappeared.

This first indication of the text about its own landscape (all reference here is verbal) projects it, however, beyond itself, to the tradition of the infernal space and the barren space. As in *Oedipus*, the guilt of the father or leader is followed by a suddenly sterile or chaotic landscape, because guilt reverses also the notion of dwelling, and the place is transformed into a wasteland. In Juan Rulfo's novel the figure of the father (tradition is nothing other than the functional change of the figures) condemns the land to die. Pedro Páramo decides to "fold his arms" and destroy Comala. But this condemna-

*Juan Rulfo, *Pedro Páramo*, translated by Lysander Kemp (New York: Grove Press, 1959). Originally published in 1955.

tion is also a self-destructive gesture, the gesture of a feudal history that refuses to uphold a natural order, which no longer upholds it either. Hence, whereas the destruction of the patriarchal authority is associated with the desert, the deterioration of its natural order is associated with hell.

The infernal space is nothing other than religion itself. One of the aspects accounting for the coherence of the text is the process of involution at work within it. Just as some of its contextual figures evolve from outside the text, from the literary tradition, the central movement of the text reduces the Catholic religion to a totalized convention. This novel makes of religion a code of conventional signs that it deliberately adopts as normative. It presents, without explaining or describing, the popular conception of the Catholic ideology as though it were the externalized form of "reality" itself. The entire novel moves within this conception taken as a systematic reference. Here that "truth" is a repertoire like any other, but *Pedro Páramo* would not have the coherence it does if this repertoire were not lived as the notion itself of an irrevocable and tragic system.

The advice of the grandmother to a young Pedro Páramo suggests this code: "You've got to have patience and, above all, humility. . . . You've got to resign yourself." But, at the same time, the coherence of this popular version of the Catholic ideology emerges, in the end, as an ambiguity, as an unresolved debate, because it contains both the code of evil and of good, or, more accurately, both terms coexist in the same code, generating at times a revealing ambivalence. Eduviges says: "Then it must have been my sixth sense. That's a gift God gave me... or a punishment, perhaps. You couldn't know how much I've suffered from it." Personal experience cannot be explained by the norms for understanding established by Catholicism, but even so it still requires these norms, because here experience finds in them its ultimate limit, its ambiguous meaning.

The ambiguity of life and death and, deep down, the identity of life and death occur within the text. Outside the text, in tradition, this movement is linked to the rich theme of the search for the father. History functions here as myth, because the account (like the redoubled space) also has its reference, its final meaning, in the recodification and criticism of literature. In effect, Juan Preciado searches for his father and finds his own death in the wasteland, while Dorotea searches for her son and in death finds Juan Preciado. The structure of this theme is evolved here similar to the way it evolved in Joyce, but this is also true for its meaning, because the new equivalencies (present in *Ulysses*) illustrate here, beyond the classical mechanisms of recognition, the loss of meaning that produces a sort of "unrecognition." The patterns of believing and knowing, the forms of consciousness, are developed ambiguously under the sanctioning Catholic code, but their final resolution belongs to the meaninglessness of arbitrariness, proposed here, however, as another order. Perversely, arbitrariness does not negate the code, it confirms it. There is no mistaking its randomness because it is the expression of a Law.

In effect, if a final debate is to be found in this novel it is in the possibility and impossibility of a Law. The conflicts of human justice and divine justice stem from this. Guilt and forgiveness imply divine justice. Father Rentería pardons Miguel Páramo but refuses to pardon María Dyada. Good and evil are thus ambiguous, because guilt and innocence are, in the end, indistinguishable in a code of salvation. In the other order, Pedro Páramo declares: "What law, Fulgor? From now on we're going to make the laws ourselves." The assassination of Toribio Alderete is the first imposition of this law. The incestuous brother and sister contradict another law. The "misdeed" of their relation "is not ordained," the bishop declares, for they should live "like human beings." The awareness of evil underlies this debate: "I'm beginning to pay," Pedro Páramo says when he is told of the death of his son. As in Flaubert's lesson, the "commonplace" states here the full meaning it renews.

This awareness of evil is carried to the extreme in Susana San Juan, but she frees herself from it at the same time that she destroys herself. Her insanity is her exacerbated conscience and also the abolition of that conscience. "And what do you think life is, Justina, except a sin?" she asks. And she adds, "I just believe in Hell." Another character comments: "Although the mystics say that crazy people don't need to confess, that they're innocent even if their souls aren't clean. Well, only God knows about that." As Father Rentería sits by Susana's deathbed, we are told: "He began to have doubts. Perhaps there wasn't anything for her to repent. Perhaps there wasn't anything for him to pardon."

Man's justice has lost its meaning. It supposes the convention of its law, its usufruct by power and its tyranny. When Gerardo, Pedro Páramo's lawyer (the intellectual of the novel), decides to leave Comala, Pedro Páramo tells him: "I envy you lawyers. You can go anywhere you want, without worrying about your lands or anything." But the mediators of divine justice, and divine justice itself, are no less ambivalent. The priest of Contla tells Father Rentería:

"Still, they say the land at Comala is good. It's a shame it's all in the hands of one man. Is Pedro Páramo still the owner?"

"That is God's will."

"I don't think God's will enters into this case. What do you think?"

"Sometimes I've had my doubts. But everybody there is sure of it."

Before this Father Rentería had said: "We live in a region where everything is bitter. That's what we're condemned to." The ambivalence of one law is reproduced, therefore, in the arbitrariness of the other.

The original paradise has become here the desert of aimlessness and the hell of guilt. This condition is compounded by the aimlessness of a Law which is not contained but is interpreted by the religious code and, in its ambiguity, is replaced by the sanctioning mechanics of power. Is there, in fact, a reordering justice behind this aimlessness and arbitrariness, or are ambiguous codes and condemnatory laws the only human measure? The novel does not answer these questions, but it implies them in its debate. It may be suggesting that human justice is as improbable as divine justice, since here they both result in a forsaking of what is human, and that a discourse about the law implies estrangement and the absence of an option. This discourse recognizes only itself, like a labyrinth with no real way out, but it is capable of the critical intransigence of its questioning.

Pedro Páramo develops all its times in a single present, the syntax of the story that the reading makes causal. In deciphering it, the reading converts that space into myth, into a textual identity. It is not by coincidence that the ending of the novel (the assassination of the father by Abundio) returns the account to the beginning (Abundio leads Juan Preciado to Comala). The text is externalized as a sort of medieval mystery play whose beginning and ending occur on stage at the same time, although here it does not take the form of a myth that is reiterated but, rather, of one that generates itself. Its symmetry is gothic; it makes of inverisimilitude a self-sufficient convention. Its illustration of meaning is sustained on itself, and in place of meaning the text gives us its own drama in the form of its enigma.

2. *Three Trapped Tigers*

A novel is sustained on the family of images it produces and on the symmetries in which it involves them. Both movements, which are the grammar of its figures, shape its code. We must add to the importance of the street as the space of fervor and chance in *Three Trapped Tigers** the importance of the textual space of its symmetries.

Whereas the ride through the streets infers the search for a celebrative temporality in the spectacle, the symmetries of the text imply the other side of this figure: the secret deterioration of events in the account and, revealingly, death as the empty center of the text.

In effect, the two paradigmatic figures in the account are Estrella and Bustrófedon. The figure of Estrella is linked to the duration of the pure spectacle, to the ritualization therefore of its emblematic material: the voice, temporal measure, and nature. On the other hand, Bustrófedon, as his name indicates, belongs to literature, but to a literature that has never been written and is fulfilled only as a game and wordplay in a recording (a parody of writing) that is a humorous jab at Cuban literature (pastiche of style). Hence, if Estrella is the glorification of oral speech, the fulfillment of a natural language prior to the demands of culture that transcends in the language's profusion the consciousness of a malaise, Bustrófedon, on the other hand, is the erudition of silence, the blank page as a permanent quotation, the shattering of the pun in the density of culture.

These two paradigms are, in this sense, opposites, but they are also correlated. In natural speech and in the artifice of speech they are separated, but in the celebration of a full oralness they are drawn together. Symptomatically, both characters die in the story and are metamorphosized in the text. They become totalized characters because they dislodge history from the story and occupy the expansion of the text. Thus the loss of meaning and the suggestion of the absurd that they introduce by disappearing generates the writing that besieges and constitutes them. More than characters or speakers, Estrella and Bustrófedon are mythical acts, figures whose death is like the signifier of their intact signification.

This function of death within the symmetry of the paradigm is not accidental in Cabrera Infante's novel. It corresponds to the openendedness that runs through the account of its speakers like a dilemma that is not objectified. In this sense the female characters are also symmetrical. The novel combines and reiterates these figures by writing with them its sensorial game, but within this game they also produce a feeling of uneasiness, that sort of anxiety of the senses

*Guillermo Cabrera Infante, *Three Trapped Tigers*, translated by Donald Gardner and Suzanne Jill Levine in collaboration with the author (New York: Harper Colophon Books, 1978). Originally published as *Tres tristes tigres* (1967).

in their aimlessness. *Three Trapped Tigers* is clearly a novel full of humor, but its vitality does not obscure the signs of its underlying grief.

In this regard, almost all the symmetries imply the loss of meaning. The girl involved in erotic play with Cué later becomes in his eyes a grotesque woman sustained by a fragile disguise. The woman who talks with a psychiatrist about her encounter with a girl from her village at her boyfriend's mansion discloses a more internal and dramatic symmetry. This woman suggests clearly the distance between the spectacle and the underlying grief when she asks: "Doctor, do you think I should go back to the theater? . . . At least, when I was in the theater, I could imagine that I was someone else." Malaise is produced in the solitude of consciousness, not in the shared myth of the performance.

There is, however, a central point at which the family of images (the street as a mythical reference) and the symmetries (the recurrence of the malaise) meet as versions of the same question, because in spite of its clear rejections and radical adherences everything in this novel has the overtones of a question. We are referring to a tacit and persistent theme: the search for a genuine norm.

With the exception of Estrella and Bustrófedon, who are fulfilled in the radicalized option of their spoken destiny, the other characters are fulfilled or fail to be fulfilled through derivative activities or mediations. Before their careers in advertising, journalism, translation, and acting these characters were perhaps close to the more radical paradigms of Estrella and Bustrófedon, closer to a life of art in which they could be liberated from their own selves. Only Eribó appears to liberate himself in his music, improvising a rhythm that transcends him. The others act in the ambiguity of a consciousness that instead of taking the form of criticism is established as alienation, which is why they pursue the spectacle, yearning for the fullness of impersonality and fervor. But even though the game does not have a norm within itself, it refracts, in the end, the loss of meaning surrounding it.

The bourgeois characters (the family referred to by the woman who talks to the psychiatrist; Vivian Smith Corona and her circle) and the American tourists represent a certain lack of authenticity because their conventions are detachments. On the other hand, even the simplest conventions of the spectacle, such as the rhetoric of the cabaret show, contain in their own artifice their certainty and, in the end, their innocence. That is why there is no irony or criticism directed at these forms of popular culture, which instead are consecrated and ritualized by the text. Even the nightclub dancers are recovered in the sensorial glow that authenticates them behind their masks.

Literature itself shares this underlying debate; parody is a mocking of style because style freezes the speech that the text seeks to articulate, at the other extreme of style, as a liberating center, as authentication of language. *Three Trapped Tigers* thus challenges artifice, making of artifice its method of composition. By authenticating an open expressive system, it also bestows a genuine need on its artificial materials, returning to them the agonizing need of the untainted events, freed from the detaching and elective consciousness. This accounts also for the praise of the "contrary" character, the faith in the proliferating game, the chronicling of friendship, and the testimony of writing about its own occurrence.

Unlike the characters in *Pedro Páramo*, here the speakers lack a code objectifying their wandering. Their game is also the space that sustains them: a casual, not causal, game. This occurs in the practice itself of a pre-text, in a proliferation that pursues a redeeming festivity and the liberation of consciousness. The pre-text means that the novel generates itself as a sequence of cuts, prologues, alternations, and recurrences within the dynamics of a writing that, in turn, seeks to gain the liberated space of the text as the final site of the possible convergencies.

Perhaps the uneasiness of the characters in the narrative and the polar and dramatic symmetries of the text tell us that the code of the spectacle is improbable in its natural site, in its occupation of the plaza, the street, the city. In the urban space this celebration of culture as liberation, this perennialness of time in the perpetuity of the people and of popular culture perhaps finds its ritualized equivalencies only in the theater, the show, the cinema, and dance, which is why the genuine norm of the spectacle is polarized, in their absent emblems, in Estrella and Bustrófedon. And also because of this it is reconstructed as a questioning, as agony and desire, in the liberations of writing and in the expansions of the text.

The images convoking fervor and the symmetries that disclose the underlying malaise are linked in the end as celebration and questioning. The novel does not intend, of course, to arouse the innocence of its speakers. It wants, instead, to transcend the Spanish-American dilemma of guilt and salvation encountered in *Pedro Páramo* by generating what is for us an equally pressing dilemma: the yearning for a fullness and liberation of consciousness. Its method is sustained by a spoken time, by an unrestricted verbalization, which is what brings together its movement of authentication and its impassioned, free poetics.

Naturally, this oralness can only be porous, a discourse being consumed and consuming itself, which is why it must sustain itself on the open formalization of a unique text. In the end, it is in the text that the loss of meaning yields itself as the possibility of a new meaning, as the form gained from a questioning based on a game. Thus the brilliant paradox of this fervent undertaking: to make of the text the notion of speech.

3. *Cobra*

Rather than the process of a debate of liberation, in moving from the site of estrangement (*Pedro Páramo*) and the site of speech (*Three Trapped Tigers*) to the site of body in *Cobra** by Severo Sarduy, we find the liberation of a textual space. Here we encounter the loss of the referential site of the novel (and, therefore, the utopian equivalence of writing) and the externalization of a writing that accounts for its own productivity (and, therefore, the raising of the site of the text as a transcodifying practice). Not by accident, utopia becomes a heterotopia: the privileged site of writing must manifest itself in a deconstruction.

This novel does not have a site; the text that usurps it for the sake of the pleasure of writing deconstructs the space situated by reading as the site of verisimilitude, in other words, the site at which convention mediates and pacifies the poles of "truth" (the reference) and "untruth" (the illusion) that verisimilitude, by its mimetic nature, establishes in "literature." Deprived of a site, the text expands as an improbable occurrence, convoking its own heteroclite space and broadening in this way the act of reading.

A utopian writing emerges in *Cobra* from the fervor of its occurrence and also from its nakedness, which frees it from the need for representation by freeing the notion of its reference. The words are set in the smooth space that secures them and expand in the gratuitous space that proliferates them. In stating its materials and mutations, delaying its figures, and generating its equivalencies, writing reveals itself as an adventure of its own materiality, of its sensible production, of its corporeal hyperbole.

As though on a single page, the pages of the text open on their own theater. Written or inscripted, the words occupy the body of the text and are themselves a body. In this ritual construction the text de-

*Severo Sarduy, *Cobra*, translated by Suzanne Jill Levine (New York: E. P. Dutton, 1972).

constructs its cultural referents to question its own literary nature and transfigure its notion of a text free from the texts.

This operation can only be parodical, ironic, humorous, and constructed of quotations, allusions, and appeals because its venture decodifies the landscape of the reading, the reliable sphere of the literary text; but, at the same time, at the center of its gratuitous verbal faith it must also rigorously secure, test, and work in the midst of its profusion the meticulous crafting of the prolix syntagm, of its lucid internal parallelisms and redoublings. A language that proceeds from culture and returns as lexicography to the dictionaries finds between these two poles a first day of its liberation, which implies the plundering of its repertoires.

Hence its solitary birth as a singular text and its implicit reference to a landscape of texts in progress emerging in both Latin America and Spain, in the "comedy of the language" of Néstor Sánchez and in Juan Goytisolo's "countryless language," a discontinuous landscape in which this text by Sarduy takes shape as "another site" of reading. Starting from the dynamics created by our own present as it is deciphered, in the prospects of the reading in which other likewise radical adventures also converge, Sarduy's text signals a new departure, a self-sufficient and discontinuous sign beyond its subjectless degree zero, as the intransigent object produced by the liberated imagination of the Spanish language.

Not by coincidence, the "verbal paradise" Barthes keenly discerned in *Cobra*, the utopian language that emerges in the pleasure of writing, is sited on the heterotopia. We are confronted by the paradox of a language that in saying everything shows itself as an empty site of the world, freed from its alliances.

This operation is not evasive. On the contrary, it is a criticism of language and a recovery of its first materiality, which is why the pleasure of its occurrence is translated into the metaphor of the senses. Meaning yields to the senses, and these in turn refer to the body. Thus the paradisiacal notion of the words requires a sustaining of its materiality and the text itself grows from the feet of *Cobra* on the first page to the syllables of the mouth on the last line, because writing is a body, and in speaking of itself it covers the body. Its materiality is generated in the senses because its text is the body, which it constitutes and transfigures.

But the alternative option of an erotic text is transcended by the radicalism of *Cobra*. In being explicit and referring to the figurations and disfigurations of pleasure, its eroticism refers also to its contradiction, to its draining, to its abyss devoid of dialogue, which is why, while being the construction of a body, *Cobra* is also its meta-morphosis and, more revealingly, its dismemberment, flagellation, and mutilation.

Like the operations of the text in the occurrence of its writing, the body is also subjected to a process of festive questioning. The broad repertoire of punishment, laceration, and torture is not simply sadistic, it does not allude only to the speculations of Bataille and his paradoxical eros, but also to the corporeal analogy of the text itself, one of whose metaphors is the pleasure of the body, while the other is its subversion. The senses thus generate the language of pleasure and, in the same movement, its draining of meaning: the body likewise requires being transformed, initiated, and criticized to arrive at the metamorphosis of its textualization, there where its freedom is perpetuated. Cobra, man-woman (or more than this: body), Cobra, alive-dead (or rather: intact and always changing) is in the end the metaphor of the text itself, whose metamorphosis and freedom are fulfilled also through the sensorial stations of its present and acting *horror vacui.*

The human body as a book written by the gods has a "divine dictate": its sex. The text written by language has a different, imaginary dictate: its freedom. In the encounter of body and text, in the realm of the senses, metamorphosis frees the body and somatizes the text. But it also reveals in its own paradise the void that sustains and dissolves it. In the gained materiality of the word, the rootless language that rises on its pleasure and on the game of its allusions is shifted, therefore, toward its own need for being rooted. It moves, therefore, toward an India that in this case is the nostalgia of meaning, a Spanish-American India that, beginning with Octavio Paz, introduces to the discourse of the senses a yearning for meaning. The pleasure of the text and its enigma is reestablished from the festive and mutating scene of Cobra's feet to the final clamor for one syllable, for the "Word" that is in the infinite circle of the cobra closed on itself, as demanded by Octavio Paz.

The joy and criticism of this text are bounded only by our habits, because its radicalism still convokes us as a privileged instance of our writing in a landsape of texts in which *Cobra* is still not fully realized. Its creative powers carry it beyond a mere tribute to the avant-garde and beyond cultural labels, and its own gratuitousness finally restores to it the sense it dramatizes, its fulfillment in the literary horizon that starts anew. Against the capitalist notion of accumulation *Cobra* exerts its prodigality; against the liberal notion of coherence it exhibits its digressive and transgressive art; and, finally, against the will to truth it displays its formidable burlesque carnival.

A subverted text, it discloses a central site of the practice of our culture, the site at which the texts of subversion are produced and await us.

11. *Explosion in a Cathedral*

First published in 1962, *Explosion in a Cathedral** is possibly Alejo Carpentier's most important novel. It is also one of the first Spanish-American novels to consider critically the subject of history, although Gabriel García Márquez, in *One Hundred Years of Solitude* (1967), and Reinaldo Arenas, in *Hallucinations* (1969), also based their works to some extent on the history of Latin America, attempting to reformulate and transgress it through fiction from a more daring formal option than that found in Carpentier. Already in Borges we find an unmistakable critical concern with history. The yearning for a fuller participation in history is seen in Borges's repeated praise of the martial events of the wars for Latin-American independence, for example, and also in his preference for certain English authors, such as De Quincey and Chesterton, in whom he finds narratives invariably linked with historical meaning, with the destiny of characters that are fulfilled in the impersonal and saving integration of a shared history. At the same time, this yearning for participation is a critical activity for Borges; it denounces the lack of that possibility within the scope of the distortions of Latin-American history. In *One Hundred Years of Solitude* history is an apocalyptic apotheosis; it not only destroys the mythical time and space of the founding of Macondo, but also consumes its actors and repeats itself like a grotesque parody whose ending reveals the dream of a revolution defeated once again by the routines of politics. The dream of the *true revolution* is personified in *Hallucinations* by Fray Servando Theresa de Mier, but here also the dream is crushed by the institutionalization of the republic shortly after independence. This debate had already been announced in *Explosion in a Cathedral*. In this

*Alejo Carpentier, *Explosion in a Cathedral*, translated by John Sturrock (Boston: Little, Brown, 1963). Originally published as *El siglo de las luces* (1962).

novel, which has a broad and precise formal orchestration, the characters can be understood as figures of a code that communicates the tragic fate of the modern historical destiny. Caught between the trappings of a golden age and the dream of a revolutionary utopia, these characters are emblems of a transition, of a fissure running from history to politics, from myth to grotesqueness, from a redemptive yearning to a sheer corruption of power.

We must add, however, that in this utopian proposition, in which disenchantment slowly gains the upper hand, a broader and always renewed desire that implies the need of a personalization fulfilling itself in history can also be found, in spite of the risk of disenchantment. Taking this risk and transcending it implies fully occupying a myth. This is precisely what occurs in César Vallejo's poem *Spain, Take This Cup From Me*, where in the place of a harmonious, sufficient mythology we find a fragmentary, dying one, a tragic utopia, therefore. The same thing occurs in *Todas las sangres* (1964), José María Arguedas's most political novel, in which the possibility of participation is also the imminence of a real change. When the dream of history becomes the nightmare of politics, the novel adopts a critical perspective and, within it, a heightened skepticism. This malaise, which can only be critical, is encountered frequently in Spanish- and Latin-American poetry. At the beginning of the debate, *Explosion in a Cathedral* is perhaps one of the first novels that does not shy away from the risk of disenchantment.

On the very first page Carpentier places us within the norm of an emblematic style: Esteban stares at the Machine, the guillotine sent by the French revolutionaries to America, and compares it to a *door*, to an *instrument of navigation*. This first image is already directly at odds with the revolutionary ideals. The revolution requires effective instruments of force. In addition, as dependent countries, history itself is imposed on us from the outside by our colonizers, of whatever stripe. The dramatic irony of these implications announces the paradoxical nature of that history.

The novel itself opens with other emblems: the death of the father and the chaos of the physical world coincide as reinforcing images. Carlos and Sofía's father is also like a father to Esteban, their cousin. The death of the father occurs in a world invaded by rains and covered by slime and mud. The repeated presence of these images suggests the prevailing chaos, and starting from this shapeless world the novel is set in motion and the life of the three young characters is reordered. Thus from the first pages we notice already the almost fatalistic significance in the novel of the relationship between the characters and a correlative environment that illustrates or defines them. This significance constantly expands the present of fiction in the anachronism of the emblem. In this way the novel also discloses the inevitable process of an emblematic history as it unfolds. And, this code of representation also announces the construction itself of the novel as a parodic redoubling, as a theater that reveals itself through the emblems of its elaborate staging.

When the year of mourning has passed and the rainy season that filled the streets with "fresh mud" is nearly over, all the doors of the house shake with the thunderous knocking of Víctor Hugues. Once again the act becomes emblematic, not only because of what it presages ("Don't open it, for God's sake!" Sofía implores, "but it was too late," the narrator informs), but because that house, *terra firma* of a creole bourgeoisie, opens its doors to the invader. As in the initial episode of the death of the father and in the chaotic mud, in these doors battered by the stranger we also read an act recognized in the tradition of the novel. And this event has clear repercussions. Víctor Hugues soon transforms the life of these adolescents and initiates them into another world, the world of an activity that will liberate them. Esteban is an asthmatic, but the Frenchman also cures him of this affliction. Thus another emblem is gradually introduced: Víctor Hugues takes the place of the absent father.

Víctor suggests that Esteban be taken out of doors, and Sofía thinks to herself that "while their father was alive, austere man that he was, no one would ever have been allowed to leave the house after evening prayers." Before long, Sofía begins to feel estranged from herself and Esteban also realizes that he is changing. We are not surprised, therefore, when a storm approaches as a warning of the decisive changes that are about to take place. The "filthy water" invades the house, converting it into "broken crockery." In this episode Víctor organizes the resistance to the invading chaos, which will be transformed into a new order of things. And when Víctor Hugues exposes the executor of the children's estate, that "second father" who proves to be a "dissembling protector," he confirms his paternal role. At the end of this episode fiction gives way to allegory, not without a certain emphasis, when Sofía feels compelled to destroy "a large portrait of their father."

Hugues then proceeds to reorganize his enterprising trading business, justifying its clandestine nature by posing it as a struggle against the tyranny of the Spanish monopoly. The people of Cuba, he says, "seemed to be asleep, inert, living in a timeless marginal world, suspended between tobacco and sugar." The Frenchman's activities thus initiate these young people into a different system of values.

"Esteban suddenly felt that he had been living like a blind man on the fringe of the most exciting realities." The paternal mechanism is too obvious to need further development, but by this means Víctor Hugues imposes a different code, the new values of which are dictated by the cosmopolitan world, by a world of objects and adventures persisting or taking place outside the Cuban context, outside the colonial sphere, in an order of values that is certainly no less colonial in nature, but where the switch to a new norm confers the illusion of liberation. This new norm comes from France. The Spanish colonial world is viewed in a different light: the Spanish administration is seen as bogged down by its "habitual torpor"; Spanish maps give a confused notion of geography, and even the boats reflect this change (the *Arrow* is "slim and proud," while the "old Cuban bilander" had "patched sails and was decrepit-looking").

Having arrived in France, Esteban discovers that his previous world was "static, oppressive, and monotonous." On the other hand, he now feels "as if he had been dropped into a huge carnival, whose characters and costumes had been thought up by some great showman." Free from the "drowsiness of the tropic," he delights in the spectacle of a "gigantic allegory of a revolution . . . a metaphorical revolution." At the same time, his view of Spain becomes more critical:

> Here they were always running over the names of cuckolded Bourbons, licentious queens and cretinous princes, until Spain's backwardness was represented by a somber picture of influential nuns, miraclemongers, poverty, persecution and rags, and all that existed between the Pyrenees and Ceuta was plunged into the darkness of a conservative revival. This slumbering, tyrannized country, with its lack of progressive ideas, was contrasted with enlightened France.

"But it's not enough to take the Revolution to Spain, it must be taken to America too," Esteban declares. In large measure Esteban represents in this novel the intellectual inspired by revolutionary theories but gradually disillusioned by the actual events. However, even more interesting than this scheme, which contrasts him to the man of action, to Víctor Hugues, is the mechanics by which Esteban, and later Sofía, accepts a ready participation within a moment in history that allows him to believe in his personal adjustment to a meaningful situation. This desire to be part of a process already in motion, this drive toward personalization within the collective struggle, defines him better than his disillusionment with the turn of events. This mechanism involves a switch: Esteban abandons the marginal world of Havana and believes that he is taking part in the most meaningful events of his time, but in this case his participation also represents a very curious displacement because it implies an estrangement from himself, an ambiguity inherent in adopting a eurocentric ideology that must be fitted to specific historical times and places. The process of alienation that leads to disenchantment reflects the gap between this ideal universalism and the specific colonial region that in fact shapes the characters. Consequently, Esteban's views are reversed and his values become confused. He easily adopts the values of the messianic universalism of a liberating Paris, but as he moves away from the mirage of this ordering center his perspective becomes less clear. When he is sent to Basque territory, we are told that "the young man marvelled at the crude Basque churches, with their squat, war-like bell-towers" and also that "he had been rather disappointed by the people, as he got to know them better; these Basques, with their measured movements, their bull-necks and their equine profiles, great stonemasons, great hewers of trees . . . were tenacious in the preservation of their traditions." Esteban feels that the Basque world is becoming increasingly "alien, artificial and unstable." This feeling of alienation is a clue. In effect, this provincial world, which is equivalent in a certain sense to his own Cuban world, is "alien" to someone like him who has been captured by the illusion of a history that promises to transcend him but that leaves him with a feeling of estrangement and displacement when he is separated from the center of his new adjustment, when he leaves Paris.

Meanwhile, Víctor Hugues makes his debut with the guillotine. He is named Public Prosecutor before the Revolutionary Tribunal at Rochefort and requests—and Esteban approves—"that the guillotine should be installed in the courtroom, so that no time should be wasted between a sentence and its execution." At the end of this sequence we find Esteban feeling unimportant, losing all sense of individuality, as though he had been swallowed by the events. In his distress he remembers Sofía, whose strength is "maternal," "as if she had really been his mother." Esteban has chosen a paternal and paternalistic figure under which to discover himself, but he still lacks this "maternal" figure, this origin closer to himself represented by Sofía.

At least to this point, there is a close relationship between Esteban and Víctor. The mechanism of participation, through which Esteban gives himself over to the frenzy of the metropolis, is also at work in Víctor, who can act only by radicalizing himself to the extreme of terror itself. Víctor's destiny is, however, more typical. Drifting from the ideals of the Revolution toward the outright arbitrariness of power, we begin to sense the first rift with Esteban, who now views him as a "Leader of Men" whose first discipline is "that of having no friends." The Revolution shifts to the Antilles at a time when it has already begun to deteriorate in the metropolis. A small squadron brings to the Caribbean the guillotine and the printing press, punishment and doctrine. Esteban begins to feel reservations about Hugues. "He still hankered after the illusion of toiling in a great dimension, of taking part in Something Big," but at the same time he harbors many doubts. He realizes that Víctor is playing the role of an actor in a theater in which he wants to emulate the archetypal Robespierre. The echo of another echo, Víctor is caught in his own contradictions and gradually becomes the politician par excellence: "Everyone is suspect," he says. Esteban decides that he would like to write, but he is not sure what this work would be: "A new theory of the State maybe, or a new version of *L'Esprit des Lois.* Perhaps a study of the errors of the Revolution." He defines himself as an "arguer," and the rift with Víctor widens. "A revolution is not argued; it is carried out," Víctor states.

But the revolution that brings to the Antilles liberty by decree and human rights in a declaration is not only contradictory in itself, it is also another chapter in a widespread colonialist war. The displacement of Spain and England from the Antilles is an enterprise undertaken in the name of liberty but which ends in the imposition of another system of colonial power. Consequently, in the activity of the guillotine, from the perspective of any colonialist domination, "eight hundred and sixty-five faces were too many for him to be able to picture any one of them in particular." Like all colonialists, Víctor Hugues is also a racist. He shows very little sympathy toward the blacks. "It's enough for them that we should look on them as French citizens," he says. "Any negro accused of being lazy or disobedient, argumentative or troublesome, was condemned to death." And the native Indian populations try to adapt to the imposition of this new dependence in their own way. The Carib Indians of the island of Marie Galante ask, through their chief, for the honor of being accorded the benefits of French citizenship. Thus, in an ironic paradox, the "benefits" of colonialism are requested as an "honor." Paternalistic, like all colonizers, Víctor Hugues declares that "the Caribs are the only people," a judgment that discriminates against the blacks. Having embarked on the course of colonial subservience,

Hugues gravitates toward violence and the imposition of power: "No one is going to move me from here," he declares.

But let us turn again to what we have already defined as the mechanism of participation, which also functions as a mechanism of estrangement. In this novel it is not difficult to find a deep paradox: historical action only seems possible outside the native context of the characters. For some obscure reason, the characters of *Explosion in a Cathedral* can participate in history only when they are estranged from it. They adjust best to the possible meaning of action in foreign environments. This is true not only in the obvious case of Víctor Hugues, but especially in the more symptomatic cases of Esteban and Sofía. Esteban is able to take part in history only when he leaves Cuba. In France he is a stranger who adjusts rapidly to the new values promulgated by the metropolis. Later, although somewhat disillusioned, he continues to participate in events in the other islands of the Caribbean, although now his activity is decidedly more critical and ambiguous. But when he returns to Cuba, his activity dissipates into simple discontent, into a purely individualistic and evasive exercise. Sofía also finds that to participate she must leave Havana, breaking with her original world and pursuing the adventure of giving herself to Víctor Hugues, only to discover that, like Esteban, she is disillusioned by him. Finally, she and Esteban travel to Madrid, where these mechanisms of displacement come to a head in the apotheosis and annihilation of the events of May 2, 1808. Significantly, they both achieve the fullest sense of their participation in history when they join the mob clamoring for Spanish liberation from Napoleon's rule. By joining the crowd in the streets, they demonstrate their opposition not only to Napoleon, but tacitly also to Víctor Hugues. At the same time, they confirm their estrangement. History allows them to recover the meaning of their search in this immolation in the colonial metropolis, in Spain. Displaced from their own Cuban world, they paradoxically possess a historical meaning in the wandering of their participation, in the exchanges determined by chance, in the attainment of consciousness and in its immolation.

The universalistic ideal of the Revolution acts throughout as an errant historical notion whose critical center has gone astray. But even in the characters themselves this center is absent. History seems to act not as a link to the original context, but as a slow and progressive awakening of consciousness, as an apprenticeship that the characters can accept or reject. Whereas in this sense Esteban is the critical consciousness, the malaise of that consciousness, the look that is always observing and comparing, torn between ideal concepts and serious disenchantment; whereas Esteban, therefore, is a wandering, blank look, a look detached from more profound and radical options than the mere witnessing of events, Sofía, on the other hand, has a more complex, less obvious, more ambiguous makeup. Thus the awakening of her critical consciousness—her discovery of the imposture perpetrated by Víctor Hugues—is part of a broader process through which she discovers and liberates herself. This liberation follows a predictable progression, perhaps, but it transforms her into the character with the greatest density in this novel. This progression begins with the death of her father; continues with her sexual initiation through Víctor; pays its dues to a bourgeois marriage; follows her, after her husband has died, as she again seeks out the Frenchman, whom she thinks will share her ideals; and then shows her abandoning her lover and going to Madrid, where she drags Esteban into the streets on May 2, 1808. There they achieve the extreme and final participation, the impersonality itself of history that begins again in another direction, as though history were only willing to yield at this price, granting its evasive fullness only through a radical gamble.

In this novel the Latin Americans are the wandering strangers, the individuals who dream their delayed personalization in the possibility that history will recover from margination, granting them a sense of adjustment in place of their wandering. But this transition is not completed and goes astray. It appears possible only in the final act of the novel, in the street uprising, in the anonymous and unanimous rebellion. Meanwhile, in the malaise of this wandering the illusion of action is produced only outside the native context, in an exchange yielding an estrangement that comes close to disenchantment and deterioration. Hence the repeated use in this novel of the image of the theater and the metaphor of the spectacle. Esteban, the self-styled arguer, is above all an observer, an incessant witness, a halfhearted actor, who for this reason sees the parodic, redoubled aspect of everything. He sees a stage—pathos, imposture—where others believe they are participating in great causes. He sees a historical burlesque—a masquerade, a parody, a show—where power believes it has established its infallible norm. That is why deep down the image of the stage exposes the intimate mechanism of participation. Through this image Esteban (and the novel, of course) discloses the distance at which the historical action is taking place for this Latin-American character and this Latin-American perspective, both of which are trapped by the conditions and schemes of a history which has been imposed from outside as a reflection of its facts and decrees, a derivative history condemned, in addition, to the very ambiguity of its total promise and its fateful impossibility.

These forms of alienation—estrangement, life lived as a parody, imposture—create the most valid tensions of this novel, those shaped as a tension between frustration and critical consciousness, between a life of wandering and a postponed adjustment. It is not merely by chance, therefore, that throughout the novel we participate in a voyage that multiplies itself. The feeling of estrangement compels this perpetual voyage and propels the characters forward in this space of Caribbean islands that multiply like a permanently foreign, dispersed, and diverse cosmos of many languages, tribes, and flags. The constant presence of the sea, the images of travel, the proliferation of the frontier, the houses and encampments, the cities that are close to and far from everything, are also the space of this stage on which men go astray on their erratic voyage. "There are times made for decimating flocks, confounding tongues, and scattering tribes," the narrator suggests, but the nature itself of history is seen here as the anguished confusion that denies the possibility of finding solid ground.

This solid ground can only be a final space, as it is for the men destroyed by the Revolution who survive in Cayenne like pathetic phantoms. In that land they live their imprisonment and their fall, the sobering derision of a grandiose era. It is also the final place for Víctor Hugues, who returns to Cayenne as Bonaparte's consul, cynical and destroyed, justifying slavery as a political necessity. ("I'm a politician," he now says of himself.) But there is no stable land, no place of union for Esteban and Sofía, who we find again outside of Cuba, in Spain, where she reads the works of the forerunners of Latin-American independence. The novel suggests that in the sense of that movement they will fulfill their last emblematic act, as though that end of their wandering might in fact announce the future novel of Latin-American independence. From the midst of the Spanish people revolting against Napoleon, Esteban and Sofía act against Víctor Hugues and perhaps also against the colonial power of Spain in America. Thus, for the first time, a radical act grants them in the end the participation they have been seeking.

History, through the novel, of course, plays a final trick on them, however. Had the novel ended with the incidents of May 2, 1808, Esteban and Sofía would have lived, at least emblematically, in the plural meaning of this conscious act. But the novel (deliberately, perhaps, but I suspect otherwise) denies them this destiny. In effect, the final events are narrated by Carlos, Sofía's brother, who reemerges in the novel as a prosperous Havanan businessman and is, perhaps, an image of what Esteban and Sofía would have been had they not heeded the call of history. The novel ends with Carlos's account of the final days of his sister and of his cousin. He ties together the loose ends and closes the fiction of the novel, but above all he draws a line backwards, toward the first page. We recall that the novel opens with Carlos returning to Havana because of his father's death. He is slightly annoyed by the interruption of his retreat in the countryside, where he had been devoting himself to music, and suspects that from that moment on his destiny will be shaped by the business left by his father. The image of the patriarchal house ("All the bolts on the big door were slid to") predominates until Víctor Hugues enters the scene. Carlos begins and ends a novel in which his participation in events is actually marginal, since he represents the commercial bourgeoisie, of which Sofía and Esteban are the liberal members. Carlos is the prosperous bourgeois who lives on the edge of historical movements and contributes nothing to them. At the end of his account, when he has ordered that the boxes containing the things that remind him of Sofía and Esteban be closed, he allows the locked and empty Condesa de Arcos's house to revert to its owners. The image of the house is perhaps more interesting than the repeated and allegorical image of the painting of the "Explosion in the Cathedral," which is a quite obvious illustration of a stable world that is deteriorating. The final presence of this bourgeois house is more suggestive because it is at the root of this novel as a polar term; it is at the beginning, when the children of a commercial bourgeois family awake to the world, and at the end, when two of them have wandered and have been recovered and the other, Carlos, tells us that the most stable side of that class is closing its liberal chapter and following its own path. If Sofía and Esteban die for a history that is starting anew, at the beginning of the new struggles for independence in Spanish America, we may also assume that at the end Carlos is the more stable part of a bourgeois class that on one hand fosters the revolution against Spain and in the long run will establish its own power based on an internal domination and on mediation with the new colonialisms. This is the final defeat of Esteban and Sofía's liberalism. Their time grants them the meaning of action and exacts, in turn, their lives, but history shows that the struggles for Latin-American independence were just another incomplete revolution whose principal effect was to change the dominant groups and to transform the structure of power into an internal domination and into a new external dependence legitimized through the formation of republics. Although the novel does not directly inform us of this, the final presence of Carlos and the internal treatment of the interaction of revolution and politics allow us to suspect this final and irrevocable ambiguity and the strayed course of events.

The stable image of the house implies and reinforces, however, other images, an extensive collection of prestigious objects that Carpentier delights in naming and describing. One phrase in the novel perhaps summarizes the author's idea of what, in terms of the historic ebb and flow, are apparently innocent constructions. Praising the constructions of an "overseas Holland," the narrator tells us that Esteban admired them as "symbols of a tolerance which, in some parts of the world, men had persevered in attaining and defending, without weakening in the face of religious or political inquisition." This statement is particularly interesting because it brings out a more internal perspective within the novel: at the edge of events, and even against them, there exists a world of ideal objects that evince higher and more patient human virtues. That world is none other than the world of culture understood as an almost intemporal conquest and challenge, as a privileged and higher ground. This perspective is what permits in the novel the slow and fervent inventory of prestigious, sumptuous objects, but it also permits a nominative prolixity, the almost inexhaustible possibility of designating space in order to fix it, resorting even to synonymy. The space of its fixity thus becomes tautological, reiterating itself in a static proliferation. Perhaps that is why this perspective implies that culture is also another way of being saved from history and its perpetual change, which destroys all images of fixity, or at least attempts against it. The static image in this novel centers on the patriarchal house, although the father is absent. The image is of a static and empty house in which "the air seemed to hang motionless around the inert curtains, the withered flowers and the plants, which might have been made of metal. The leaves of the palm trees in the patio had taken on the heavy look of iron." But even there, in this wrought-iron and high-walled world, the mud of history upsets everything, and we can see in the novel this tension between the fixity of various prestigious and resistant signs—between the fixity itself of a style that resists change—and the transformations imposed by the unfolding of history. When Sofía draws closer to Víctor Hugues, who is a rather inglorious character in the end, it is not by accident that she is muddied by a herd of wallowing pigs, in the typical reductions that allegory sometimes implies.

In this space of tensions, in which fixity refuses to surrender to change, we can also perceive the contradictory relations between history and utopia. If the novel had opted decisively for utopia, its historical view would have been formed by the positive response that revolution is a permanent process; on the other hand, if it had opted for a more obvious historicism, its view would have been lost in pure chance, in meaningless adventure. By attempting to contrast utopia and history, the novel creates a more valid tension, an ambiguity which saves it from the need to offer a positive response to its own disenchanted view.

Carried to an extreme, utopia is the dream of a lost paradise, which revolution seeks to recover; and history, when taken to the extreme, takes the form of "political" degradation when it has lost the mediating possibility of being the active channel for rendering that utopian world as real. The dream of that Better World—the Promised Land sought by the Caribs—is at the root of the acts which pursue in history that original and lost space; and this yearning is what makes of these acts a restless and agonizing desire that is partial and always unfinished. This is why the utopian dream becomes a tragic nightmare. Utopia is no longer the ideal world painted by the humanists, a perfect world which accuses a depredated reality. Overcome by the inanity of events, that world is again lost. It is blurred and becomes a caricature, a farce of the ideals and their final negation. That is why the perfectible ideal is followed by a deteriorated reality. The epic is replaced by tragedy. The characters are doomed to a moldering, farcical tragedy and to a parody of events. Nevertheless, within that very depredation, the desire of historical participation gives the characters the most valid dimension of their adventures, the risk that demands meaning, the possibility of a real act in one's own destiny.

Explosion in a Cathedral can be read as a sequence of several emblems suggesting an allegorical process. But upon showing itself to the reader as a self-referential construction, the novel gains the parodic dimension that defines it. This dimension is found in the redoubled acts of the characters, in their very self, in the ambiguities of a history which duplicates and destroys itself, and in the spectacle of a farcical theater. In the emblems and allegories, in the exemplary types and topical events, and in the redoubling itself of a style characterized by enumeration and fixity, in other words, in the mechanisms exposing the permanent artifice of a precisely woven construction, we observe the parodic dimension, the redoubled life, underscored by estrangement, that destines the characters and perhaps defines the intimate critical perspective of this novel.

This novel stands at the beginning of the narrative renewal in Spanish, within which it indicates and announces the will to assume more complexly the debate of a Latin-American history questioned from the perspective of political skepticism and the utopian dream. The desire for participation is also a will to personalization. In Latin-American literature today these tensions shape the new version of an ancient dream, the real independence of countries whose own identity has been denied many times.

12. *A Change of Skin*

A Change of Skin,* by Carlos Fuentes, is a vast collage, but above all it is a happening. The collage processes of montage and simultaneity are found in this novel as action, as an improvisation convoking the feast and its theatricalness. *A Change of Skin* stands out among the important Latin-American novels because it shapes into a narration all the possibilities of a metamorphosis based on a collage constructed in the space of a happening; the essay, the feast, the simulacrum, and techniques interact in this novel in a single narrative sequence, in a language that fuses all levels and transforms them into fiction. This intense and unbounded novel combines, to a greater extent than any other, the deepest concerns of the new Latin American narrative. *A Change of Skin* is a younger relative of *Hopscotch*.

The story of the novel is simple but totalizing: On April 11, 1965, a Sunday, two couples—Javier and Elizabeth and Franz and Isabel—take a wrong turn on their way to Veracruz and end up at Cholula, where they visit the Aztec pyramids. Another character, the Narrator, follows them, stopping also at Cholula. Six young people arrive in a Lincoln. They appear only at the beginning of the novel and at the end, when they return to play a central and allegorical role. It is Palm Sunday, and the characters find themselves in a village which was once an Aztec religious center and the site where the Spanish *conquistadores* killed the Aztec princes before marching on Tenochtitlan. Time and space are thus double. The time of the novel is double because it convokes a celebration and feast on this allegorical Palm Sunday—the festive arrival—on which the characters find themselves in a desacralized place where, however, they will consecrate another ritual, another Passion play. The space of the novel is double because the ritual of the novel will merge at that site in a par-

*Carlos Fuentes, *A Change of Skin*, translated by Sam Hileman (New York: Farrar, Straus & Giroux, 1968). Originally published as *Cambio de piel*.

able of the encounter and transformation of the culture of civiliza-
tion and the culture of myth by making of Cholula the place where
other cultures converge, perhaps in an uncertain judgment and revenge of each against the others. The underground chambers of the
pyramid are the vortex in which the two couples see their own lives,
failures, and tensions in the double mirror they are to each other and
that dramatizes the part of the world each one reflects. Hence the
chance of this accident—within the mechanism of the journey—
also recognizes the possibility of order, which is here an instant of
chaos. Confused by the old roads and having lost their way, the characters descend into the hell of their own face-to-face encounter. This
is why the concentric pyramids are in the middle of Cholula and
why the galleries of those pyramids converge on a center that conjugates the lives and deaths of the characters in their doubles. The galleries are a "labyrinth," like the novel itself. The labyrinth, however,
is not chaos; it is its form and, in one instant, its order.

Three different sequences shape these interactions and this game
of mirrors. Each sequence is a double web of opaqueness and clarity,
mystery and evidence in the relationship of the characters and in the
encounter of their worlds, because each world is a topic disclosed
through each character stretched to the limit. The web of opaqueness and evidence is also found in the formulation and passion of the
verbal development, in a nervous writing, in a fervor at once contained and encouraged, in a generous energy docilely applied to details that are then immediately questioned. The first sequence is
titled "An Impossible Feast" and begins with a quote: "as though we
were on the eve of an improbable catastrophe or on the morrow of an
impossible feast." This quote warns about this very brief space and
time from which emerge much vaster coordinates in the conflictive
instant of a character, of writing itself, a juncture that in the narrative field created by a one-day stay in Cholula breaks up the novel
into brief fragments, incisions that bring into this space other times
in Buenos Aires, New York, Mexico, Prague, and Terezin, convoking
the other faces of the four characters. But this eve and this morrow
are also the novel as a whole, in the instant of one day. The probable
catastrophe and the impossible feast, which the novel borders, also
point to its ritual thrust, to its need to consecrate the events of a
spoken labyrinth under the tense gaze that reveals multiplicity. This
first segment, which is like an overture to a complex symphony, introduces the two worlds and two times that will face each other
in their tension, in their battle, in the Palm Sunday that is also the
Day of Judgment and the Day of Passion and Death. The writing
presents on the same level the characters entering the streets of

Cholula and Hernán Cortés entering the "sacred city" he later subdued. The invasion of Cortés is paralleled by the invading presence of the Narrator and the young people. The budding culture brought by Cortés somehow will confront the modern culture of the leading characters, who are figures of a dying twilight.

The second sequence, "In Body and Soul," combines the Narrator's versions of the characters and different incidents attributed to the characters themselves. The characters are thus defined at various levels, especially by connections and disconnections with the Narrator. The Narrator is totally involved in the world of the characters because he functions both as the internal author of the work and as the nucleus or mirror of the characters. Javier, a Mexican writer, and Elizabeth, an American Jew, are a couple redoubled in Franz, a German architect, and Isabel, a young Mexican girl. In this redoubling Isabel represents the absence of the dramatic nature that characterizes Elizabeth. She is a young, free woman who falls within Elizabeth's configuration in the sense that she is a moment of her life and a possibility that also negates her. Elizabeth is more complex in relation to her own world, which also determines the world of her husband, Javier. This is also why she is defined by different possibilities, by different names, of which Isabel is one and Betty, Beth, Liz, Lisbeth, Liza, Bette, and Betele are others. Javier calls her Ligeia, and the Narrator calls her "Dragoness" to distinguish her from Isabel, whom he calls "Novillera." These different possibilities point to her transformations. At the end, after witnessing the almost lyrical construction of her world, we learn that this construction is false: she is actually a Mexican Jew and has invented a world of obvious facts to replace a world of mystery, or vice versa. Elizabeth invents her adolescent world; she makes it mythical to highlight the moment she met Javier, because, fearing that she will be abandoned, she also needs to feel free in that past. "Imagination is identical to its desires . . . in other words, their only possible freedom," Carlos Fuentes has said in a conversation with Emir Rodríguez Monegal (*Mundo Nuevo*, No. 1) about this fiction that is also redoubled in this novel. These possibilities of evidence to produce mystery and of opaqueness to pursue clarity also lead Fuentes to concoct a jumble of objects and details for each character. Literature, journalism, and the cinema are other possibilities of bestowing on the characters that fiction within the fiction denoted in Elizabeth. She is central in this expansive mechanism. The center of the kaleidoscope, Elizabeth determines Javier, invents Isabel, summons Franz, and opens a window to the Narrator. Elizabeth's fictional reconstruction of her own past is another way of involving her husband because, while she

determines him, he also defines her; hence her fear of being abandoned. The relationship of this couple in the story offers more tension than complexity because it is reduced to the demonstration that
Javier—"form and background" of a "style" that Fuentes himself has
labeled "romantic"—seeks The Woman, not in opposition to his
own wife but exploring her own potentiality in the mutual tension
that attracts and repels them. Aside from this demonstration, the
complexity lies in the various faces and names of Elizabeth, in her
tenuous and pious mystery, which the narration allegorizes in the
pebbles of the beach at Falaraki:

> You never know which pebble to choose. There are so many and
> when they lie on the soft sand where the beach enters the sea
> they are all beautiful. They are of the sea and of the land also,
> and when brought ashore they become like the land. But within
> the sea they reproduce all its lights and shadows, all its colors.
> They are the gentle teeth of the sea fastened in the land to allow
> the sea to hold itself to the land, and without them the sea
> would be different, a different world, faith, dream, the promise of
> a different millennium. You sit on the beach entire hours finger-
> ing your pebbles, staring at them. You have found every color
> except blue.

This paragraph is at the center of Elizabeth's world. Like the pebbles of Falaraki, which reproduce the sea in the sea, Elizabeth's faces
and changing possibilities also reproduce her. She plays at lying
through her many faces just as she plays at imagining precious
stones in the pebbles. But the pebbles, like her many faces, retain
their own opaqueness even in the sun:

> You sort your pebbles out. You know that each of them will
> change color as the sun moves. Noon's yellow becomes orange as
> the afternoon lengthens, is red at twilight, beneath the moon is
> violet, a fusion of red and blue. But not beyond that: a clear and
> unmixed blue never appears. It is there, that blue, buried within
> the tight concentric circles of the little pebble, you believe. And
> every day the pebble must withstand the attack of the sun,
> which would like to force the blue out into sight. The pebble
> allows itself to be overcome and transformed, from yellow
> through orange to violet, then to white at dawn and at noon back
> to yellow again. But only darkness is permitted to see the se-
> cret blue.

These are, precisely, the realms of evidence that veil the mystery,
the possibilities of discourse that struggle with the unrevealed core

of an individual or of his no longer reflective development. That is why Elizabeth is the center of the narrative mechanism of this novel. Like her, in the light of the reading the novel reveals different colors, different possibilities of transforming the pebbles of a Greek beach into imitation jade, granite, or rubies for the game of constructing four parallel worlds in a single conflict. The mechanism by which Elizabeth invents her world without revealing her own opaqueness is also in the other characters, so that the fiction within fiction (the sea in the sea) creates possible certainties of a central mystery: the mystery of making a novel, that parable of writing itself. Hence, after the description of the pebbles, the Narrator tells Elizabeth: "Now I must quote you a classic: *What you say to me is not true but nevertheless, simply because you say it, it reveals your being*" (italics added).

Javier is a frustrated writer who planned, but never wrote, a novel entitled *Pandora's Box*, although this novel is also *A Change of Skin*, or *A Change of Skin* is a novel the Narrator writes through *Pandora's Box*. More accurately, Carlos Fuentes writes *A Change of Skin* through a Narrator who through Javier writes *Pandora's Box* in order to write *A Change of Skin*. The three narrators all narrate starting from Elizabeth. *Pandora's Box* was to be a novel about "secret love," because, according to Javier, it is a lie that one loves more the more one knows one's lover. "What a proud and foolish lie. What you love is the unknown. What you haven't possessed yet. And maybe to stop loving when you begin to know the other person is... well, necessary for sanity. Because if we loved and knew each other, yet went on loving, we would all be out of our minds," he says. This is Javier's dilemma. Elizabeth's is just the opposite: "I loved you. But you have never loved me or any woman. You've loved Woman. Capital W. Phantom. That was how you could go on feeling free and unchained. A real woman of flesh and blood would have been too much burden for you. Whatever her name, Ligeia or Isabel."

This posing of the problem—an area of certainty in the process of becoming a mystery—achieves its form and expression in the theme of the face, the double, and the mask. Love, for Javier, is a furious battle, an endless copulation that is equivalent to "binding one another, killing one another, robbing our solitary identity, Ligeia, our secret mask." Thus love is also guilt, and Mexico is also a mask. "It hides us from the world, from what we left behind. Dragoness, this is only a place of exile for aliens, no one's home. You are also a prisoner of this country. So captivated and in love with your mask, that if the mask broke, light would blind you." Elizabeth replies, "No, it isn't true about the fog and the sun. I didn't come here looking for that... Not in search of the sun, but the sun as a mask, which is quite different." The sun and the sun as mask once again evoke the light transforming the pebbles into evidence and mystery. Here, when love has lost its drive and given away to frustration, the sun is also another mask, another opaqueness; it is no longer the light that brings out the names and their faces. At this point the masks have fallen away and this couple face each other in their naked and dramatic reality. That is why Elizabeth says, "Do you think I've been anything else, Javier? Do you think I'm still Elizabeth Jonas, the girl you met in New York? Don't you see that I've become you yourself? What you've wanted me to become. That I speak and think now not as myself but as you? That my own being has vanished?" In another passage the Narrator tells her: "You didn't want me to love your lovable mask but the other, whatever it might be, what you yourself ignored, also another mask. And if your mask also transformed you, your twin gestures would be reflected in his twin gestures and that love would be richer." Thus the evidence of love and its mystery would unite in that secret mask, in that secret identity. In one of his verbal fireworks the Narrator says, "Drop dead, corpse; every character is another character, himself and his mask, himself and his counterpart, himself and his own looker-on, victim and executioner at once."

Javier, a romantic at heart, is also the product of a masked Latin America and of a postwar period that pathetically demands change. As a young man he recognized himself in his innocence, in other words, in a tenuous individualism: "violence was created by the innocent when he burst into a world that had not wanted him." Elizabeth liked John Garfield "because he looked like Javier, because he lived between humiliation and danger, because he was, in the end, a living contradiction, the hero-villain, the saint-assassin, the artist-vulgarian." Javier will flee from this mirror, from this "dumb good guy" heroism, but she will have read in that mask the face of her husband. The adult Javier recognizes himself in a different perspective: "We learned that we're all guilty. Maybe that was the only lesson of those days." He adds that during those days: "Not even justice was ambiguous. Nor dream itself: dream was only the light cast by a darker reality. History was idea and politics was morality. . . . Everything was so clear." And also: "The revolution was the unity of all humble human beings, Dragoness. All artists, all men of justice, all over the world. A unity that transcended governments and nationalities. Politics had to be moral, history had to be conscience." The strong adjustments have given way to maladjustments; the individual is no longer comfortable in history because history also raises ambiguities and contradictions. In his first poems Javier saw a world explained by will and reason. Reason triumphed, but only because "it did not understand what was taking place around it." "A world that is incomprehensible has to be ordered by reason. And only a world that cannot be understood, neither at its irrational edges nor in its core, can be an object to be acted upon by the will, the strength of maturity," he says.

Javier demonstrates the failure of his reason in the larger failure of contemporary reason. Now, in the present time of the novel, history and human relations are governed by irrational interrelations, which is why the will struggles to elucidate this world. The playful clue of this will is a ritual consecration, parabolic thought, an incandescent will at the very center of the novel, a will of form. The paradox is rebelliously played out in Javier, who pursues the redoubling of love in Isabel, the redoubling of reality in a novel he does not write, and his own redoubling in Franz. It is also played out in the Narrator, in the mask that on the last page of the novel claims to be "Freddy Lambert." But here the Narrator pretends to be marginal, when he is actually a central figure, and to have traveled along a different highway and to have arrived voluntarily at Cholula without getting lost. His language and the show of making pastiches with culture in the baroque essays he writes suggest the margination of the mask that besieges his many faces. Creator and judge of the characters of the novel, by also being a character the Narrator is the grand witness, executioner, and opponent of the world he recreates. In his exasperated and pale defeat Javier would seem to be a univocal character, an individual condemned to himself, to the first step of his contradictory search. Javier proceeds from the same line as Oliveira, the other Latin-American terrorist of postwar culture, and like Oliveira, Javier is also a well, a void. His verbalism is different from Oliveira's, but their makeup is similar. Through Javier we see two periods: one filled with the nostalgic mythology of the movies, the 1930s, and the other filled with the mythology of development, the 1960s. The frustrated attempts to write and love lie at the core of his personal conflict. This Latin-American victim of modernism is the silent movie comic who gets hit by all the pies. Fuentes seems to censure a period at the same time that he consecrates it. Through the Narrator and through Javier himself, the novel seeks to make of its will to form a form different from that represented by Javier. The novel wants to go beyond innocence—the world explained by reason—and beyond culpability—the world accused by the guilt of the "I." In the sacrifice and summary consecration of these confronted lives, *A Change of Skin* also seeks another world, another time, the new space in which reality is reshaped, because, as Javier writes in his novel, "A novel discloses what the world has within itself but has not yet discovered and may never discover."

A Change of Skin is also sensitive to the cultural dualisms of life, to the fragmentation of a reality established as failure in the individual. "Better to keep silent," Javier tells himself. "Who will save himself? He who must sing the glories of labor or he who must sing the glories of the products of labor?" The Narrator tells Elizabeth:

> "you were merely taking pleasure in the awareness that incompatibles no longer exist, that the old Manichaeism which has led us by the split nose since the time of Plato, obliging us always to make choices, always to create blacks and whites, has taken a step that cannot be reversed toward the only position that matters today: a position not midway between external good and evil, objective, clearly separated, but between the moral options that are found only in subjective unity."

Fuentes is suggesting a step beyond the perception and dramatization of contradictions, not at the level of Cortázar's metaphysical knowledge nor in a synthesis of the instant, as in the poetry of Paz, but in the fullness of what is subjective: personalization perhaps, the defense of an area still not coopted by culture or society, a resolution of opposites in the intimate analogy of the personality. This is perhaps insinuated through the pure energy of myth and the nature of individuality: a festive zone of Renaissance overtones looms in this interaction.

The Narrator sees the Beatles as heralds of a different age because they are free figures who reject the established dualities:

> "And so they sing, setting us free from all the false and murderous dualisms upon which has been built the civilization of the judges, the priests, the philosophers, the artists and hangmen and merchants, and Plato dies drowning, surrendering, entangled in their long hair, mesmerized by their drowning voices, trampled upon by the sound of their rhythm as the Beatles, liberated, leap high to their heaven and slowly float down again, like Antheus, to the new earth where there are neither men nor women, good nor evil, body nor spirit, substance nor extension, essence nor accident, where there is only the dance and the rite, the fusion and the flowering mask of Arcimboldi which grows continually around everything and is the being and the nothingness of everything, its own moment seen from a helicopter that comprises the totality, the unity, in which die the old schizophrenias

of the Greco-Christian-Judaeo-Protestant-Marxist-industrial dualism."

This festive pastiche mocks the dualisms of our culture from a point outside their own drama. It is a parody of this drama because now these dualisms are combatted by the open-endedness of form (dance, rite, fusion, and mask), by the will to construct with it a new and free space, the new novel itself.

But the Narrator is aware of his game, of his space determined by the nearness of the improbable catastrophe and the morrow of the impossible feast, coordinates that in any event are inserted in a space impregnated by the world that is to be exorcised. That is why his speech becomes a pastiche and why he is a parable of the real narrator. He says: "Ah, Elizabeth. Between participation and escape there remain to us only our individual maladies, our personal cancers, our parodies of the great synthesis." He also speaks of "the Black Mass of the great synthesis, the great game of opposites outlawed by the judge called rationality and the hangman called morality and the jailer called history," a mass officiated by the new priests, the young people who in their pure joy reflect a world infinitely simplified by all humanisms. The following passage refers to a renaissance and to the Renaissance, "the New Renaissance, the renaissance of the Only Faith, that of body and soul fused upon the cinder ruins of a Dark Age of bankers and munitions makers and Talmudic commissars and Pentagonic marines, all the planners and orators of the crusades for collective death and individual degradation." The young people's world is therefore the other world, the world of the feast consecrated by a new mask over a new earth.

But for Javier the contradictions that make him remain silent are still found in the premonitions of fragmentation:

"My unity was overcome by divisiveness: words could not conquer the fragmentation of reality, a fragmentation that was there already, before I tried to write it. Then once again only the determination to make everything fixed, and again the failure to fix the past, to devour the present, to accept all of the future's premonitions."

But this program, which he satirizes in himself, is the thrust of the novel itself, its curve and tension, because through fragmentation *A Change of Skin* tends toward totalization, toward a simultaneous presence. Realizing his dramatic vein, his solitary, agonistic vocation, Javier says:

"Within me the search for the absolute, the failure of incompleteness, the creation of that incompleteness which, simply
because it is all that can be attained, is converted into my tiny
absolute."

Between Javier and the Narrator there is thus an opposition that
opens a passageway. The Narrator is like a turn of the screw of Javier.
Javier is obvious, something the Narrator does not want to be. Instead, like Elizabeth, he wants to invent another world in which to
find a face among the complexity of his own.

Franz, the German architect, is the analogical contradiction of a
univocal Javier. Franz constructed part of a concentration camp and
allowed Hanna Werner, another Jew and a Nazi prisoner, to be killed
because he refused to recognize her. Franz is Javier's double by opposition. His frustration is his guilt, but also his way of assuming his
own life, his way of claiming another innocence as the object of a
history in which he went astray. Franz is the potential victim found
in Javier, his other side, inasmuch as he is the victim of a concrete
history, a victim of it but also guilty within it. Franz also searches for
Elizabeth and Isabel because he wants to confess his story in order to
pursue his innocence, although his guilt appears to him in a tragedy,
in the heroic world, more than in the drama that characterizes Javier. A double in the mystery of being an object of time, guilty in the
innocence of change, Franz must succumb as Javier's mirror; his
death is also the death of his dark age, the evidence of another dark
age, Javier's.

Franz is assassinated at the pyramids of Cholula. The novel does
not reveal the assassin but suggests it might be Jakob Werner, the
son of Hanna and one of the young people traveling in a Lincoln in a
seemingly casual manner that is perhaps determined, however, by a
secret persecution, by the will to exchange one time for another.
Franz's death is double; it implies the death of Javier (in other words,
his possible resurrection) and the death of his own heroic and fatal
representation. The young people and Jakob are the other time killing Franz's time. The death of this double also requires the death of
the other double: Isabel. Javier strangles her with the shawl Elizabeth had given her young double. This final exorcism, this resurrection in the darkness, is also the death of the innocence that pursues
Javier, making him guilty and also victim. The outrageous parody at
the end of the novel takes place, parabolically, in a brothel, which
happens to be the former house of Javier's parents.

This second part of the novel brings together several languages
and conjugates them in the instant of the four lives confronted in a

mirror. These languages range from a very descriptive realism to poetic metaphorization, from a succinct schematism to euphuistic verbalism. They are impregnated with life and fuse in the coherence of
the novel, in its narrative course, and in its relentless will to find a
total form.

The third and final section of this novel is titled "Visit Our Cel-
lars." The characters descend into the infernal space of Cholula, into
the labyrinthine galleries of the superposed pyramids. In this section
the novel suddenly catches fire. It sets itself on fire to search for a
synthesis of the times and spaces represented by its characters, to
abolish and recover them, as well as to find the other narrative synthesis of the arrival and the encounter, of the feast. The synthesis is
also double. In Cholula the characters explore the galleries of the
"seven ancient pyramids that form the great hill." Like in a rite or a
play, the four characters are thrown into alarmed confusion when
one of the galleries caves in, separating Javier and Isabel from Franz
and Elizabeth. On the way to the hotel, after the labyrinthic immersion, Javier realizes that he prefers Elizabeth "with her barrenness
and her routines, because she is violent and given to extremes, to
some other barrenness and routine . . . tender and compassionate."
He then kills Isabel. The other space of the synthesis is more complex. It refers to Mexico City and to the six young people in the Lincoln, who return to Cholula, and is a parody of the novel itself. The
six young people represent, in a parabolical trial, the four characters
of the novel. The trial has a judge, a prosecutor, a counsel for the
defense, and an accused: Franz. This delirious and richly ambiguous
sequence synthesizes in the fullness of play and in the feast of the
doubles the contrasting situations of the characters, transforming
them into a masquerade. But the trial has a dark purpose. Jakob
Werner is the prosecutor, and he wants to kill Franz. This extraordinary parody reveals a baroque, expressionist language, a verbal fusion that creates a masked language. Here the young people are like
puppets, or the characters are like puppets in the hands of the young
people.

In a different role, that of the accused, Franz is also represented as
a sort of Christ. His failure is his answer to a history that subsumed
him:

"The accused wanted to prove that the strength of the ancient
heroes is still possible, that it can be the strength of feeble modern man if he will only give up his comfortable myths of common sense, his golden life in the miserable mean, his mask of
decency and decorum."

His counsel then parodies this failure:

> "That true freedom to accept all, not only what man is but what he may be. All the powers of Man, of Man, of Mangy, Maniac, Manacled Mannequin Man."

The woman who represents Elizabeth also accuses Franz of having treated her just like Javier:

> "at least he never tried to deceive me... I always knew what he wanted, that I had to pretend to be another woman... He made me play games... I had to go late to a party so that he could come even later and find me there and pretend I was a new love... A love he had never known before."

The accused responds:

> "No, Lisbeth. I didn't want you for that. I swear it. Not to wipe away a guilt I never felt for a moment."
> "Then why?"
> "To possess again a girl I had lost years ago."

That girl is, of course, Hanna. The parody fervently continues in a brothel. Javier says:

> "And the point is, a few minutes ago the attorney for the defense spoke about rediscovering the unity we have lost. About desire fulfilled simply by being desired. And I realized . . . that both the poets and the criminals . . . could be born of the same mother. Sade is named Auschwitz. Lautréamont is Treblinka. Nietzsche is Terezin. . . . And our dream, the dream I could never write, was born of the spirit of those times . . . and was part of those times and had to die with those times . . . to end with the end of that world which had crippled all of us . . . and the only way to destroy that world was to do just what the attorney for the defense said. Put everything to the test. Compel reality to submit itself to will and our purpose. Our desire that no man had dared to feel before. . . . So there had to be two revolutions instead of one. One in the world. One within ourselves. . . . Victory for will and desire at last. At last an end to the terrible oppositions that for centuries had isolated us from each other. Yours and mine. Word and action. Dream and waking. Body and soul. Homeland, flag, family, property."

Thus Javier's dream parallels and is a double of Franz's dream, a searcher also for "the tragic life." This parody of the characters and of the novel itself becomes a carnivalization in the fake birth of a child to Elizabeth and in the birth of a two-bit Savior. This supreme and ferocious mockery is also a coherent rebellion. Finally, in another parody of the novel, the Narrator opens a trunk—Pandora's box—and takes out objects associated with the other characters, with Javier's parents, and with Franz's life in Prague. He also pulls out a live puppet, the strange dwarf called Herr Urs, who Franz, as a young student, had known and had seen die. In the total trial to which Franz is subjected the appearance of this dark dwarf must represent the mockery of his own history, of his guilt and innocence defeated by a different world. Like in an expressionist film, here representation rests on variations of a self-reflecting fiction. Finally, in the dark Cholula night we know that the Narrator has led the procession, that he has declared Franz guilty, and that Jakob Werner, the assassin of Franz, who is perhaps his father, returns from his act of revenge and announces his freedom. This revenge is also metaphorical: a different time replaces the life of a guilty time.

The evidence and mysteries of *A Change of Skin* fuse in this tremendous parody, in the extraordinary play that is a mirror of the novel and its solution in a game. At the conclusion of the novel, the Narrator is in the mental asylum at Cholula, or rather, in the house of Lazarus, a place of resurrection. Another mystery surfaces at this point. Elizabeth relates that she and Javier stuffed Franz's body into the trunk of the Lincoln and that there she saw a wrapped bundle that stirred and whimpered and that "behind those bandage-like wrappings there was life, perhaps there was even more than one life." She took out the bundle and left it at the gate of the asylum. Already in the first part of the novel the Narrator has said, "But I could hear only the whimpering and sobbing, soft, fused, that I knew came from the trunk of the car." Also, during the masquerade of the trial, when the trunk of the Lincoln is opened, something inside this mysterious wrapped bundle whimpers. The last passage of the novel reads: "But the yellow, foaming dog of Cholula is about to turn from his snack; he is going to tear the dirty rags that still tie him and then, Dragoness, and then . . . I know that his hunger is far from sated." Another symbol, another parody. The dogs of Cholula, like its pyramids, are present throughout the history of this central village. They surrounded the *conquistadores* and they now surround the visitors. The hungry dog of Cholula thus suggests another form of resurrection, another possibility of ceremonial revenge.

13. *Three Trapped Tigers*

An Open Novel

Three Trapped Tigers* poses literature as a game, and within this context the game has a more decisive role than literature because for Guillermo Cabrera Infante the infinite possibilities of the game compromise in a fundamental way the shaping of reality. This novel is a spiral of that game; the game is its perspective, its development, and its unity. Of course, the novel as a game amounts to a game the novel plays with itself, because this spiral is also the novel; in other words, all of literature and culture, reality, in short, are the contents brought into play in a writing that thinks of itself as a game of mirrors. Cabrera Infante's radicalism is also a synthesis and a departure. His novel recognizes Lewis Carroll's appeal in the carnival of its paradoxes, Joyce's paradigm in the delight of its wordplay, and Borges's influence in the transcendence of even the smallest events. But *Three Trapped Tigers* is above all a novel with a fervent Latin-American baroque character. This baroque quality underlies a new departure defined by an antitraditionalism that rejects plots and conventional unities, verism, suspense-filled episodes and psychological insights in favor of its free verbal festivity and of a will to convert it into oral forms. From its first page to its last, this novel is a conversation, a multiple dialogue.

A belated novel and an early open work, *Three Trapped Tigers* rejects an obvious structure and refuses the rigidity of a reconstruction through reading. Cabrera Infante has avoided the novel as construc-

*Guillermo Cabrera Infante, *Three Trapped Tigers*, translated by Donald Gardner and Suzanne Jill Levine in collaboration with the author (New York: Harper Colophon Books, 1978). Originally published as *Tres tristes tigres* (1967).

tion and poses instead the novel as a river, as a free and liberating flow. Its freest internal and external rhythms flow from the swift movement of conversation, from a total verbalization creating a porous, live, thick language, which is why a nervous vitality, the physical sensation of the world recorded by the word, emerges beyond this euphuistic, popular, elaborate, and spontaneous game. Drawing from literary and demotic speech, from the melodramatic and from true anguish, and through the richness of urban popular culture, this novel reveals a world of appearances transformed into the rules of a game. It records an immediate world in the sensations and a mediate one in words, an intense and irrepressible space and time of a Havana attacked by language, the nights of the city registered by the fervent duration of the word.

The novel posed as a river rather than as geometry, as time more than as space, finds also in the flow of conversation, which is more immediate than "dialogue," and also more arbitrary, its most unifying rhythm and duration. Every game has its rules, and the rules of this game (the rules of reading) are based on perceiving this duration, on allowing it to involve us freely in its spiral. *Three Trapped Tigers* is a novel that also permits an open reading. The world of the novel has been, therefore, forged as verbal time and as oral time. The novel is almost like an orchestra or a sound track. This is why in the prologue the master of ceremonies of the Tropicana nightclub opens the show (of the novel) and introduces several of the novel's characters who are in the audience, setting in motion in the book the festive and theatrical nights of Havana. This game with the novel also implies, incidentally, the posing of a deep contradiction: on one hand, the novel attempts to blur the traditional schemes and to carnivalize culture itself, while, on the other hand, it plays with its own formulation, with the fact itself of being transformed into a novel. Its literary field is thus a double literature, or a double attempt at producing antiliterature.

The tongue-twisting play of the title and the epigraph by Lewis Carroll ("And she tried to fancy what the flame of a candle looks like after the candle is blown out") suggest, but do not exhaust, two possible means of access to this fascinating narration. The title, by its popular oralness and irony, also points to the word game evoking in the novel the nights of Havana and the infinite richness of the various languages, languages that are also a sort of tongue twister. The epigraph indicates the imaginary and contradictory realm in which this game (and reading also) will develop. Commenting on Carroll's phrase (*Mundo Nuevo*, No. 13), Cabrera Infante describes it as "one of the most felicitous phrases of English literature, a summary of man's metaphysical need and of the crystallized nostalgia that is one of the names of poetry." In effect, the entire novel oscillates between nostalgia—not of the past but of the nervous present of reconstructed speech—and the metaphysical need to transgress the immediate reality through this language. Cabrera Infante's recognition of this metaphysical need is quite revealing and surprising, as in the novel the characters constantly satirize the threat of the word "metaphysics" entering consciousness as a terrorist act against the flow itself of speech and the events of speech. This suggests also that the pervasive ridicule in the novel is the shaded line of a more serious line; in Cuba, one of the characters states, laughter is the most serious thing of all. This may be true for all of Latin America, and especially for a Latin-American literature rebelling against the conventional formulations of tradition and seeking to liberate art in a new space of questioning.

The title and the epigraph, small clues, add to the many possibilities of play suggested by the prologue set in the Tropicana. They introduce us into an essentially dialogical world and advise us that the rules of the game or of reading are based entirely on the shaping of this verbal world, on its absolute independence from any reality other than that represented by words.

The lengthy, detailed verbalization of the nights of Havana does not attempt to recreate a social atmosphere or situation or a disclosable plot. It seeks, simply, to capture the experience of that world through oral memory, through a verbal nostalgia in which the chatting actors, rather than individuals to be analyzed, are verbal points of view, speakers implicated in the festive and flowing novelizing of this recreation. The spiral of this novelization is animated by a relentless drive, by an almost frenzied rhythm struggling with breathing and, certainly, with time. In this novel words live the adventure of replacing with their associative sound the other life of opaqueness and confusion, capturing the blind momentum of a somnambulant-like existence, inebriated by their own duration. This novel is a rite and an auto-da-fé. Even more than the phoenix and its rebirths, it evokes the magician with his robes and paraphernalia. Rhetorical and festive, this one-night magician displays his powers. At times he perhaps trips over himself, but he is his own greatest game. The intense tension of the novel rests, therefore, on its mechanisms of verbal reconstruction starting from oralness. In this chorus of voices time reveals its docile and fleeting substance.

As the chorus rises, the reader is pulled deeper into a novel that requires giving up the search for a plot or a unifying subject. The readers are forced to relinquish the sensation of a plot created by the author, who has trapped them with the intention of later releasing them in the free flow of his verbalness. The trap is set by the author in the short chapters at the beginning of the novel, in which various speakers insinuate the outline of a plot. But the plot never materializes, and the reader is left with a series of truncated adventures. Hence the clues to an open reading are reduced or expanded through motivations, more or less anecdoctal, and through points of view (or of speech) that again take up situations and characters that are as many other voices of a single verbal urge. The paradox of *Three Trapped Tigers* emerges when the reader realizes that this novel does not have the traditional fabric. The verbal fascination holds our attention, incited by a sort of "suspense" of verbalness, and we realize to our surprise that it is necessary that nothing "happen," that the novelistic spiral continue to spin. The lack of a central theme or even of a central problem, as well as the absence of a visible structure, constitute, by virtue of the oral rules of the novel, the freedom of its reading, which is here the freedom of the reader and, certainly, that of the author himself. A rite of memory and an auto-da-fé of the mechanisms of memory itself, *Three Trapped Tigers* is free on each page because of its total presence in language.

The narration continues, of course, to set traps for the reader by systematically reintroducing several of its characters. This is especially true of the female characters, who in one way or another are the enclosure or the landscape of the novel—sometimes even allegorically, as in the case of singer Cuba Venegas, who is also called Toda Cuba or Cubita Bella. "It's better, much much better to see Cuba than to hear her and it's better because anyone who sees Cuba falls in love with her but anyone who hears and listens to her can never love her again," one of the characters says about this singer, who in some allegorical way stands for Cuba, although the statement of the character is also a double love, another obsession of love.

The characters of this uninterrupted conversation are mainly Arsenio Cué, an actor, Silvestre, a writer, Eribó, a bongo player, Códac, a photographer, and Bustrófedon, an oral poet and master of punning and paraphrasing who has died and is a legend among the other characters. Bustrófedon—like his name in jest—is reflected in the other characters as a central mirror. His continual verbal humor is a mechanism among the speakers, who quote, imitate, or reproduce him, and it is also the mechanism of the novel itself, because Bustrófedon is the pole of the metaphorical possibilities of language and of words, a man-word, words as game. Silvestre, who is the horizontal line of the novel, the mask of the author himself, is also involved in the broad game of language. He is a chronicler of this myth of speech replacing reality. Perhaps the word *Tradittori* he sees at the end of a dream is a double accusation, traitor and translator, not only because of his literary translations, but also because of this other translation of oralness into writing, because of this desire of total poetry. Through the open line of an infinitely accumulative verbal game, Bustrófedon is also the archetypical equivalence of this total poetry, which is why his death transforms into reality Lautremont's definition, the umbrella and the sewing machine on a dissection table.

In this poetry of speech simulating reality "literature is no more important than conversation," and "The Great Novel of the Air" that Bustrófedon and his friends have recorded on tape is also *Three Trapped Tigers*, whose "sound pages" record the "noises which is what we all have been of Bustrófedon," nucleus and law of this mythical language.

All Bustrófedon ever "wrote" was a recorded tape of a parody of Cuban literature, "The Death of Trotsky as Described by Various Cuban Writers, Several Years after the Event—or Before," through which Cabrera Infante pokes fun at the most famous Cuban writers, from Martí to Guillén. But he does this starting from the central dread of his novel, style, that other translation of reality in written language. From the perspective of this novel, style is the negation of an exclusively oral, spoken reality in which time is alive and myth has its place at the same time that it slips away. This explains why Bustrófedon paraphrases and exaggerates the stylistic traits of these Cuban authors. This dread of style, of the second operation of written speech, also explains why the chapter entitled "Some Revelations," which could be expected to be Bustrófedon's written clue, consists only of blank pages. This radicalism is a clue in the form of a joke, because Bustrófedon, the author's alter ego, never wrote a page. He only spoke them, just as the novel attempts to speak by requesting, in one of the author's introductory notes, that it be read aloud.

Remembering the image of a young woman, Silvestre knows that:

"That moment . . . will not return and this is exactly what makes moment and memory precious. This image assails me violently now, almost without provocation, and I think the best way of recapturing time past is not one's involuntary memory but the violent irresistible memories, which don't need any madeleines dunked in tea or the nostalgic fragrance of the past or an identical faux pas, but which come up suddenly like a thief by night and smash the window of our present with a blunt memory. It is then not uncommon that this memory induces vertigo:

that sensation of being on the edge of a precipice, that sudden, unpredictable journey, that bringing together of two planes by the possible violent drop (the planes of reality by a vertical physical drop and the plane of reality and memory by the imaginary horizontal drop) shows us that time, like space, also has its laws of gravity. I would like to marry Proust off to Isaac Newton."

This description of memory, which pursues the idea of dynamism as law, could also be applied to the novel as a whole. Here memory is immediate; it does not require Proust's stimuli and is, therefore, successive. It implies an immersion in the vertigo of duration, a converging of time and space. In this novel memory is the totalization of the instant, another path for making present a whole reality.

Musician, writer, actor, photographer, and the supreme poet, Bustrófedon, god and mask of this tropical Parnassus, these characters practice their professions as though they were forms of a single exorcism in which appearance and reality are fused or confused in the same somnambulistic present. Talking about Arsenio Cué, Silvestre states that:

"He didn't want to eat up the miles as we say here . . . it was more like he was going over the word mile and I thought his intention was the same as my pretension to remember everything or as Códac's temptation wanting all the women to have a single vagina . . . or like Eribó's who got an erection whenever he heard distant drums or the late Bustrófedon who wanted to be a living language. We were totalitarians: immortals to be by uniting the end and the beginning. But Cué was wrong (we were all wrong, all of us except, perhaps, Bustrófedon, who could well be immortal by now), because if time is irreversible, space is irreducible and, what's more, infinite."

But this contradiction is the scope and risk of open-endedness, as occurs in the novel itself.

Through Silvestre the novel establishes a category: contradiction, the "contrary" man who wants to explain, or to stop explaining and assume, an image of passion and its faces, play and commitment in the parable of an existence that runs its own risks by following its own rules, a notion that comes close to the idea of personality as destiny.

Characters such as Sherlock Holmes and Don Quixote and authors such as Hemingway and Rabelais are "contraries," but Gargantua, Pantagruel, Julian Sorel, Ahab, and Billy Budd are not. The "contrary" is an unpredictable and antirationalist individual. He is obviously the opposite of a univocal or topical type. "Sorel is French and as you've seen for yourself the French try as hard as possible to be rationalists to the point of madness. They are deliberately anti-contrary. Even Jarry wasn't a contrary. There hasn't been one since Baudelaire." Julius Caesar, on the other hand, is a "contrary" and besides that a modern man. Caligula was perhaps the greatest of all contraries. The only contraries in American literature are the "half-castes," or people who behave like "half-castes." The most contrary of the contrary Americans is, of course, Ezra Pound. Lewis Carroll is clearly one of the great contraries.

> "Not talking about, *playing with* literature."
> "And what's so bad about that?"
> "Literature, of course."
> "That's better. For a moment I was afraid you were going to say the game. Shall we go on?"

From this point of view the characters belong to a breed for whom contradiction does not imply a dichotomy or some other form of dualism but, rather, a multiplicity within unity, a sort of resourcefulness, an open-endedness, if one might say so, an open availability of the face in its masquerades. As opposed to the univocal character—a child of verism—and to the dualistic character—a child of schematization—, the "contrary character" is a risk of himself, more unexpected than ambiguous, more probable than obvious. The convergence of so many characters within contradiction as a category also reveals the metaphor this term implies. This category is a metaphor because it seems to point to the nature itself of the character as a literary entity straddling the book and reading. The character does not have a reference in an obvious scheme (his possible model in reality) or in an ideal scheme (his possible literary development). Deliberately set midway between all forms of realism and literary classifications, this novel announces its paradigmatic character within contradiction because, as a spiral, as a rite with no formulas, it poses itself directly in contradiction with established literature and with explanations of reality. Flowing between both shores, the course of this novel-river is fervent, nervous, and warm. Thus the novel itself can be a character, or, as it states, it could have been a pistol.

The vast and fervent arbitrary game of *Three Trapped Tigers* is somehow also a pact and a truce. A belated novel and an early example of an open work, it announces in its own way the creative ambition of the forms that designate a Latin-American art that has reached its creative maturity.

Additional Notes

I.   The prologue of this novel, in which the master of ceremonies of the Tropicana cabaret introduces the show, is also an invitation to the spectacle the book itself proposes. At the center of the book, participation in all the possibilities of the spectacle (from the extreme "camp" of the cabaret to the ride through the city) represents the need to identify the faces of time or, rather, its masks. Time appears to consecrate itself in every form of spectacle. From its most trivial performance to its mythical irruption, time is always double. Unfolding, it gives the measure of its duration and the promise of a grasped fervor.

II.   The events and voices, the fortuitous and proliferating acts, and the accumulative and wandering dialogues of this novel are animated by the proximity of the spectacle. They enter, abandon, or pursue the sudden animation of a broader rhythm within whose patterns any act, including even the simplest, suddenly recovers the wild innocence of its duration.

III.   This accounts for the proliferating speech characteristic of this writing. All notions of line and all traces of internal restraint are overtaken by the loquaciousness of a speech competing for time. This speech unfolds sumptuously, playing with its own emphasis. This comedy of speech is so uninhibited that it overwhelms us with its reverberating din and plunges us also into the extraordinary confidence of saying everything.

IV.   The spectacle, therefore, is the mechanism of composition of this novel. Bustrófedon, its mythical character, the writer who refused to write, leaves only a recorded tape containing a long parody of Cuban literature. Through this parody the novel also discloses its own root: it is a game it plays with itself, a joke meticulously devised to liberate the consciousness of the world in the spectacular redoubling of spoken time. The writer, Bustrófedon, whose name stands for an inverted writing, never wrote a page. He is thus the negation of fixed writing and the longing for spoken writing, which, however, lacks substance and has only the reflected nature of parody. In its profusion speech is also a parody of time, a masquerade, a labyrinth to manifest its temporality. The absence of a center producing a constitutive substance yields a proliferating spectacle. This spectacle has no beginning and no end and implies the excess that drowns the conscience, the extreme speech of the tongue twister, the fatigue and anxiety of humor, the vague moment at which night becomes a new and almost intrusive day. Bustrófedon refuses to write in order to avoid being responsible for time. He speaks so that time will occur in his place. Hence he is also a spectacle—as his name indicates—a redoubled time: feast and consciousness, excess and alienation.

V.   Every spectacle implies a space of its own in which its nature is defined. As time in motion, this rhythm requires its reference, its solid ground or desired land. In *Three Trapped Tigers* this space is obviously the street. The bars, theaters, and nightclub dance floors are the chance that the street and its doorways consecrate and promise. On the street everything happens as an inciting, unpredictable possibility. In this novel the street is the site of the promise, the center of a universe that lacks a center.

VI.   At the start of the novel the two girls who are the spectacle of the town "played with each other's things" under a truck parked in the street. Their experience of the world emerges starting from a shared curiosity. Later, the two boys going to the movies experience the spectacle of the city when they choose the Santa Fe trail. Their pilgrimage is an adolescent rite implying enchanted stations. "Who would think of eating when the road is so long and patience so short—or was the reverse more true—and when in Santa Fe we would find adventure, freedom and dreams fulfilled?" But on their way to the movie theater the two boys encounter a different possibility of the street: one man shoots another man to death. "On the corner there is a black pool of blood under the street light and a crowd has gathered around it, staring and making comments." A crack has opened in the pure spectacle of the street.

VII.   As in much of the book, the street is also the point of reference of the section entitled "Bachata." The characters ride through the city, contemplating, making, and being the spectacle. "Cué had this obsession with time. What I mean is that he would search for time in space, and they were nothing but a search, our continual, interminable journeys along the Malecón." An urban Heraclitus, Cué substitutes the street for the river, vertigo for consciousness. "When Cué talked about time and space and when he went over all that space in all our time I thought that he did it to divert us, and now I know: it was to do something different, to make one thing of another, and while we were going over space he succeeded in evading what he always avoided, I think, which was to go over another space outside of time. Or to be precise—remembering." According to this version, Cué flees from himself and is entertained by his own flight. But Cué is also a spectacle, only in this case his redoubling is deliberate. He is an actor, but, surprisingly, he does not participate in the gratuitous innocence of the spectacle around him; his awareness makes him almost an impostor. The others are the actors; they live a basic life with full fervor and feel only the shadow of an anguish similar to that of a breach between a spectacle that is passed and one that is probable. Still talking about Cué, the narrator adds: "He said that there were times when the car and the road and he himself disappeared and the three became one and the same thing, the ride, space and the destination of the journey." This narrator thinks in terms of Zen Buddhism (the archer, the arrow, and the target). But does Cué actually seek to deny himself? His gamble is different. If he were to gain the space of the spectacle, his life would no longer require the spectacle itself. He would have possessed the place. The fact that Cué's method is unorthodox is another form of Cabrera Infante's *permanent humor*; his characters live the comedy of the nocturnal paradise, the derision of time, and the substitutive masquerade. These characters would be absurd if they did not speak. After their loquacity they do not know—or suspect—the stifling embarrassment of their own silence. Their reality is constituted in speaking; in the spectacle they find their passion, and in the street they encounter their *comic destiny*.

VIII.   In an essay on Baudelaire, Walter Benjamin has written about the images of the street and urban crowds in late nineteenth-century literature. He describes a hostile street in which the individual comes face-to-face with horror. Benjamin omits in his account a story by Maupassant in which a man, suddenly terrified by the absolute void, roams the nighttime streets of Paris. Benjamin was interested in capturing the crushing effect of the crowd, but the other side of this emptied spectacle, the "hollow men," is found in the void itself of the street, in the irrevocable indifference of its fixity. Unreality can also penetrate the image of these excessively real streets. As in one of Octavio Paz's poems, our footsteps seem to imply some other place. But the street is not only unreal when it is empty at night. The crowd also lends the street its code in its pact of mutual indifference. In Paris, during the period between the wars, it seemed possible, or festively credible, on the other hand, for a person attempting suicide to jump into the Seine (in a movie by Jean Renoir, of course) and for a servant girl to shout "An accident!" while a crowd gathered and several people jumped in to help, thus producing the spectacle of a widely shared dialogue. (Perhaps the cinema has tried to move us through the scandal of that dialogue, now that the notion of the public square has been lost.) When Breton tells about his visit to the flea market and describes a map of relations and assumptions, the street —or the streets of his city—would seem to allow the operation of an objective chance because it is a converging of a familiar world, which he views, nevertheless, with amazement. In one of Borges's stories, on the other hand, a street could be the Acheron itself.

IX.   In *Three Trapped Tigers* the street is a nocturnal topography. Its points of reference are the nightclubs, the spectacle that toward midnight, after the theatricality, begins to take on the curious feeling of a lingering duration. In this profane hall Cabrera Infante consecrates a ritual time, a duration with the rhythm of memory and contemplation. But prior to this, the street is the promise of open-endedness. To roam the streets is to recover chance. Its claims have the power of a spell. The other side of the random, festive search is a series of encounters and answers that are also incidental and indistinct. This mechanism is also present in *Hopscotch*. The character wanders about the city and, suddenly, by chance, he reads a poster announcing a piano recital. By chance he goes to Berthe Trepat's concert, and consecrating this chance, the author narrates the episode. It could have been left out of the novel, its character could have turned at some other corner. This is an example of a proliferating mechanism, of an accumulative composition. Occurring, writing pursues its center. In this search writing invents itself, and its center can emerge or be deferred. The street episode in *Paradiso*, in which José Cemí is caught in the middle of a student riot with the police, has other repercussions, not so much in the meaning of the episode itself as in the direction given to it by Lezama. At the height of the scuffle, a hand grabs Cemí and guides him to safety. The battle thus has a mythical substratum. As in a typical Homeric episode, a god saves the character from danger, and in this case this gesture is an indication of friendship as another initiation. An episode thus implies several webs, a direction, a center. This is far from a necessary event; it only indicates that representation is articulated in its "fictionality."

X.   In *Three Trapped Tigers*, however, what stands out is the free festiveness of the street. Unlike the characters of *Hopscotch*, who expect to be helped by chance, the characters in this Cuban novel already live at the center of chance; they are chance itself. This confers on them the innocent vigor and elemental charm of open-

endedness, the vitality (of the Latin-American city?) of attachment
and detachment that the Cuban tradition designates, at least in part,
as *choteo*, a making fun of someone or something. But if the exuber-
ant life of speech occurs as a subjecting of time it is because the
street permits this raised voice, this chain reaction of a game ver-
balizing culture, conferring to it the tone of the street and converting it in turn into a parody, into puns and humor. All the possibilities of adventure can be found in the open-endedness of a street at
night, and the characters seek the innocence of the spectacles in order to participate in a fuller communication, or perhaps to flee from
themselves, or to find themselves alone in a common setting. But
the street also contains an element of malaise: the assassination in
the street narrated at the beginning of the novel; the poster pro-
claiming *President Batista's Public Works Plan, 1957–1966*, which
the characters put off but in which the reader recognizes the irony of
the dates. And this is another dilemma. The Havana of this book
belongs to one of the branches of science fiction or archaeology, because the street will encounter history, and the spectacle will disclose another of its ritual phases, as Cabrera Infante himself recognized in his vignettes in *Así en la paz como en la guerra*. But perhaps
the street in itself is only the visible or mediating image of some
other implicated space. Perhaps Havana itself has been transformed,
but there is another zone that belongs to literature and to the oral
speech of Havana, and that zone emerges as another possibility that
history and literature will continue their dialogue, because the oral
exaltation of this book recovers the drive of certain specific individuals toward a fullness that is unfulfilled and deferred. But this drive is
not only individual, it is not only the longing of an author for his
favorite streets. It is perhaps a norm held in common by a group of
individuals, by a defined or undefined age. In some way this is a collective book, and as such it has the rare value of not attempting to
prove anything. It is, in its own way, a novel about the art of the
novel; it does not show us the process of its figures but the results of
the process, the options of its figures. In other words, it demonstrates itself; it sustains itself on its own spectacular nature.

This implicated space, of which the street is the mediating path,
is, of course, language itself, speech and its duration. This is the
point of encounter of the searching of the characters and the malaise
of the future, the indetermination that does not find answers in a
future that for them is equally indeterminate. Judged from the outcome of history, the "guilt" of this novel is unlikely, but so is its innocent vision of the streets of Havana. That Havana is impossible,
its "innocence" is scandalous. We are left instead with the drive of

an inexhaustible energy, through the oral metaphor, toward its fullness. Meanwhile, at the heart of this book, or in its probable center, this drive chooses the spectacle of its own occurrence. This novel can be read, therefore, as a dialogic chapter of Cuban speech. That language has gone through other stages, some very different from this one, but it also speaks for itself in the fervor of these pages.

14. *From Cuba with a Song*

From Cuba with a Song,* by the young Cuban writer Severo Sarduy, is a novel that carries radicalism of form to a new level in the Latin-American novel. It is a novel, an antinovel, and a scrapbook of a possible novel. It strikes the reader first as a jumble of innovations, but it actually possesses a self-induced program within its obstinate will to transgress. This program takes the form of the draining of the traditional novel in new variations of the reshaping of cultural forms.

The book consists of an introduction followed by three segments, each dealing with one of the three racial components of Cuban culture:

(a) "Curriculum cubense," a sort of prologue, poses the idea of the text as iconographic writing. Through this writing, Sarduy will attempt to make visible the different and conjugated components of the Cuban world.

(b) The first segment, "By the River of Rose Ashes," is a mirrored recreation of the Chinese world of Havana. Its detailed descriptions, enumerations, and transformations are not intended as a snapshot of this world but as its possible metaphor: the masks are switched in this feverish transgression of its own design, in the play of its verbal fireworks. The humor found here is a form of criticism, of self-questioning. This text is, therefore, a brilliant pastiche sustained by the code of its baroque gratuitousness and is valid in its own right. The glossed world of this novel is drained—by the act of glossing itself—of signification and even of materiality, because the baroque line of this work is light and airy and the sensation it distills is an insinuation, a trace of desire, rather than the full sensation of desire itself.

*Severo Sarduy, *From Cuba with a Song,* translated by Suzanne Jill Levine in *Triple Cross* (New York: E. P. Dutton, 1972). Originally published as *De donde son los cantantes.*

(c) The second segment, "Dolores Rondón," is a pastiche of the Black component of a "Cubanness" brilliantly reduced by Sarduy to a myth of sensible forms. Whereas the Chinese spectacle implied a world of objects, a happy confusion of changing characters and masks, the Black spectacle implies a theatrical oralness. The tragic game of a feminine character sarcastically followed through the popular legends about her is developed here in another literary game. Through a popular theatrical performance we witness the lost cause of this Cuban mulattress who has been elevated to a national symbol. Sarduy once again constructs a rhetorical parable, a baroque, oratorical pastiche, intended as another mask of reality within language.

(d) The third segment, "The Entry of Christ in Havana," is the most accomplished part of the text. It too is a verbal parable, but its object is the Hispanic component of this "curriculum cubense," which we now realize has critical implications and a dynamics of festive interrogation. The hallucinating creation of a language as a totally imaginary adventure, a process whose very nature implies a radical criticism of the tradition of this genre and of representation, reaches it expressive culmination in this text through gratuitousness. Its most beautiful creative energy emerges from the play of free verbal invention.

This ethnic and cultural anthropology turns out to be a proposal for an antianthropology, so to speak. The conjugation of "cultural" and "ethnic" elements is presented here starting from a different perception: the pictorial and theatrical possibilities of language. The three glossed components are seen as pure spectacle; thus their essences are disclosed through appearances, through faces represented as masks. Hence the Chinese is only a repertoire of objects; the Black is a full-bodied voice; and the Hispanic is a rotting wooden statue (of Christ), a parable of signification. Pastiche and inversion, the novel's secret Sadian or satirical festivity provide the touchstones for an ironic criticism of the three cultural components and the key to the possible reshaping of popular creativeness in a textual fullness. This popular imagery is reduced to a few sensuous signs, and the novel thus becomes a radical rejection of the meanings of culture in the name of the liberation of the senses provided by art.

Appearance is inevitably also a cultural form in Sarduy's literary game. It is a form emptied of meaning but infused with another proposition, the baroque in this case. The baroque aspect of Sarduy's work is not, however, the allegoric and sensorial baroque encountered in Lezama Lima or the solar baroque of Octavio Paz; it is, instead, a hyperbole of pure form, a spiral of metaphorical accumulations, a double mask, perhaps because the pastiche implies a total suppression of density and at the same time a pure presence of language. Deprived of a signifying connection with all referents, Sarduy's baroque requires a formal relationship with them based on its own medium: the word, the phrase, the text. Therefore, this baroque is almost a parody of itself, because Sarduy longs for the idea of the baroque as a kind of verbal absolute. The text is thus produced as a recodification by the image and as a recovery of the world through the senses. Repeatedly proposed as an erotic activity, Sarduy's writing is also the nervous or tense desire for a fulfilling eroticism, which is found here as suggestion, as a beckoning. Thus, even if the lack of density does not imply an aleatory eroticism (as in Lezama Lima), the origin of writing does. For Sarduy, narration amounts to liberating meaning through the senses, to posing a parody of the world through empathy.

This reduction of reality to the image produces various rhythms and scenes in the novel, from the image constructed and then displaced ("By the River of Rose Ashes") to the spectacular and sonorous image ("Dolores Rondón"), and to the image playing with the irony of symbols ("The Entry of Christ in Havana"). A warm and festive current runs through the novel in these sequences. This festive energy suggests the continuous displacement of the text's own findings, because the reader himself loses, in the barrage of images, the course of its reference; the text thus continues to unfold in a constant imagistic beginning.

Sarduy has found a way to reconcile the surrealist method of figurative exploration by the image (especially in the delirious final text) with the *nouveau roman*'s method of detachment and objectivity.

Through this dual method, his writing evinces a pictorial base that is immediately transformed into a theatrical space and then converted into a dream. Hence this novel is nothing other than the dream of an innocent apocalypse.

Guillermo Sucre has written as follows:

Sarduy's novel is a metaphor, and this metaphor is nourished, above all, by art. Sarduy looks through art at what is real. Art is his mediator and it is knowledge, but not in the sacred way it was for Proust, Joyce, or Thomas Mann, for all of whom art was still an absolute. Although Sarduy superposes art on all his perceptions, he does it in a playfully ironic way. (*Imagen*, No. 20)

This accurate comment also points to the place of this novel within the Latin-American narrative. The baroque aspect of Sarduy's work is rooted in a transgression of culture in the name of art as a sensuous resumption of reality through words.

But this novel also engages in an obstinate effort to destroy the pathos of the everyday world and attempts, instead, to rescue the world through the possible formal purity, in the full simplicity of its sensible evidence. "The Entry of Christ in Havana," in particular, suggests a critical zeal in its progressive hollowing out of the great myth (myth of Meaning? of Humanism?). This amused rage is the patient and final reconstruction of reality, its reformulation in the synthesis of dreaming and verbal actions. Through its changing images and the playfulness of its forms, the radical criticism of this operation also suggests a parody of traditional works, but this parody finally becomes a fervent reconstruction of the pure spectacle of sensible forms, of language as an infinite metaphor of tradition.

The verbal action or the verbal liberation have the same motivation, the reshaping of the world in the pleasure of the word, the desire for a conjugated perception arousing the desire to live reality anew as though it were a language of feelings. The freedom of the word is also the freedom of desire in the fleeting perception that conjugates them through the magic of writing. But the lucidity of this dream in *From Cuba with a Song* carries with it the inevitable ambiguity that goes with creative criticism: when it is critiqued poetry is destroyed and empties its references in the neatness of sensoriality. In this case poetry perhaps sees itself as a mask, as gratuitous appearance and, therefore, as ironic criticism of its own poetic game. Perhaps more critical than poetic in nature, this novel consumes itself as its own excessive example. Thus, its creative resolutions lie in the radical position gained by its own textual drama, because this novel is also on the cutting edge, on the edge of culture. But Sarduy's imagistic fervor and verbal passion will undoubtedly reveal to us that *culture* itself is just another form of the more radical art he is proposing.

Some More References

Critic Emir Rodríguez Monegal has given us a key to the creative work of Severo Sarduy in an interesting interview with him (*Revista de Occidente*, No. 93). Referring to *Cobra*, the title of his best-known novel, Sarduy establishes various possibilities of association with it that are based on reference and allusion and imply an interplay between a given structural system and a peculiar mechanism of writing.

From Cuba with a Song (1967) also shares in this multiple interplay. The title in Spanish (*De donde son los cantantes*) is a line from a popular Cuban song, in which it is heard as a question, but in the novel it appears as an answer. In the song the singers are from Havana, but the novel tells us they are from Cuba. This phrase is thus an epithet. In addition to establishing an association with the song and Cuba, the title establishes an association, through popular culture, with the reader. The title is thus the first phrase of the book: its metaphor and its incitement.

In effect, the association is established through allusions, and this is the point at which writing formulates its design. As in *Three Trapped Tigers*, in *From Cuba with a Song* allusion operates actively and permanently, although in Cabrera Infante's novel it tends to the direct, obvious pastiche, to the play on words as proliferating material. In *Three Trapped Tigers* the allusions serve the novel; they are one of its levels but are not necessarily the basis of its structuring, which is to be found instead in the unfolding of a parody that alludes to itself. On the other hand, in Sarduy's novel the three-part structure itself is referential: the *curriculum cubense* implies the Chinese component, the Black element, and the Hispanic factor (names that are places, races, cultures). Hence the three levels of the novel allude, in the manner of a gloss or masquerade, to these "anthropological" components, which are stripped of their traditional meaning.

Sarduy realizes that the only way to speak separately of these three components is to approach them from a detached point of view and through the effusiveness of play and sensorial empathy. Thus the system that creates the novel (three "full" worlds that are emptied exultantly) permits the release of a writing that always alludes to a potentially "infinite," presupposed objective correlate.

The allusion can refer to literature but, above all, it begins by referring to the visible and formal characteristics of those three festive worlds. Consequently, this writing achieves the brilliance of a formal play that is ironic in its perspective and sensorial in its choices. These detached points of view and the approximations in the structure of the narrative allow the work to be self-sufficient, to require only the spectrum of its artifice, of its illusional game: sleight of hand, magic word, and final switch. We can say, then, that this novel is critical in its antitraditional formulation and "poetic" in its ritualization of the fantastic paraphernalia adopted by the three texts-worlds-glosses.

Therefore, the reductive activities of the novel (the sharp humor of its parodies and its "draining" of the meaningful levels) are countered by an accumulating and masquerading activity (the novel chooses to carnivalize the signs of a festive and spectacular reality).

Notwithstanding its lack of density, which is precisely what makes it a mirage or a chorus of echoes, *From Cuba with a Song* contains several books: first, those that are part of the basic structure, whose common space is the exalting parody constructed by empathy, by identification; second, the substratum of the three "full worlds" that are simultaneously present and absent and imply the area in which the author cuts, selects, and reassembles; third, the writing that constructs with masks, that is, on the "surface" levels of a purely verbal deduction; and, finally, the other book, the one with critical implications, because this play of unrestricted, gratuitous appearance—this pageant of appearance—implies the irrepressible and systematic criticism of literature and of the traditional need that explains by "meaning" while overlooking the "meaninglessness" of the "artificial" forms, which are no more and no less artificial or gratuitous than desire and its labyrinth.

In *La Maison de Rendez-Vous*, a novel by Robbe-Grillet, the sensuous nuance of the Chinese scene is also produced starting from a repertoire of objects relevant to a Western outlook: a dancing woman in a clinging silk dress, for example. The erotic suggestion emerges, in this case, from a very clear notion of femininity: full presence, pure object. In the Chinese chapter of Sarduy's novel, on the other hand, the sensuous suggestion emerges from an expectation, a proximity, a light touch—from the postponement, therefore, of the act itself—and from the successive incitements that permit the disguising and imagistic proliferation of what in the end is not a woman but an empty mask. Robbe-Grillet prefers to design the unhurried sensuality of a repeated and formalized scene duplicated in the sumptuous tradition of typical objects. Sarduy opts for a bric-a-brac, delirious, and multiform China stripped of its tradition and reduced to a game, to a buoyant spectacle.

In so doing Sarduy places himself within a characteristically Spanish-American tradition. His critique of literature operates by expansion. He selects a formal and imagistic repertoire that goes beyond verism and the need to correlate words with the "reality" that supposedly underlies them. Lezama Lima had already brought images of snow close to his tropical landscape, but Sarduy goes one step further: he makes it snow in Havana. This mechanism has come to us from the baroque. The first Spanish-American baroque poets pretended to see European flowers among our own. This act is more audacious than comparing an Araucanian girl with some mythological goddess, or the environs of Mexico City with some classical longing.

The greatest audacity is not, however, the inducement of an imaginary reality; it is the attitude toward language, because the use of words becomes as decisive as the knowledge of the world: language seeks to be the final transparency. This use of language reveals, above all, a nominal faith: the poet need only say the names of the world to believe that the world is inexhaustible. Names, therefore, are the images, the birth of metaphors and figuration. The mechanics of Spanish-American Modernism are not much different: a nominative repertoire becomes a fantastic paraphernalia; the world is transformed into a series of prestigious images.

Like Lezama, Sarduy has developed a variation within this tradition. Lezama's dense baroque, full of symbolic implications, is followed by the light baroque constructed on pure figuration that characterizes this novel. But the exultation itself of its artifice discloses its critical slant. In the end, in its draining of the meaningful levels, Sarduy's writing acts significantly based on the irony of a questioning, demythifying criticism.

The component aspects of "Cubanness" expose in this novel the other side of their full appearance: their empty appearance. The Chinese factor exists only as a carnivalesque masquerade; the Black factor exists as a chorus of voices (a mulattress reviews her "career" from the vantage point of her death, of her legend); and the Hispanic factor is seen from the perspective of the traditional and meaningful symbol par excellence, a statue of Christ on the cross, gradually and spectacularly destroyed during a religious procession. Along with the festiveness of the characterizing images and the masquerading, we find again a reduction of the mirages. Thus, the celebration of "Cubanness" is also the discovery of its significant "nonexistence," in other words, of the sole *presence of its forms*, which language consecrates through a reuniting eroticism.

15. On the Text of History

"It is not a game, but an enigma," we are told by the narrator of *Morirás lejos* [You will die far away], the memorable novel by José Emilio Pacheco, which has recently been reprinted by Joaquín Mortiz with revisions by the author. That riddle, which implies inquiry and rigor, is a good definition of this exceptional text. Published first in 1967, a rereading of it confirms one of the paradoxes of that enigma: the text is more current today than ten years ago.

Morirás lejos was published during a privileged time of reading. The Spanish-American literary text seemed to be saying that our own social and political history was legible, decipherable and, perhaps, transparent. Literature moved ahead to promote that change and, with it, a political liberation, two processes that supposedly were also legible and predictable. However, in *Morirás lejos* José Emilio Pacheco had posed a prior question: How can we keep history (barbarity) from repeating itself? Thus this novel is today a different novel. Barbarity, in fact, has repeated itself, and this question again confronts us. Hence it was not a game but an enigma, the enigma of reading itself, in other words, the rigorous formulation of a pertinent question.

History moves in the text like a destructive machinery. Titus and the Romans demolished Jerusalem and the Nazis destroyed the Warsaw ghetto, but in this novel it is not the same fire, the victims are different. Hence the relevance of this lucid inquiry. History repeats itself because power—the power of the hegemonic culture over the dominated culture, the power of the colonizer and his sanctioning discourse over a marginal speech branded as guilty—usurps and decides it. The victims do not end in death—the holocaust shifts from Jerusalem to Warsaw and, during this time of imprisoned, tortured, and *desaparecidos*, to Latin America. History repeats its violence: the Jews of the concentration camps illustrated this violence; the *desaparecidos* in Latin America now cannot even document it. Carlos Fuentes has keenly observed that the historical metaphor of *Mo-rirás lejos* is the updating of a model, and its demand is that we not forget, that we remember, in other words, that we make legible our response to violence.

Giving a form to that response demands here that the text inquire into itself. It must determine how to write from fiction a current history of fascist violence. The response that the text formulates is the development of that same question. In other words, the text is produced as the inquiry into a reading. The moment of fiction is the text itself; writing acts as an operation of reading on the facts of history. This is why the account must be virtual: from a window a man observes another man who, in turn, apparently watches him. This is the exchangeable axis, the perspective that opens a combinatorial alternative that is left with no possible outcome. The narrative is, thus, a not knowing of the text. Both men are many men and, among them, they are M (the ferocious Nazi torturer) and Someone (the pursuer disguised as all men).

The narrative presupposes that the reading will decipher the riddle, but the text in fact only multiplies its game of alternations, which are implications, while at the same time surrendering to reading the proofs of a history that is both abominable (and this is the knowledge of the text) and thorough (a knowledge that does not yield or fix). This renewed violence accumulates with hallucinating precision the evidence of the crime. History is thus impressed on us as the reconstruction of reading: reading is the greater knowledge, the work of consciousness. Its notion of truth is extended in the fictitious nature of the narrative. To read from fiction implies, in the end, to search for reading the central site of its meaning.

The reading that watches M in the narrative is the beginning of the judgment. Immediately, reading recognizes the evidences of the crime, one of whose subjects is M. Thus the reading constructs its own drama; it is inserted in history because it has a decisive role in the fiction, which is why it must add its own evidence to the judgment and be itself the final outcome of the text.

The text, of course, does not culminate in a mere response; its inquiry continues. Within its genre this is a frontier novel; it proceeds from history but does not simply document or pay tribute to it. Its repertoire of facts is a model, a summary paradigm of the destructive machinery that comes from afar and, transforming itself, continues. But *Morirás lejos* is also the chronicle of a novel. Its plural narrator is also the axis of a changing reading, and the text notes its own variations disclosing its nonmimetic composition, the skillful and pleasant exercise of a rotating form. Historicity, therefore, is generated in the construction of this form that rejects fixity. The adventure of reading assumes the nakedness of the story as an object of meaning. In another paradox, we are confronted with the form of a novel whose narrative is the absence of a novel. As Noé Jitrik has observed, the text is a production that inquires into its form of production. The *mise-en-abîme* and a system of incisions, which Margo Glantz has discussed, are the process of this inquiry.

History and the narrative are, then, the work of the reading, whose drama is the form itself of the text. That is why the narrator changes. Someone observes, someone reads, and someone erases what he has read. Someone notes the certainty of that reading and immediately questions it. Imagining the form of a novel is tantamount to a totalizing narrative that would include us. Reading multiplies itself: the plural subject intervenes, underscoring the facts, criticizing the report, occupying possible speakers. To narrate is thus to surrender the final responsibility to language. The narrator is an ellipsis which the text returns to the axis of these permutations, to the "you" of the reader, in other words, to the hypothesis of an identity constructed by our capacity to make history legible.

"Hypotheses are ventured," the text announces, but its writing composed of "digressions" arrives at another simulacrum: the possible conclusion. In effect, the story of M has gradually been formulated, his guilt is obvious, and the punishment looms. But even in the end we find another redoubling, other endings. The "disrepresentation" thus continues. The narrative can conclude in several ways (or in all possible ways at the same time) because its inquiring purpose is, precisely, to have opened this scene in the writing so that by asking about its meaning it could interrogate us about violence.

Between the look of a character who is observed and the vigil of another who observes, the text has produced its denunciation as an enigma of fiction. In this way fiction also forms a consciousness of meaning whose moral sensibility is another sign of the relevance with which the text has questioned us.

16. A Book on Death

(Translated by William L. Siemens)

El zorro de arriba y el zorro de abajo [The fox above and the fox below] (Buenos Aires, 1971), José María Arguedas's posthumous novel, is a complex and extraordinary document. One must ask at the outset how to take this passionate book. The first page, dated May 10, 1968, announces the author's determination to commit suicide; Arguedas had already attempted to kill himself in 1966, and he does not wish to fail this time. He is writing under doctor's orders, "because people never tire of telling me that if I manage to keep on writing I will recover my sanity." But at the same time his decision to kill himself seems to be without appeal. These two motions—to kill himself and to save himself—are strikingly combined in a single impulse: with unconcealed fervor ("This preoccupation of mine is wondrously disquieting"), Arguedas writes while foundering in that strange paradoxical region in which a page both hastens and retards the final act.

The book consists of three diaries and a "Last Diary?" in which, in effect, the author achieves the final balance and decides on his death. Between these diaries there has grown, with agonizing difficulty, a novel that is to remain unfinished. There are no fictional relations between these diaries and the novel as such; the relationship is more an internal one. Arguedas writes his diaries when the depression or the profound uneasiness he is suffering prevent his going on with the novel. The first of them opens with his decision to kill himself, but it is evident that the act is being postponed by the novel that has imposed itself upon the writer and that, as a consequence of this fervent exorcism, is beginning to take form. The "Second Diary" (February 1969) seems to indicate that the author has deferred his suicide because, in fact, he has in hand a novel, one that is growing despite his enormous difficulties; it is curious that Arguedas should say here that the desire for suicide originated in his exhaustion, but in part also in his fear of the difficulties of writing a novel about the port of Chimbote, an industrialized city, which he suddenly believes he does not know well enough. At the end of this diary two lines announce that the author has managed to take up his work again.

The "Third Diary" (May 1969) states that "suffocation" is detaining his work of fiction; nevertheless, his uneasiness does not demand suicide here either, but rather the recourse of travel: Arguedas writes these pages, and the novel itself, between Chimbote, Lima, Arequipa, and Chile. But once again, a postscript announces that the author is finding it possible to resume the work of fiction. Still, the "Last Diary?" (August 1969) puts an end to this process: "I have struggled against death, face to face, in writing this faltering, complaining tale." Suicide reappears, ineluctable now. An epilogue, added by the editor, collects the final letters and messages, which reveal the sober meticulousness with which Arguedas attempted to order the facts before shooting himself on November 28, 1969.

Perhaps it is not coincidental that the "Last Diary?" should carry these questions, because in fact the novel was being composed in the midst of a fight with death, as its postponement, but perhaps also as its exorcism. Perhaps Arguedas knew that salvation was no longer possible, but his having attempted it, in a passionate struggle, endowed his novel with a fervent, if desolate, character. The book can be read in this way, as an agonized attempt to play one last game. An unsettling reading, to be sure, since the novel is obviously truncated and, even more important, a dramatic failure. It has noteworthy moments—scenes and dialogues of great dramatic intensity, in addition to the vertigo with which he manages at times to communicate the hell of a port whose life revolves around perversity and annihilation—but the tension of the work steadily declines and the text loses its form. How, then, can we evaluate literarily a book that by its very imperfection transcends literature? That very lack of fulfillment is another level, and not only of the fiction, but of the documentary aspect of this book. Because, in the final analysis, the book reveals to us Arguedas's faith in the act of writing: perhaps he felt that writing could in some manner accomplish his salvation. To save oneself by words: this gamble, dark and tortured, presides over these pages. A complex wager, nevertheless, now ballasted by the malaise that was undermining the creative power of this man; thus, salvation by means of words could only be the reverse side of a salvation by death. There is a moment when words forsake him: he writes the last diary questioning whether it is in reality the last because—as he himself understands—the fact of being in the process of writing even about his own failure, the very act of being in the process of using language, retrieves him in the continuity of a writing that in some manner exceeds and prolongs him, as if his life were being sustained in that final possibility of following a phrase through. But now the plot of salvation and death could have no other outcome: the novel itself is, at bottom, a metaphor of the internal uneasiness that was overwhelming him; not only on the surface of its incompleteness, but above all in the image of deterioration that he proposes for a city where worlds parallel to his (characters from the Peruvian Sierra, victims of rootlessness) are destroyed in the distortion and perversity of the industrial city.

Thus one might say that the wager on saving himself by means of words is in reality the final preparation for taking death upon himself. From the perspective of his suicide ("this theme, the only one whose essence I live and feel"), after the "First Diary," the book surrenders to him for the length of two chapters that establish several characters and their setting. The "Second Diary" reveals the tremendous difficulty of writing about the city and its chaos, and in the confession of this burning impotence Arguedas finally says that his fear of the theme was another factor in his suicide as a strange (but perhaps symptomatic) statement that would indicate precisely that for a moment he is living the work as a postponement because words avert the outcome. But here the central paradox of this work is revealed to us: it is the diaries, in directly taking upon themselves his uneasiness and failure, that avert suicide, because they constitute the fall and the transition, the recovery each time of the work that had stopped. And it is upon the resumption of the work that suicide seems to return, no longer as a theme, but arising from the metaphor of deterioration and in the lonely frustration of writing. From this springs the relationship of necessity between the diaries and the novel: on the simplest level they are the confessions of a man writing a novel with a sense of bold helplessness; on another level the work demands to be stopped, interrupted, so that its frustration may take on a sense of incompletion, because the work leads toward the tragic conclusion while the diaries recover the energy of postponement within that same helplessness. At the end, the diaries forsake the author and he forsakes the work. The last confession also tells how the plots, the lives of the characters would have continued if the author had gone on with the work. But this not only is no longer possible, but no longer seems necessary. The questionings, the doubt, in the final diary suggest that the author perhaps still hoped to find new strength at last. But why go on? If the work had concluded like any other novel we would then find ourselves before a fraud or before a simple psychological process, and not in the presence of a tragic text.

In fact, not even the last diary (because of the question mark) is the last; the work and the diaries thus remain incomplete and the book founders (like the reading) in the solitude of unfulfillment. Nevertheless, a writer—even in losing this battle—has gained the resonance of his own tragic destiny. At the end all that remains is for him to kill himself in order not to deny himself; he dies paying off all the accounts, trusting in the destiny of his country and its peoples, trusting in his own work, denying to himself only the uneasiness that has undermined it.

In the "Third Diary" Arguedas finds himself lacking the energy to go on and says, "Perhaps it is because I have entered the most intricate part of the lives I seek to tell about, in which my own involvement, instead of working itself out, threatens to get out of hand or cloud over."

Thus in the text are found the two great difficulties inherent in this adventure: the complex existence (even more complex for Arguedas) of the people of the new industrial city, as well as his own personal situation. The novel, that is to say, and the diaries. His life would have to penetrate other lives; there would have to exist a functioning continuity between confession and fiction, or, perhaps better, between the fragmented autobiography and the expository chronicle. It is interesting to observe that to the worsening situation he is living at this time (and which his sudden trips reveal as well as do his confessions), Arguedas is to oppose the almost naïve will to coherence of the narrative: not only have the characters been chosen as types, but it is clear as well that the very situation of the industrial port (the image of a semi-modernized, capitalistic Peru, which Arguedas rejects) appears explained or schematized, as if the author wished to expound for himself a complete and coherent understanding of this social hell, which attracts him with its human chaos and repels him with its dehumanized origin and present state. Capitalist mechanics have converted the port into an enormous urban sprawl into which people from the entire country are pouring, attracted by the illusion—ludicrous to be sure—of industrial progress: that social vertigo fascinates the author and he wants to tell the story of certain peoples, understand the destiny of certain characters who have taken the road he himself followed: from the mountains to the coast, from the traditional communal society to the class-oriented urban society, although the former does not fail to suffer also from depredation, as well as injustice. In that exchange a metaphor of uneasiness is established: the port is fundamentally perverse; it has been turned upside down by industrial exploitation, and thus the infernal metaphor is the new context of that inhabitant who has lost a potential place of residence. Already in his previous novel, *Todas las sangres*, capitalist industry (in this case mining) was destroying communal life and announcing the distortion of a nation forced into dependency.

But the mere attempt to explain that painful situation to himself in a coherent manner is, to be sure, insufficient from the author's perspective; the work demands to be more than a chronicle, although the chronicle is the initial impulse that permits this work. Since its inception Arguedas has acted out of that impulse: to make known a hitherto unknown world was a point of departure for fiction. Therefore it is revealing that he warns, in the last quotation, that his search for expression, his labor with the literary work, "instead of working itself out, threatens to get out of hand or cloud over." It clouds over because his own uneasiness has for him a dark zone that in some manner is liberated by fiction as it takes upon itself that uneasiness in a broader process, now involving the various "countries" that make up Peru, because the work seldom, if ever, achieves the vertigo of poetry translating these relationships. It is for this reason that the uneasiness threatens to "get out of hand." This statement is essential to the composition of the work because it alludes to its central impulse; in fact, from its hellish perspective, the work demands of the author another language, another discourse, a writing that should stand ready to serve the fever of its urgent and compulsive dilemmas.

It is for this reason that alongside the intended coherence of the story the work imposes a delirious discourse: the dialogues soon drift toward a frenzied vertigo where speech seeks to capture that unattainable reality within the living chaos of the industrial city, that infernal labyrinth so resistant to reason. It is a discourse of this sort, about to break loose, about to lose its bearings, that appears as the central impulse of the work, as its appeal and also as its best poetic possibility. A discourse burned by agony, impelled by the necessity of totalizing a speech that embraces that variegated and discordant reality of the city. In the diaries, too, that discourse began with the fervor of suicide, with the arbitrariness of summary judgments, with the necessity of reasoning unconventionally and freely about the author's vital situation, following the discontinuous flow of facts, memory, or ideas of hope and redemption. That heated discourse also takes upon itself the situation of the writer who develops from his early regionalism a well-delineated perspective; not without ingenuousness, Arguedas feels the necessity of stating precisely his vision of literature, thus running the risk of oversimplifying the evident complexity of his writer's world. That complexity makes him a contemporary of the Inca Garcilaso, César Vallejo, and us at the same time, because his work develops within the context of a Latin-American debate that concerns us in the questions we ask about ourselves.

The delirious discourse is thus at the center of the work in progress. This impulse toward vertigo also reveals how the author wishes to violate a principle of fiction, to amplify it by questioning it, thereby putting pressure upon rational discourse, not only delineating that social chaos but also desiring that poetry say of its own accord what the narrated chronicle can no longer say. To say more—perhaps to say it all. It is possible that with his discourse the author was searching for a total understanding, one that would be critical, social, poetic, and, in some measure, prophetic.

The dialogues submit to delirium, and sometimes conclude in a sort of dance of characters, complete with songs and new voices. One of the characters, Tarta, is called "the poet," "the intellectual," but is, revealingly, a stutterer. More important is Moncada, a madman, who "preaches" in the streets and marketplaces, bearing a large cross. Arguedas takes pains to make this character, who is drawn from the life situation of the Chimbote countryside, stand out. The speech of a madman allows him to confront the work and the city by way of a discourse that, while it is delirious, is also critical, out of a sort of holy wrath, as a total accusation that is at the same time an internal rending. That discourse finds its echo in Esteban de la Cruz, ex-miner, now terminally ill; the dialogue of both characters exacerbates the vision of the industrial city, provides the keynote of the drama of those lives wrecked by the penury of the nation. De la Cruz says, "When drunkard speak truth, true truth, about justice her foundation God, then authority cop, injuneer, etcetera, say, 'You drunk, you drunk, you under arrest, dammit,' An' they arrest you, they beat you. Fucked up. Word of drunk, even if it's true truth, very heart and body of the Lord, no good. . . ." This marginal speech, this language of the madman, the drunkard, the man condemned to death, opens up the exacerbation of the discourse in a total protest, in an agonized appeal; in Moncada's preaching that appeal becomes accusatory, the delirium of a sorely wounded discourse. It is no coincidence that at the conclusion of the novel a character reads from the Bible a flaming paragraph from the pen of St. Paul.

The fox above and the fox below are characters drawn from the mythology of Huarochirí; in the novel one represents the mountain region and the other the coast. At one point they engage in a conversation about the novel, and they also intervene in the fiction behind the faces of certain characters. But this mythic plane is never developed; it appears only as the possibility of what is perhaps a choral dialogue, of another suprarational discourse, between the two zones of a divided Peru.

Novel, document, text about the work that makes and unmakes us, this book by José María Arguedas is, at its deepest level, an unusual testimony concerning the tragic destiny of a man who lived the beauty and discord of a cruel country. On the last page he wrote, "In me you will bid farewell to a time for Peru whose roots will forever suck juices from the earth to nourish those who live in our nation, in which any man not chained and brutalized by selfishness may be a citizen, and a happy one, of all nations." All of Arguedas's books speak to us of the happiness and the desolation with which he lived that country; his work unveils for us a world torn between utopia and despair, fed by the dream of redemption through the exercise of criticism. Even though this novel is not, as such, on a par with his previous books, as a document it possesses a value of a different order, and its peculiar intensity and character confer upon it a heightened and deepened life. In Latin-American prose fiction the voice of Arguedas is our "consciousness of misfortune," but also the dream of another time.

Index of Names